W9-DGP-756

COLLABORATIONS:

Meeting New Goals, New Realities

JUNE K. PHILLIPS, Editor
EILEEN W. GLISAN, Chair
1997

National Textbook Company
NTC a division of *NTC/Contemporary Publishing Company* • Lincolnwood, Illinois USA

1997 Board of Directors

Published by National Textbook Company, a division of NTC/Contemporary Publishing Company.
© 1997 by NTC/Contemporary Publishing Company, 4255 West Touhy Avenue,
Lincolnwood (Chicago), Illinois 60646-1975 U.S.A.

ISBN 0-8442-9156-0

7 8 9 0 VP 9 8 7 6 5 4 3 2 1

In Memoriam
A. Ronald Walton
1943–1996

The Board of Directors of the Northeast Conference on the Teaching of Foreign Languages dedicates this volume to the memory of A. Ronald Walton. Ron served as a Director of the Northeast Conference from 1990–1993. He was also a member of the National Standards Task Force and in that capacity helped shape the standards upon which the Northeast Reports in this volume are focused.

Contents

Collaborations: Meeting New Goals, New Realities

June K. Phillips

Weber State University

C ollaboration, literally working together, has characterized developments over the last few years in foreign language education; thus, collaboration serves as a powerful theme for the 1997 Northeast Conference *Reports*. Collaboration does not mean that our common labors embrace a single approach, a single curriculum, a single vision of how students learn languages other than their first one. Rather, collaboration implies working together to discover and agree upon the best practices for teaching languages in the classroom.

Professional Standards that Challenge

A renewed vigor permeates the profession as it has established, and now seeks to aim toward, standards for learning the world's languages, standards that challenge students and teachers, standards that are positioned to carry us into the 21st century. Standard setting takes place at many levels: the national standards are not federal mandates imposed by authority; they represent goals and standards determined through a three-year professional dialogue and, if espoused, accepted voluntarily. While the national standards were released to the public in November 1995, numerous states were and are in various stages of standards design, and classroom teachers are considering how standards relate to their programs today and into the future. The National Standards (1996) link together five large goal areas, the Five Cs of language education:

Communication in languages other than English
Cultures, the acquisition of perspectives of other cultures
Connections with other disciplines
Comparisons with one's own language and culture
Communities and the use of new languages at home and abroad

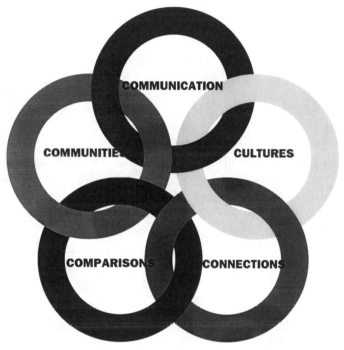

Figure. The Five Cs of Foreign Language Education (Standards, 1996, p. 28.)

Eleven standards were specified in these areas. States currently working on standards have drawn heavily from the national standards and have taken them to a next level of specificity in terms of student outcomes and sometimes assessments.

The standards framework does not prescribe an instructional approach or methodology. Instead, it reflects more broadly conceived purposes and objectives for language study for all the nation's students. It advocates quite clearly that students should have opportunities to begin their study in early grades and to have extended sequences available to them. For a profession firmly ensconced in a curriculum where the model of two years of high school remains the norm, movement toward welcoming all students into our classrooms, articulating among elementary, middle, and high school students, not to mention the transition to higher education, and preparing to teach advanced learners will be cumbersome, challenging, and most importantly, rewarding.

Collaborations to Develop Effective Classroom Practices and to Reform Curriculum

As the profession takes up the invitation to address the standards in their classrooms and in curriculum design, the need for experimentation, reflection, and reform will be great. Feedback from the classroom, successes and failures, will inform the content standards (what students know and should be able to do) as to challenging but achievable performance standards (how good is good enough?) For experimentation with approaches, materials, and new strategies for diverse learners to be productive, there must be greater collaboration among professionals and their constituencies to advance the vision created in the standards effort. A striking reality arises from the greater complexity in language instruction than was engendered in the paradigms of the past. Gone forever are the days of narrowly defined outcomes and prescriptive approaches derived from a neat but inadequate theory of learning.

The contexts for collaboration are many, yet the changes envisioned by the national standards will have to be explored, reviewed, observed, and revised in the context of the classroom. At first blush, it seems so obvious to conduct research in actual school settings, yet a review of the literature in the field of second-language acquisition indicates that far too few studies have actually taken place in that whirlwind of uncontrolled, uncontrollable variables called a classroom. If high standards are to serve as a challenge to all students, and if all the Five Cs are to be visible in curriculum, then teachers and researchers together will have to develop penetrating observational methods to uncover successful learning scenarios where the outcomes lend themselves to global assessments and not just discrete measures.

For the 1997 Northeast Conference *Reports*, Eileen W. Glisan, Chair, and the Board of Directors decided to focus on the newly born standards in full knowledge that their presence in classroom learning is yet to be deeply felt. In addition, the Conference sought to facilitate collaboration among professionals for the purposes of conducting classroom action research projects. Three interlocking elements form the basis of the 1997 *Reports*: Research teams/ collaborators; goal areas or standards; action research. The collaborators were to examine a particular goal area/standard (e.g., *Communication* in the Interpersonal Mode) through the design and implementation of short action research projects. Thus the *content* of the project is a standard, the *vehicle* and thread tying the project together is *collaboration*, and players are researchers, teachers, students, and community members.

Each of the projects generated research questions specific to its focus, but several questions related to all projects.

- How do various groups of professionals come together for effective collaboration?
- What types of research will best address implementation of the goals and standards within the classroom setting?
- How do we transform the goals and standards from written texts to the realities of classroom interactions?

Cases of Collaboration in the *Reports*

The *Reports* appropriately begin with a message for foreign languages from our colleagues in mathematics who have been about the business of standards-setting for a decade. Mary Lindquist, a university professor and officer of the National Council of Teachers of Mathematics when the standards were being created, and Linda Rosen, Executive Director of NCTM, collaborate to relate a virtual case study in the development and promotion of the mathematics standards. One can almost substitute the phrase "foreign languages" for "mathematics" in both the history they present for their discipline and the future directions they foresee. While many foreign language teachers might think our disciplines are quite different given the solid place of mathematics in the core curriculum and our tentative clinging to the fringe, strong parallels arise as one explores concepts such as elitism, professional development of teachers, and a public with views of the curriculum not necessarily in alignment with our own research and goals. Their *Report* concludes with five valuable lessons that we, as a profession, should thoughtfully consider.

The National Standards Task Force had also planned for collaboration even as the standards were being drafted. In order to ascertain the fit or the leap of the new standards in today's classrooms, it was decided to pilot the draft version in a number of schools. Kathleen Riordan, a district foreign language supervisor, and Rita Oleksak, a K–12 world languages resource teacher, capture the voices of teachers in their school who collaborated with the Task Force and with one another to provide input into the discussion of standards. Teachers identified current classroom activities that they felt were standards oriented; subsequently, descriptions of these scenarios were included in the publication, *Standards for foreign language learning: Preparing for the 21st century* (1996). At the pilot stage, teachers, quite naturally, were desirous of verifying practices in line with the emerging standards. As we move toward implementation, it becomes critical to our professional dialogue that the standards continue to be at the core of reflection, discussion, and informed, targeted critique of instructional practices.

The five central *Reports* were designed as projects that share the following common elements as appropriate:

- The project involved collaboration of at least two people from different contexts.
- One of the standards goal areas stimulated the design of the project.
- Each collaborative team explored a standard or goal area as it played out in teaching and learning.
- The project involved small-scale action research that could be conducted for a limited term (e.g., one semester).
- The project was descriptive in nature and aspired to provide information concerning ways in which the targeted standard or goal area might be addressed through innovative practices.

The first project was conducted by Bonnie Adair-Hauck, a university teacher educator and second-language researcher, and Philomena Cumo-Johannsen, a secondary teacher of French. Their project targets the Communication Goal, and in spite of an original intent to focus primarily upon the Interpersonal Standard, the reality was that all three standards for communication were integrated in teaching and observed in student performances. The reader of this *Report*, through the vivid protocols of classroom interaction found in the article, are inducted, with the teacher, into the instructional model presented, PACE, a Whole Language/ Guided Participatory approach. As the teacher and her students work though lessons together, the "negotiated meaning" that underlies the Interpersonal Standard comes to life.

Ana Marie Schwartz, a university professor and developer of video magazine materials, collaborated in every sense of the term with Mark Kavanaugh, a high school teacher of Spanish. Not only did this team plan together, but they both taught parts of a cultural unit that used video, feature length film, library research, and many other resources. Their theme was immigration, and readers of this *Report* will be astounded at the growth exhibited in student knowledge and attitudes at the end of the unit. The standards framework of the study of practices and products of a culture leading to new and expanded student perspectives is clearly demonstrated through this project.

The *Report* that focuses on the Connections Goal with its interdisciplinary focus is the only project not conducted solely for this Northeast Conference volume. However, the extraordinary and longer term collaboration described by Eileen Lorenz, a county foreign language supervisor, and Pierre Verdaguer, a university French professor, responds so clearly to teachers who pose the questions: "How can I do interdisciplinary work when I don't know the other disciplines?" or "How do I find someone in my school with whom to do an interdisciplinary unit?" The Connections Goal should not be so narrowly interpreted. The collaborative project in this Report was conducted under the auspices of a grant from the National Endowment for the Humanities. Divergent groups — specifically elementary/middle school teachers and university faculty specializing in cultures —came together to design a scope and sequence for the teaching of culture where there had been none. The pedagogy and appropriateness of materials was the decision of the teachers; the content was worked on two levels by participating university faculty, one purpose to build the teachers' knowledge base, the other to create accurate teaching materials. The advantage of this funded project is that the collaboration has made available materials that enable language teachers to teach effectively from the arts, history, geography.

Zena Moore, a university second-language researcher and teacher educator, collaborated with a graduate student, Mark English, to create a middle-school exploratory language course for a group of young people who had never had the opportunity to study another language. The researchers targeted the Comparisons Goal area as they challenged themselves and a class of at-risk youths with the learning of Arabic language and culture. The standards have advocated language for *all* students within all goal areas, but in particular the Comparisons standards have a long-range objective positing that learning about other languages and cultures opens the learner to insights *about* languages and cultures as systems. Even though this case was only a two-semester experience, student journals illustrate that these young people did find success; they took pride in their learning and recognized their own ability to work with new codes and practices. One essential key used by this instructor lay in his willingness to build positively on the language students brought to the classroom.

Mari Haas, a teacher educator and folk art author, collaborated with Margaret Reardon and her seventh grade Spanish students to make the world their community. These two educators put in motion a number of devices to pair students from a town near New York City with their peers in a Chilean village. The project demonstrated the multiple meanings of "community" in ways that should assure teachers that this goal area does not mean that students have to be physically transported to other countries or neighborhoods. While students did take a field trip to a local bakery, that was not the primary means of illustrating language and culture for the concept of community. The *Report* lets us see how students negotiated meaning within their electronic community, how they pictured their respective communities through folk art, and how they experienced another culture within their home community.

Reflections from Outside the Collaborations

The final *Report* is a unique blend of spoken and written language in an edited version of a videotaped conversation between Dale L. Lange, noted university researcher and teacher educator, and Joe Wicczorck, a mid-career, professionally active secondary teacher. In the spirit of collaboration and reflection, Eileen W. Glisan, 1997 Northeast Chair, moderated a discussion of their insights and reactions to the *Reports*. After all, short and intense projects generate ideas and stimulate innovations. At the same time, replication may be difficult, and the results of collaboration are most powerful if readers discern the larger implications of what they show us. Our discussants noted, for example, that one of the anticipated, yet significant, findings from these projects lay in the observation that targeting one standard or goal area envelops them all. The linkages in the graphic for the Five Cs illustrates that the circles are complete in themselves, yet they connect and overlap one another. Both educators saw patterns, identified problems, raised questions, and shared perspectives from their own experiences in a thoughtful and provocative *Report*. It will be the responsibility of us all to continue that dialogue.

In his comments, Joe Wieczorek asked at one point the perennial question: "Is there going to be another paradigm shift in twenty years?" And of course, the answer is "yes, absolutely," for even as we create a new knowledge base surrounding the new standards, as new snow sets off the avalanche, the paradigm will shift once again. Our field is not static; change is inevitable.

It is the hope of all who worked on this volume that the projects and case studies presented will not be seen as ends in themselves. Rather they present us with examples of how, in the era ahead, questions must be posed, expertise must be shared, problems must be solved, experiments must be made. This group of collaborative action research projects is only a beginning of a long effort to change the face of foreign language instruction for our students. Before we can do that, we, as professionals, must read the research and seek to understand it, we must analyze our practices, revise our approaches and ways of thinking. We must invite new students into our classrooms and grow as teachers of the world's languages and cultures.

June K. Phillips, 1997 *Reports* Editor
Weber State University

Reference

National K–12 Standards for Foreign Language Education Project. (1996). *Standards for foreign language learning: Preparing for the 21st century*. Yonkers, NY: Author.

Professional Collaboration: A Perspective from the Mathematics Standards

Mary Montgomery Lindquist

Columbus State University

Linda P. Rosen

National Council of Teachers of Mathematics

Ongoing dialogue with diverse groups of people is necessary to the change process, and insights from the dialogue must be considered in subsequent decision-making.

66 But this is only the beginning." This poignant, simple sentence in the introduction to the *Standards for Foreign Language Learning: Preparing for the Twenty-first Century* (1996) summarizes the most important perspective on standards that those of us in the mathematics community can share after our ten years of experience. It is true that developing the standards is only the beginning—the excitement and hard work are yet to come.

It is a pleasure to share with the foreign language community some of the activities associated with the National Council of Teachers of Mathematics (NCTM) *Standards* as well as some of the lessons that we have learned over the past decade. Some would say that these are not new lessons, that we have not learned these lessons well, or that we have many other lessons yet to learn. We do not disagree with these viewpoints, but some of the experiences and challenges we have encountered may help the foreign language community move its agenda forward in the decade ahead. (To avoid having to write *mathematics* and *foreign language* repeatedly, we shall henceforth use *we* to refer to the mathematics community and *you* to refer to the foreign language community.) One of the lessons we have learned is that discipline-based organizations must work together in our common efforts to move ahead. We welcome the opportunity to do so through this chapter.

As described in the introduction to your standards, language study has special features. Because the place of foreign languages in our schooling process is different from that of mathematics, our lessons need to be interpreted in the light of what makes sense in your community. The chapter opens with background information about the mathematics standards and our efforts. After sharing this information, we discuss those lessons that may be relevant to you.

The NCTM *Standards* and Associated Activities

You need some context about the standards-based movement in the mathematics community. What follows is an illustrative, rather than exhaustive, account of our efforts. It begins with a brief description of the origin of the documents and their development and then discusses the main messages of the NCTM *Standards*[1] as well as the major shifts in learning, teaching, and assessing that are indicated. Although many lessons were learned in the development phase, you have already completed this part of the task, so our development discussion is brief. The chapter focuses on the associated activities of awareness, professional development, monitoring, and connecting. This section concludes by discussing current and upcoming activities of NCTM and others.

The *Standards* and Their Development

Education is often in a state of flux as it attempts to meet optimally the needs of students and the communities to which it is responsible. The past decade, however, has seen unprecedented effort on many fronts. The portrayal of the disastrous state of education in the 1980s by publications such as *A Nation at Risk* (National Commission on Excellence in Education, 1983) spurred many of these efforts. Such descriptions played some part in the decision of the National Council of Teachers of Mathematics to take a leadership role in setting the vision of mathematics education needed for the remainder of the century. These external documents, however, were only part of the impetus; there was already widespread acknowledgment of the need within the mathematics community (NSF, 1979; NCTM, 1980; CBMS, 1983; Romberg, 1984; McKnight et al., 1987). After a fruitless search for outside agencies to underwrite the cost of developing standards, the NCTM Board of Directors in 1986 allocated the funds to develop the *Curriculum and Evaluation Standards for School Mathematics* (NCTM, 1989). They established the Commission on Standards for School Mathematics and charged it with the following two tasks (NCTM, 1989, p. 1):

1. Create a coherent vision of what it means to be mathematically literate both in a world that relies on calculators and computers to carry out mathematical procedures and in a world where mathematics is rapidly growing and is extensively being applied in diverse fields.
2. Create a set of standards to guide the revision of the school mathematics curriculum and its associated evaluation toward this vision.

Each of four Working Groups—Grades K–4, Grades 5–8, Grades 9–12, and Evaluation—consisted of a leader and five additional members. The commission and the leaders began planning during the school year of 1986–87 so that writing could begin in the summer of 1987. The Working Groups included schoolteachers, mathematics supervisors, postsecondary mathematics educators, mathematicians, and evaluators from across the United States and Canada. After two two-week writing sessions in which all members of the Working Groups were brought together away from their everyday routines, a draft was produced for reactions. The following year was alive with conversation at open sessions held at the Council's regional and national meetings and with specially designated focus groups. Written reactions were also received from individuals and groups. Historically, most of our documents had been written by appointed groups and then presented as finished products to our membership. The interactive approach used for the *Curriculum and Evaluation Standards*, although different, was ideally suited both to refining of the final document and to stimulating awareness within the community. The writers listened and responded to what they heard, and the membership and others had the opportunity to think seriously about the issues and offer their perspective for consideration. For a complete discussion of the development of this document, see McLeod et al. (1996).

As a teachers' professional organization, we understood the importance of teachers and teaching in making standards-based mathematics education a reality. If the *Curriculum and Evaluation Standards* described what should be taught, it was equally important to describe how it should be taught. An initial positive community response to the first set of standards encouraged the Council to move quickly to develop the second set, the *Professional Standards for Teaching Mathematics* (1991). A slightly different development process was used whereby lead writers were appointed who, in turn, relied on the input and reaction of a working group. Again, the entire team was small but representative of the broad community of mathematicians and teacher educators. The writing, begun in the summer of 1989, produced a draft to which reactions were solicited during the following school year. The final document was released in the early spring of 1991.

Since the success of standards-based mathematics education is crucially linked to successful student performance, the need for a third document that focused on assessment quickly arose. The Council wanted to describe *Standards*-based assessment strategies and practices that would enable teachers and others to assess students' performance. By the summer of 1993, assessment working groups had been appointed and asked to work collaboratively in a manner similar to that used with the first document. Once a draft was available, a year of review was undertaken. Using voluntary comments from more than two thousand people as well as using solicited reviews from a broad spectrum of individuals, the writers revised the document. The *Assessment Standards for School Mathematics* (1995) was published in the spring of 1995.

Main Messages of the *Standards*

The NCTM *Standards*, like the *Standards for Foreign Language Learning*, are neither detailed curriculum guides nor courses of study. They simply set goals and principles against which curricula, instruction, and assessment can be examined. They provide a vision—but not a prescription—of what students should know and be able to do, of the kind of teaching that will help students reach those goals, and of the types of assessment that teachers must use in making instructional decisions to help students reach those goals.

The three documents (NCTM, 1989, 1991, 1995) present a coherent vision of school mathematics. One of the main messages is that all students should have the opportunity to study sound mathematics that will help them become productive members of society. It has almost become a cliché that mathematics is for all students, but, as with foreign languages, this has not always been true. Instead, for centuries, mathematics was the province of the intellectual elite. Many students were relegated to studying only a tiny part of mathematics—arithmetic—and in a way that did not encourage mathematical thinking or useful applications. The *Standards* represent a significant change in our view of who deserves the opportunity to study mathematics and why they need to study it.

Another central message is that mathematics must be understood as a sense-making subject. For too long, many of our students saw mathematics as a series of rules to which only the teacher was privy: as long as they remembered the rules and followed them carefully, they would be successful. The *Standards* emphasize the need for student understanding.

Many shifts in expectations and practice are recommended in the *Standards*. The discussion in the *Assessment Standards* (1995, p. 2) summarizes the shifts in content, learning, and teaching. In content, it is a shift toward more extensive study of mathematical concepts and procedures and their uses for today. In learning, it is a shift to more active involvement of students in making sense of mathematics and being able to use this knowledge now and to learn more mathematics. In teaching, it is a shift to creating classrooms that are stimulating learning environments in which all students have the opportunity to reach their full mathematical potential. This document ends with a description of the shifts in assessment (p. 83); since they are applicable to any discipline, they are included for your consideration in the table below.

Awareness Activities

The *Curriculum and Evaluation Standards* received a great deal of attention from the Council's membership through the distribution of the draft and the special sessions scheduled at regional and national meetings in the year prior to its release. NCTM members were eager for the release of the final document. The public, however, was completely unaware of the effort, and a public-relations firm was hired to assist in the press release and initial efforts. This firm helped train Council leaders to speak about the *Standards* and develop speakers' kits for distribution to others.

At about the same time, the Mathematical Sciences Education Board (MSEB), part of the National Research Council, which is the operating arm of the National Academy of Sciences, released *Everybody Counts: A Report to the Nation on the Future of Mathematics Education* (National Research Council, 1989). This document, written for the lay public, presented an account of the weaknesses in the current system of mathematics

Table. Major Shifts in Assessment Practice	
Toward	*Away From*
Assessing students' full mathematical power	Assessing only students' knowledge of specific facts and isolated skills
Comparing students' performance with established criteria	Comparing students' performance with that of other students
Giving support to teachers and credence to their informed judgment	Designing "teacher-proof" assessment systems
Making the assessment process public, participatory, and dynamic	Making the assessment process secret, exclusive, and fixed
Giving students multiple opportunities to demonstrate their full mathematical power	Restricting students to a single way of demonstrating their mathematical knowledge
Developing a shared vision of what to assess and how to do it	Developing assessment by oneself
Using assessment results to ensure that all students have the opportunity to achieve their potential	Using assessment to filter and select students out of the opportunities to learn mathematics
Aligning assessment with curriculum and instruction	Treating assessment as independent of curriculum or instruction
Basing inferences on multiple sources of evidence	Basing inferences on restricted or single sources of evidence
Viewing students as active participants in the assessment process	Viewing students as the objects of assessment
Regarding assessment as continual and recursive	Regarding assessment as sporadic and conclusive
Holding all concerned with mathematics learning accountable for assessment results	Holding only a few accountable for assessment results
Source: *Assessment Standards for School Mathematics* (NCTM, 1995, p. 83).	

education, the reasons that mathematics education in schools and colleges must be improved, and the strengths on which the changes could be built. In particular, it called attention to the *Curriculum and Evaluation Standards* as the centerpiece for reform. This document was widely disseminated to leaders in education, science and engineering, business and industry, and public policy.

A collaborative effort of NCTM affiliates, spearheaded by the Association of State Supervisors of Mathematics and funded by the National Science Foundation, was also instrumental in spreading the message. This effort, entitled Leading Mathematics into the 21st Century, consisted of five regional conferences for teams from each congressional district within the states in the region. Conference organizers developed materials that described the central messages for different audiences, such as parents, businesses, and school boards. During the conferences, there was time for the teams to plan and to share their ideas. On returning to their states, many of the teams carried through with their plans; it was a time of much activity.

The awareness efforts have varied in intensity with each new document. After the *Professional Teaching Standards*, for example, a commercial video highlighting several main messages was produced; this footage furnished material for several infomercials for national television. Many states, through the affiliates and through the state coalitions sponsored by the MSEB, conducted their own awareness activities. These coalitions, begun in almost every state, sought to become statewide steering committees, linking school and postsecondary mathematics education as well as state and national goals.

One of the key audiences that must be addressed is parents. The MSEB cooperated with the National PTA, for example, in developing, testing, and disseminating *Math Matters: Kids Are Counting on You*. This kit of parent-tested materials was designed to be used by a school's PTA to help parents help their own children learn mathematics through simple at-home activities. The success of these kits eventually led to the demand for a Spanish-language version. MSEB also sought to engage the business and industry community in mathematics education reform by sponsoring discussions about the mathematics education needed for the workplace, both then and in the future.

In summary, efforts were made to inform the NCTM membership and the larger public through Council-sponsored activities and through the activities of other stakeholders in mathematics education. This communication must be ongoing in order to keep the messages fresh in people's minds and address any misconceptions that may arise.

Professional Development Activities

As the first document went into production, all the Council's committees and editorial panels were asked to plan activities that would provide significant professional development opportunities for a *Standards*-based mathematics education. (Because the *Standards* were such an integral part of the Council's activities, it is difficult—and probably unnecessary—to separate these efforts from other activities.) In response to the need for materials that illustrated the messages of the *Standards* in action in the classroom, for example, an extensive effort, affectionately called the Addenda project, produced a wide variety of grade-level and topic booklets with *Standards*-based classroom activities. Summer workshops built around these materials were subsidized with small grants to pay for the booklets. The resulting workshops exemplified not only the content of the *Curriculum and Evaluation Standards* but also the instructional messages of the *Professional Teaching Standards*. Similar addenda efforts are under way for the *Assessment Standards*.

Changes were also made in the NCTM-sponsored conferences: longer sessions at the regional and national conferences, "conferences within conferences" that allowed for a day of sustained attention on one topic, and special conferences were begun. Speakers were encouraged to model the teaching standards by encouraging discussion, active participation in activities, and subsequent reflection on the activities.

Although NCTM is a K–12 teacher organization, historically it was often those from the college or supervisory levels who wrote articles and spoke at meetings. With the release of the *Standards*, however, came a stronger role for teachers: more teachers became involved as speakers, writers, and leaders both in the national organization and in its local and state affiliates. This is probably one of the most powerful, but not widely recognized, forms of professional development.

The Council also sought to influence the work of others. For example, with concurrence from the National Council for Accreditation of Teacher Education (NCATE), NCTM revised the guidelines for the review of pre-service programs in colleges and universities nationwide. The Council worked with the Mathematical Association of America as it updated its guidelines for the mathematical preparation of teachers in *A Call for Change* (Leitzel, 1991) and with MSEB as it produced *Counting on You* (1991), a short document that described the kinds of support teachers need from different facets of the educational community.

NCTM also encouraged many massive professional development activities. Some of these arose at NCTM's urging; others were initiated by people inspired by the potential of the *Standards*. One of the common pleas from teachers was to see the standards in action. The Public Broadcasting Service's MATHLINE is one response to this plea. It provides an opportunity for middle school teachers to watch videos of their colleagues teaching lessons that illustrate the content of the various curriculum standards. After watching each video they have the opportunity to discuss the lesson by electronic means with other colleagues across the country. Such discussions may focus on the mathematical tasks, the pedagogy, the students' reactions, and the appropriateness of the lesson for their situation as well as on other issues of interest to the network of colleagues. The Annenberg Video Project has produced a series of videos at the grades K–4 level and is currently developing a series for high school as well as several that focus on assessment.

Connecting Activities

The MSEB's role in the whole process has been a crucial one. Formally launched in 1985 "to provide a continuing national assessment capability for mathematics education," the MSEB (1991, p.2) sought to provide:

- *leadership* of continuing efforts to improve mathematical sciences education nationally;
- *coordination* among existing mathematics education projects;
- *service* to localities and states, through assistance in determining curricular goals and higher standards for all students, and improving teacher preparation;
- *recommendations* of ways to strengthen weak parts of the infrastructure of mathematics education;
- *information* to increase public understanding of the rapidly changing missions and character of the mathematical sciences; and
- *advice* to federal, state, and local agencies on long-range goals and needs in mathematical sciences education.

Perhaps most powerful was the implied "third party endorsement" of the NCTM's vision of mathematics education by the disparate groups that the MSEB brought together. Its strategy was to form alliances between the many stakeholders in mathematics education, to provide exemplars of high-quality mathematics education that were meaningful to these groups, and to stimulate and support ongoing efforts to improve the mathematics education offered to all students. For example, presentations and exhibits were organized at annual meetings of more than thirty national associations, ranging from the National Alliance of Business to the Education Commission of the States, to the National School Boards Association, to the National Association of Elementary School Principals, to name just a few.

The NCTM, acknowledging the linkages that the MSEB was working to sustain, also realized there were other constituencies to reach. In particular, the publishers of texts and tests played a significant role. For about six years, publishers were invited to special conferences hosted by NCTM that were often jointly planned by the publishers and NCTM. This was an opportunity not only to describe the vision of the Standards but also to listen to the concerns of the publishers and through them, the opinions of many who purchase and use textbooks.

Other groups used the NCTM *Standards* as a starting point for the development of their own standards or guidelines. Many NCTM individual members were instrumental in these efforts. Sometimes the Council was asked to participate as an organization. For example, states or localities used the *Standards* to different degrees in developing their state or local frameworks. The Council jointly sponsored a conference focused on mathematics literacy for adults, out of which an organization of teachers of adults was formed and standards subsequently developed (Lindquist, 1994). The American Mathematical Association of Two-Year Colleges (AMATYC) launched its own effort to create standards for its diverse populations. Building on the NCTM's *Standards*, AMATYC is now planning a series of awareness and implementation conferences across the nation. The National Association of Educational Progress (NAEP) used the draft version of the *Curriculum and Evaluation Standards* to develop the framework for its 1990 and 1992 mathematics assessments and the published version to update the framework for its 1996 mathematics assessment.

Monitoring Activities

Recognizing the lack of information about the impact of earlier reform efforts, including those of the "new math" era, the Council sought to monitor the implementation of the *Standards*. Early in the process, several monitoring proposals were submitted for funding, unfortunately without success. The possibility that MSEB would monitor implementation was discussed at length as well. It was, however, difficult to secure funding in the magnitude required for such projects. One project (Ferrini-Mundy, in press), funded by the Exxon Education Foundation in 1992, used ethnographic research methods to study the mathematics programs of seventeen school or district sites. The results describe the change process, including the struggles, the driving forces, and the successes. Reflection on the complete set of stories is a valuable learning tool for NCTM members and for others facilitating the process of change. Part of this project also collected information about the landscape of change as well as how teachers throughout the nation perceive change. The Weiss pilot study (1992) gave some indication of teachers' awareness of the *Standards*. A follow-up study (Weiss, 1994) gave a more complete picture of the attitudes and practices of teachers.

Although many studies of reform, some centered on the efforts to reform mathematics education, have been made, no documentation or careful study of the overall impact has been done. We hope this void will be addressed soon by an impartial group. Although NCTM has the greatest need for the information, an examination by an outside group will be unbiased and most believable.

Future Activities

As we approach the twenty-first century, we recognize the rapid rate of change. For example, the power of today's technology was only dreamed of ten years ago when work began on the first volume of the *Standards*. And technological change is not likely to slow in the next ten years. Hence, the Council continues its efforts to clarify *Standards*-based mathematics education further through careful dialogue with its members, with the wider mathematics community, and with other stakeholders. We will continue to respond to the needs of our members, providing support for their positions and evidence of progress. At the same time, we have begun the process to reexamine the three *Standards* documents in view of pulling together the present documents and moving forward. The projected date for completion of the next "document" is the year 2000.

Lessons Learned: Change and Challenges

Writing the *Standards* may be the easiest step in the change process. Professional associations such as NCTM and the foreign language organizations have historically provided guidance to their members and to their professions. Implementing a standards-based education, however, requires more than guidance. The organization must become active in turning recommendations into realities. This is the challenge.

Lessons that follow are drawn from the personal experiences of the authors[2], not from a collective position of the Council. Other individuals would certainly have other perspectives. The authors acknowledge that some of these lessons are observed more in the breach than in actuality. Nonetheless, these lessons seem central to the continued progress of making educational change. They are offered here as starting points for reflection and discussion as the foreign language organizations carry forth with their own standards.

Lesson 1: Ownership and Openness

Many voices must be invited to join the chorus to ensure a rich, vibrant message. What emerges, however, must resonate with those who consider themselves responsible for the mathematics—or foreign language—education of young people. This tension—between ownership and openness—requires careful attention and nurturing.

The bold movement to produce the *Standards* breathed new life and purpose into NCTM as an organization (McLeod et al., 1996). The message of excellent mathematics education was more in the national spotlight than ever before. Nonetheless, it was a "homegrown" message that evolved from the personal experience and beliefs of many teachers. NCTM has a parent's stake in its offspring, the *Standards*, with all the predictable responsibilities, joys, and challenges of parenthood. Even as the *Standards* were put up to public scrutiny, the NCTM continued to fine-tune and explain the message.

From the beginning, a small group of members were willing to give their time to reflect carefully on the rich and varied comments made about the draft documents and to revise the documents accordingly. Members asked to be involved—very few had to be recruited—and they asked in ever increasing numbers. Similarly, the Council's Affiliated Groups expressed interest in, and enthusiasm for, participating in the standards movement. Given their close proximity to the membership, the affiliates' activities were essential to spreading the word and to sowing the seeds of change on the local level.

With many stakeholders in mathematics education, NCTM recognized early that it had to share ownership and responsibility for the *Standards* with other individuals and groups. However, it was not an easy task to bring other groups to the table; they had their own agenda and their own jargon, and mathematics was not always foremost on their minds. Nonetheless, their views, needs, and methods had to be listened to and respected. When their perspectives diverged from NCTM's, compromise became necessary.

This blend of initial ownership and subsequent openness to others requires a new way of thinking and acting as an organization. It is helpful to distinguish between negotiable and nonnegotiable positions when working with others. A remaining challenge is to listen to those who have contradictory views, even on nonnegotiable topics. Oftentimes, these views enriched our own understanding and helped point the way toward the productive exchange of ideas. This process is far from over and leads to the next lesson.

Lesson 2: Dialogue and Digestion

Ongoing dialogue with diverse groups of people is necessary to the change process, and insights from the dialogue must be considered in subsequent decision making. The discussion of discourse in the *Professional Teaching Standards* (NCTM, 1991, p. 35) is appropriate here:

The teacher of mathematics should orchestrate discourse by—

- posing questions and tasks that elicit, engage, and challenge each student's thinking;
- listening carefully to students' ideas;
- asking students to clarify and justify their ideas orally and in writing;
- deciding what to pursue in depth from among the ideas that students bring up during a discussion;
- deciding when and how to attach mathematical notation and language to students' ideas;
- deciding when to provide information, when to clarify an issue, when to model, when to lead, and when to let a student struggle with a difficulty;
- monitoring students' participation in discussions and deciding when and how to encourage each student to participate.

Except for the fifth point regarding mathematical notation, each recommendation can easily be translated into guidelines for sustaining conversations with members and with other groups. NCTM is now holding open forums to gather ideas about the current documents as we plan for the future. Although the conversation often flows freely, one of our challenges is to design questions that elicit deeper thinking about the issues.

Perhaps it goes without saying that we need to listen carefully to all ideas, but this task is a difficult one for many. We hear what we want to hear. With diverse groups, a shared vocabulary is rare. For example, parents often think of problem solving as dreaded pages of story problems from their old arithmetic books whereas teachers may be thinking of richer, deeper, and more involved problem settings. Periodically, a vocabulary check is needed to be sure that the listener is hearing the intended message.

The sixth recommendation must be considered carefully. When is it useful to provide more information or clarify an issue? We have, for example, charts in our *Curriculum and Evaluation Standards* that highlight some topics for more emphasis and some for less emphasis. All too often, *less* is interpreted as *none*. We continue to struggle to explain these charts without sounding defensive. It is hard to predict in advance where misinterpretations will arise. Certainly some of what you've written will be misinterpreted. Our advice is to address these misunderstandings directly and forthrightly.

As you gather information on your progress, you need to digest the many ideas that are forthcoming and to decide which to pursue in depth. We have found electronic means helpful in organizing and characterizing the responses. When a high percentage of respondents maintain the same viewpoint, a corresponding decision is easy to make.

One of our purposes in creating standards was to raise the level of discussion about mathematics education. Given the widely held goal of improving education, the documents have provided an excellent platform for important discussion. They have given a focus for many workshops, presentations, articles, and books. Indeed they have helped us take the necessary step of posing challenging questions.

Lesson 3: Coherence and Comprehensiveness

The standards must be coherent, and a comprehensive plan must be developed for their implementation. We realized from the beginning that more than content had to be addressed. What was to be taught, how it should be taught, and how we could measure success were all vital components. We also learned that we needed to keep the messages of reform few and simple:

- All students can learn mathematics.
- All students need to learn more mathematics.

- Reform requires national standards with local implementation.
- Learning must become more active in order to engage all students.
- Technology must be used throughout schooling whenever appropriate.

Finally, we revisited old recommendations and positions of the Council that were not consistent with our new vision for mathematics education.

Along with coherent recommendations, it is important to have a comprehensive plan of action. We cannot yet claim to have a comprehensive plan, although our efforts are ongoing. The difficulty of such planning must be both acknowledged and overcome. Any plan, of course, should be subject to midcourse adjustment but should also serve to focus and prioritize work. To be successful, a comprehensive plan must be developed with the needs of change agents clearly in mind as well.

One aspect of the comprehensive plan should center on professional development for K–12 teachers and administrators and also for college instructors. The mathematics community has been fortunate to have support through both the Eisenhower Education Act and the National Science Foundation. The Eisenhower money has been used to offer opportunities for focused professional development to teachers both in institutions of higher education and in schools. The National Science Foundation supports longer-term projects in both curriculum and professional development. On the whole, we have had a positive impact on individual teachers and on some school systems but have yet to see major accomplishment in a large system.

It is important that professional development target the initial preparation of teachers as well as their continuing growth. Whenever possible, more than one teacher in a school should receive professional development. Sustaining new ideas is easier when others are implementing similar ideas in the same setting.

Lesson 4: Partners and Professional Help

Partners and professional help are essential ingredients to realize the vision of the *Standards*. We, as you, were fortunate to have many partners in the process. There is no doubt that our own affiliates are our most powerful partners; do not neglect the state and local groups in your discipline. The collegiate mathematicians have also been essential to our progress; we value their participation and are still learning to build the needed respect and the communication channels that will support continued growth. We have spoken of the leading role that MSEB had in paving the way for the *Standards* and for connecting with administrators, business leaders, and others.

Acknowledging the need for partners is only the first step. We still have a long way to go to learn how to collaborate. Moreover, we need to forge stronger ties with two groups, parents and the general public. Although many members have produced isolated activities for parents, NCTM has not provided a sustained program to reach parents with information about a mathematics education different from the one they experienced. Yet, we need the support of parents in changing mathematics education, and we have to go more than halfway in the process. Likewise, we need to reach the general public. In setting the need for standards, *Everybody Counts* (National Research Council 1989, p. 80) enumerates what effective change requires of the public:

- Conviction of the need for change
- Consensus on high-quality mathematics education for everyone
- Skepticism of "quick fixes" and simplistic solutions
- Awareness of the general nature of needed changes
- Support for investment of the necessary resources
- Recognition of the need for continuing leadership at the national level

Since few of these points are discipline-specific, all the professional organizations should work together to convince the public of the need of higher educational standards.

One aspect of this lesson is that partners we had never thought of before appeared with interest in, and enthusiasm for, our message. We had little experience in working simultaneously with diverse organizations. Another challenge was the many individuals and groups who sought the Council's imprimatur on proposals and its advice on oversight committees. Look for these new partners, and be ready to adjust your policies while protecting the integrity of your organization.

We have learned that we need more professional help in this complex endeavor. For example, we need public relations advice and expertise, we need training on public presentations, and we need more technological assistance. Professional help can be expensive and must be used judiciously, but resistance to its use can be costly, since progress is slowed. A new vocabulary is often needed when outside expertise is brought to the table, although the accuracy and appropriateness of the message remains with the professional organization. New methods of delivering the message and identifying new audiences for it are often enhanced by professional help.

Lesson 5: Assessing and Adjusting

Throughout the process, there is a need to assess the status and adjust the course of action to fit the changing times. The comprehensive plan for implementation called for in Lesson 3 must include ways to assess progress and changes in the educational climate. This assessment, as described in the section on monitoring activities, has been one of our greatest challenges. Without convincing, widespread evidence, our critics find us fair game. Moreover, it is difficult to reflect on progress and make the needed midcourse corrections when one does not have the necessary information. In fairness, we note that it is not only expensive to gather this information but also difficult to define what information is needed.

In retrospect, we had the advantage of beginning in a gentler time, a time when no one much cared about standards. This has changed radically, as you well know, which is both an advantage and a disadvantage. You have not had to fight to gain credibility for the very notion of standards, you have had the work of many other disciplines as models, and you have managed to avoid some of the public brouhaha other disciplines have encountered. But you also have to fight to capture the public's interest and imagination.

The tensions in today's political climate surrounding the reform movement should cause all of us to examine the role of professional leadership.[3] This is not the time to retreat, but the time to build greater understanding of our knowledge and beliefs about our disciplines. If we learn Lesson 2 well, we will be able to help build this public understanding.

In mathematics, we are struggling with the tension of balancing a need for dynamic, changing standards with the practical needs of those in the process of change. Our *Standards* were never meant to be carved in stone but instead were documents that would stimulate discussion and spur new professional decisions. Standards must be vibrant enough to sustain change as more is learned and as the needs of students, society, and the discipline change. Yet, a moving target is a hard aim. There is a need to support those in the process of change by not moving too far ahead of the educational system.

By the time this book is published, the first results of the Third International Mathematics and Science Study (TIMSS) will have been released. This complex study will give us much information about other countries in terms of the context of schooling, curricula, instruction, and teachers' beliefs, knowledge, and working conditions. It will also give achievement results of the almost fifty countries involved. It will provide a rich source of information on which to make professional decisions and should influence, as the second study did, the *Standards*. It also can and should influence policy decisions, but the profession needs to help interpret and direct those decisions. Too often they have been made on achievement results only. If the standards-based movement has accomplished anything, it has reminded all of us that educational change in a democratic society is a complex challenge that requires leadership and persistence. We will need to adjust our plans to take into account both what we learn from this study and the political fallout that may follow.

Technology is having a profound effect on mathematics education: it enables the study of some mathematics heretofore unattainable at the K–12 level; it makes some mathematical learning obsolete and other learning more important. For example, an ordinary calculator performs long division quickly and accurately. The complementary skill of doing complicated division computations by hand is no longer needed in today's world. What is needed is the ability to estimate answers to such problems and a greater facility with magnitudes of answers. As before, students need a conceptual understanding of division to help them know when to use it appropriately, and they need to be able to do straightforward division by hand.

As in your discipline, research and practical experience help us understand how students learn mathematics and how teachers can help support this learning. The growth in knowledge should also motivate us to consider carefully the recommendations of the past. Education—like many vast enterprises—has the tendency to fluctuate between competing pedagogical recommendations. In our zeal for reform, we often neglect successful practices of the past. For example, the need for students to know basic facts automatically is often neglected in our zeal to build understanding and power with numbers. This is often interpreted as ignoring basic skills. Since that is not our intent, we need to adjust our message.

Central to all these lessons is the need to remember why we, the mathematics and foreign language professions, are committed to this process of change. We are teachers who have as our mission the students we serve; we want the best education for these students that we can provide. This holds for each of our students in each of our classrooms and collectively for all students worldwide.

We are ourselves learners with a thirst to keep learning. We recognize that we have much to learn about mathematics, about learning, about teaching, and about change. We know that many of our practices are ones that have served us well, yet we yearn for more effective ways to meet the changing needs of our students and our discipline. We know that we can learn from the many excellent teachers in our schools and colleges, from the growing knowledge base, and from our own reflections about our successes and our failures.

We are professionals who are willing to take the risks and responsibilities associated with educational change because we are teachers. We chose this profession to fulfill our desire to work with students, to help them change, and to grow intellectually. We chose this profession for the opportunity to continue to change, to continue to grow in our knowledge of our subject specialties. We each approach these opportunities in our own way, and yet with common goals we can progress together. Standards provide this common bonding for many; our challenge is to continue to question, to learn, and to expand our views of a standards-based education.

When young children learn to walk, the first step is a momentous occasion. You should be proud of your efforts in taking that first step, the development of your standards. Our closing advice is to plan a path that you will follow both as individuals and as organizations. Stop and take stock of the progress you are making and be ready to take side trips and modify your routes. Keep the vision in mind, but remember that it will grow and change as you make your journey.

Notes

[1] *Standards* will be used to refer to all three documents: *Curriculum and Evaluation Standards for School Mathematics* (1989), *Professional Standards for Teaching Mathematics* (1991), and *Assessment Standards for School Mathematics* (1995).

[2] Lindquist served on the NCTM Board at the time of the approval of the *Standards* projects, was a member of the K–4 writing group of the *Curriculum and Evaluation Standards*, served on the Standards Coordinating Committee, was president of NCTM during the development of the *Assessment Standards*, and is presently chair of the Commission on the Future of the Standards. Rosen was on the staff of the Mathematical Sciences Education Board during the development of all the *Standards*, ending her term there as associate executive director. She had staff responsibility for most of MSEB's publications, especially *Reshaping School Mathematics, Counting on You, Measuring Up*, and *Measuring What Counts*—documents integrally liked to the three Standards documents. She is now the executive director of NCTM.

[3] The authors would like to acknowledge Michael Kirst and Robin Bird for describing these tensions in a draft document.

References

Conference Board of the Mathematical Sciences. (1983). The mathematical sciences curriculum K–12: What is still fundamental and what is not. In *Educating Americans for the 21st century: Source materials* (pp. 1–23). National Science Board, Commission on Precollege Education in Mathematics, Science, and Technology. Washington, DC: National Science Foundation.

Ferrini-Mundy, J. (Ed.). (in press). *The recognizing and recording reform in mathematics education project. Journal for Research in Mathematics Education* Monograph Series, Number 8. Reston, VA: National Council of Teachers of Mathematics.

Leitzel, J. R. C. (Ed.). (1991). *A call for change: Recommendations for the mathematical preparation of teachers of mathematics.* Washington, DC: Mathematical Association of America.

Lindquist, M. M. (1994). Lessons learned? In I. Gal & M. J. Schmitt (Eds.), *Proceedings: Conference on adult mathematical literacy* (pp. 9–197). Philadelphia: National Center on Adult Literacy, University of Pennsylvania.

McKnight, C. C., Crosswhite, F. J., Dossey, J. A., Kifer, E., Swafford, J. O., Travers, K. J., & Cooney, T. J. (1987). *The underachieving curriculum: Assessing U.S. school mathematics from an international perspective.* Champaign, IL: Stipes Publishing.

Mathematical Sciences Education Board. (1991). *Mathematical Sciences Education Board strategic plan.* Washington, DC: Author.

McLeod, D. B., Stake, R. E., Schappelle, B., Mellissinos, M., & Gierl, M. J. (1996). Setting the standards: NCTM's role in the reform of mathematics education. In S. A. Raizen & E. D. Britton (Eds.), *Bold ventures: U.S. innovations in science and mathematics education: Vol. 3. Cases in mathematics education.* Dordrecht, Netherlands: Kluwer.

National Commission on Excellence in Education. (1983). *A nation at risk: The imperative for educational reform.* Washington, DC: U.S. Government Printing Office.

National Council of Teachers of Mathematics. (1980). *An agenda for action: Recommendations for school mathematics of the 1980s.* Reston, VA: Author.

National Council of Teachers of Mathematics. (1989). *Curriculum and evaluation standards for school mathematics.* Reston, VA: Author.

National Council of Teachers of Mathematics. (1991). *Professional standards for teaching mathematics.* Reston, VA: Author.

National Council of Teachers of Mathematics. (1995). *Assessment standards for school mathematics.* Reston, VA: Author.

National Research Council, Mathematical Sciences Education Board. (1991). *Counting on you: Actions supporting mathematics teaching standards.* Washington, DC: National Academy Press.

National Research Council, Mathematical Sciences Education Board. (1989). *Everybody counts: A report to the nation on the future of mathematics education.* Washington, DC: National Academy Press.

National Science Foundation. (1979). *What are the needs in precollege science, mathematics, and social science?: Views from the field.* Washington, DC: Author.

National Standards for Foreign Language Education Project. (1996). *Standards for foreign language learning: Preparing for the 21st century.* Yonkers, NY: Author.

Romberg, T. A. (1984). School mathematics: Options for the 1990s. Washington, DC: U.S. Department of Education.

Weiss, I. (1992). *The road to reform in mathematics education: How far have we traveled?* (Pilot study) Reston, VA: National Council of Teachers of Mathematics.

Weiss, I. (1994). *A profile of science and mathematics education in the United States, 1993.* Chapel Hill, NC: Horizon Research, Inc.

The Teacher's Voice: A View from a National Standards Pilot Site

Kathleen M. Riordan

Rita A. Oleksak

Springfield Public Schools, Massachusetts

One might well ask how serving as pilot site teachers for the National Standards in Foreign Language Education project did anything but complicate further the lives of teachers in the classrooms of Springfield, Massachusetts. Certainly, the pilot site activity was work added to already busy schedules, but it was work that caused us to make time for reflection on our teaching.

Even in the formative stage of drafting standards for foreign language learning, the Task Force charged with creating the standards knew that it had to follow a path consistent with the advice given in the opening chapter of this volume by our colleagues in mathematics: "Many voices must be invited to join the chorus to ensure a rich, vibrant message. What emerges … must resonate with those who consider themselves responsible for mathematics—or foreign language—education of young people" (Lindquist and Rosen, p. 12). As the first drafts of the foreign language standards were emerging, the desirability of involving classroom teachers in a focused feedback situation became clear. The term "pilot site" was used to designate the school districts whose teachers were called upon to reflect upon the standards in their draft forms and to provide feedback to the Task Force.

Pilot Site Selection Process

Six pilot sites were selected from among eighty applicant schools or districts. The Standards project directors sought sites which would represent the diversity of American K–12 education and foreign language programs in the United States. Consideration was given to geography, size, and district support structure. One site offered only a single language in grades 8–12; other sites offered multiple languages at many grade levels. One site involved a single school while others involved a large number of schools in a mid-sized or large urban center. In addition to national geographic distribution, teacher and student diversity was also a factor. The goal was to have, among the six sites, as broad a representation as possible of American K–12 education. The Task Force anticipated that it would be valuable to engage practicing classroom teachers in the formative development of standards in order to gauge the clarity, the focus, and the challenge inherent in this professional enterprise.

Each pilot site was matched with one or two members of the National Standards Task Force. The Task Force members worked with the site teachers and served as the liaisons to the full Task Force regarding feedback from the pilot sites. The Task Force members scheduled visits to each site to present workshop sessions where teachers learned more about the development of the Standards, the content of the draft document, and the expectations of the pilot site teachers. Each site named a coordinator to organize the work at the local level. Each site also identified specific aspects of the Standards project for input. For example, the Edmonds School District (Lynnwood, WA) was in the midst of district-wide reforms in assessment; foreign language teachers in one school there wanted to study how the new oral testing procedures matched with the draft Standards. Sites designed a variety of report forms and procedures to capture particular information regarding local activities in standard terms. These forms provided sites with an organizing process for the written feedback which the Task Force members had requested. This written information helped teachers focus on actual lessons and reflect on the question: "What is it that I want my students *to know and be able to do* with the target language?"[1] The goal for pilot sites was to establish two-way communication for teacher input and discussion at a local level as well as feedback to and from the Task Force and among pilot sites. (For further background on the role of the pilot sites, see Phillips, 1996.)

The Springfield, Massachusetts, Pilot Site

Demographics

Springfield offered a site in an urban setting, with a racially and economically diverse student population and a large language program. Springfield is a mid-sized urban center in western Massachusetts. The Springfield Public Schools serve 23,535 students of diverse racial, ethnic, linguistic, and socioeconomic backgrounds. The student population is approximately one third Spanish surnamed, one third African-American, and one-third White. Almost 70% of the students qualify for free or reduced cost school lunches. Transitional and Two-Way Bilingual Education programs are offered in Spanish and Russian. Transitional Bilingual Education programs are offered in Haitian Creole and in Vietnamese. The school system is intensively engaged in many aspects of education reform including curriculum development and assessment and school governance. The school system currently offers a long and strong foreign language program and has begun to implement a K–12 program for all students. Multi-year language offerings are available in Chinese, French, German, Italian, Latin, Russian, Spanish, as well as special elective courses for native speakers of Spanish. Advanced Placement courses are also offered in French and in Spanish. The foreign language teachers participate actively in generic and foreign-language-specific, district-wide, professional-development workshops on topics such as inclusive teaching practices, activity-based teaching, cooperative learning structures, proficiency-based teaching, performance-based instruction and assessment, and the integration of technology into foreign language instruction.

The national effort was a perfect complement to state and local work already in progress. Springfield teachers were already reviewing the draft documents of the Massachusetts World Languages Curriculum Frameworks. As part of the district's work in instruction and assessment, foreign language teachers were in the third year of a five-year project to develop district wide learning outcomes and assessments for all courses, grades, and students. Springfield's foreign language teachers would now be engaged professionally not only on a local and state level, but on a national level as well.

Teacher Participants

In Springfield, thirty-eight of the sixty-five foreign language teachers volunteered to participate in the Standards pilot. They represented grades K–12 in Chinese, French, and Spanish. Some teachers were fairly new to the profession, while others were experienced language teachers. Springfield teachers were able to document their classroom research work for consideration as part of their professional portfolio towards Massachusetts teacher recertification.

The Project Focus

The Springfield pilot site focused on writing learning scenarios that linked current classroom instructional practices to the goal areas that organized the Standards.

"Learning scenarios" under different labels (e.g., classroom vignettes) have appeared in most of the disciplinary standards publications. In the initial drafts, the Task Force had provided some of these glimpses into classrooms. Even though the activities described had been drawn from actual classroom observations, reviewers found them to be less than credible. Consequently, it was hoped that teachers in pilot sites, after having been part of intensive discussion of the standards, would be able to design, teach, and describe classroom activities or units that targeted specific standards. Chamot (1994) recommends keeping a journal as a good way to capture ideas and reflections on teaching and learning that might otherwise be forgotten. Reflecting on a variety of classroom activities and referring back to the journal, or teaching moment log (TML) as we called it in Springfield, provided a way in which classroom teachers could discover a particular area or topic which peaked their curiosity for further investigation about the Standards as reflected in their teaching. The TML is not only a way to record ideas and impressions, but it is also helpful in exploring ideas and developing insights through the writing process (Chamot, 1994, p.1). For Springfield, the TML served as the vehicle through which our teachers explored further the classroom implications from which the learning scenarios were drawn. For example, comments from a middle school teacher's teaching moment log reflected the opportunity for greater *interdisciplinary collaboration* around the theme of the "Day of the Dead." While the actual activity took place within the Spanish classroom, student interest motivated the teacher to think in a more interdisciplinary way. The TML indicates he or she may collaborate with art or social studies teachers the next time. Another pilot site teacher shared her impressions when working with a classroom visitor whose meaningful speech highlighted the possibilities that exist when the participants are able to identify with the information presented. In this case, the teacher reflected upon how students learned content, i.e., about Togo, its history and status today and how they related to this French-speaking person from a distant country. (The learning scenario from this class can be found in *National Standards*, 1996, p. 79.)

The classroom forms which we used to record specific information about individual lessons, and the Teaching Moment Log, which was used to reflect on the lesson just completed, gave us a focused and systematic way to provide deeper insights into the curricular content and classroom interactions. The forms used to record detailed classroom information were closely aligned with major focuses of the draft Standards. One form required teachers to identify a *goal area* and *standard* from the draft. They then designed a *progress indicator* to mark student performances indicative of the targeted standard. The next stage was to describe the classroom activity and assessment, if applicable. Since a content standard for Goals 2000 purposes is defined as "What students should know and be able to do," one might call this form a record of the "doing" in a content standard. The second form concentrated on identifying the "knowing," that is, it took four elements of the *curricular weave* in the Standards (*National Standards*, 1996, p. 29) namely the language system, culture, communication strategies, learning strategies. (See the Appendix for copies of these forms and the Teaching Moment Log.)

As a pilot site we were careful to explain our work and share information with parents and guardians through letters and classroom discussion. The students were cooperative and shared our belief about the importance of this project. Students felt empowered as we told them that their involvement in this process would make a difference in foreign language education. Teachers also gave students an opportunity to process and reflect on their work and drew on student insights as part of their own reflections.

Findings from the Field

The goal of the pilot site component of the work was to field test the standards in real classrooms, with real teachers, and with real students.

Input at this developmental stage of the standards work was very empowering for the teacher participants in Springfield as at other sites. Teachers and students tested the standards, goals, and progress indicators in day-to-day classroom life. The written feedback included comments on the text of the draft document as well as suggestions for possible progress indicators and scenarios. Springfield teachers were very pleased that some Springfield site work was reflected in the *Standards* (1996) publication. While the National Standards Task Force members valued and validated the professional expertise and classroom experience of the site teachers, the former group strove to go beyond present practice to develop challenging standards for the next century. The combination of today's reality and a vision for tomorrow combined to strengthen the final document.

What did we discover as we worked for several months as pilot site researchers for the National Standards project? We verified that we do deliver and can describe classroom instruction and classroom scenarios where the teaching of culture is woven into language instruction. Our reflections helped us see how we could improve instruction, revise curriculum, and aim higher in terms of goals. We successfully wrote up classroom scenarios that are presented in the *Standards* document (e.g., pp. 79, 85). This was good news for our pilot teachers. The classroom data supported not only our initial instincts, but also the professional literature that shows the importance of meaningful materials and communicative practices. We found that the use of the classroom reporting forms and the Teaching Moment Logs (TML) helped us pause to reflect on our classroom teaching. This process also helped Springfield teachers to determine if we were, in fact, providing a balanced program for our students of Communication, Cultures, Connections, Comparisons, and Communities, the five broad goal areas defined in the *Standards* document. As teaching professionals, we rarely find this objective and non-judgmental commentary on our work. The descriptive data provided us with evidence and feedback on our district curriculum and our state frameworks. We also felt that this contribution to the National Standards was very important to our professional growth and program improvement.

Below we have included some of the pilot teachers' original comments as they reflected on classroom scenarios through the teaching moment log. The teachers briefly described classroom activities along with their reactions as its effectiveness (See the TML form in the Appendix). For example, several teachers had focused classroom lessons on grammar points rather than on topics themselves with grammar as part of the curricular weave, the support system. One teacher's reaction and reflection demonstrated that he or she was beginning to sense the necessity of changing from focus on form to focus on meaning:

> **Context:** Elementary school lesson on *-ar* verbs in Spanish
>
> **Description of the activity:** "I introduced a group of -ar verbs. I had them written in Spanish and English on the board. I introduced each one by acting the verb out and then saying it in Spanish. ..."
>
> **Reaction — How it went:** "This was a great class! Everyone participated. Everyone enjoyed it."
>
> **What I learned:** "I thought, wow, this is great! They learned some verbs. However, when I tested them the next day, nobody could remember a single verb!!"
>
> **Other comments:** Elementary students learn quickly but there needs to be much repetition, and many opportunities must be given in different ways for the language to be acquired in the classroom.

This TML allows us to see how a teacher's initial response becomes more tentative as assessment of the learners fails to support the original assumptions. The teacher's comments also pinpoint areas for future professional development. Is more repetition the answer? Or should teachers in the district be investigating alternative classroom approaches such as the PACE whole language model discussed by Adair-Hauck and Cumo-Johannsen (this volume)?

A ninth-grade Level II Spanish teacher had students conduct videotaped interviews with one another. The task was to learn about their partner's elementary school and early childhood experiences, a task that the teacher hoped would provide meaningful practice with the imperfect tense:

> **Reaction — How it went:** "Well, they were thrilled to interview each other and report to the class on what they had learned."
>
> **What I learned**: "Students really like to 'take over' the situation and 'run the show.' They grasped the value of the *imperfecto* best here. I should have done the interviewing earlier in the unit."
>
> **Other comments**: "Many students were strangers to each other in this diverse class. Building respect for other was a prime goal from day one! It took a while for them to become comfortable with each other ..."

These students, by focusing on a real life communicative task acquired facility with a verb tense, but more importantly they actually worked toward the *Interpersonal Standard* in terms of sociolinguistic and linguistic power. The teacher was also realizing the goal of reaching all students.

Teachers' comments reflected the importance of organization and provisioning in the classroom, the need to recycle and spiral information throughout the curriculum at all levels, and the value of authentic materials in the classroom. Teachers' comments also revealed the need for professionals to recognize the importance of cooperative learning, TPR, and shared decision making in the classroom.

Springfield: One Year Later

Reflections on the National Standards Pilot Site Process

Springfield's pilot site teachers were asked to reflect on the pilot site experience one year after the intensive work. Teachers responded in narrative form to several questions about the impact of the pilot site work in their practice.

When asked about what they learned about *language teaching*, because of their involvement in the project, teachers shared some varied insights. Their thoughts included:

- The clearer my focus, the more reachable is the students' goal. Clarify, clarify, clarify, and then realize that some days have more peaks in them and other days, more valleys. Whimsically, so little is linear anymore.
- I must keep an open mind to change.
- Foreign language curriculum must be connected to other subject areas and, at the same time, student centered.
- Interdisciplinary cooperation helps students realize that everything they are learning is relative and connected in order for meaningful application in many aspects of their lives.
- Colleagues are interested in what happens in the classrooms of others—more than I had thought.
- The information which we provided is significant because it is the result of real educators' experiences in contemporary classrooms; it is not just theoretical.

Teacher researchers felt that they grew as *language teachers* as a result of their involvement in this work. Teacher comments were varied and insightful.

- Language teachers need more reflection time in their day. A risk-taking skill needs to be fostered in me as I work with other disciplines, like theatre. It sounds easy enough.
- Language teachers need to learn to be risk takers.
- I need to provide students with genuine feedback and support at the same time.
- I must learn more about using technology effectively.
- I saw *again* the importance of interdisciplinary learning.
- It takes more planning and energy to implement the National Standards.
- It's fine to have opposing ideas about teaching. It's expected that teachers should voice opposing views … to each other, to administrators, to national leaders. Teachers provide the 'reality check' inherent in this whole process.

Did the involvement of Springfield's teachers and students in this pilot site work *change foreign language instruction* in the Springfield Public Schools? The answer from the teachers is a resounding "absolutely"! They saw the need to use technology as an instructional tool. Several teachers now include content readings more often. Classes are more active, more vibrant, and noisier. Good noise, of course! Teachers are more open to trying new techniques and less afraid of failure.

Springfield teachers also shared thoughts about the *significance of their involvement* in this national level work. They appreciated learning about the excellent work being done in the classrooms of colleagues. They felt that the collegial and professional interaction provided by the project kept their spirits alive, fresh, renewed, recharged, and refocused. One teacher shared that she is "more convinced than ever that *all* children can be successful in a foreign language class."

Conclusion

The pilot site work offered the foreign language teachers in Springfield, Massachusetts, the opportunity to grow and be challenged as professionals. Additionally, they contributed to a national effort which will influence foreign language education into the distant future. The contribution occurred within a collaborative, collegial, supportive environment of professional growth. Participants felt that their professional contribution had made a difference. Isn't this a true reward for a professional?

Note

[1]This question is derived from the definition of a content standard as specified in Goals 2000 projects. A *content standard* answers the question: What should students know and be able to do? A *performance standard* answers the question: How good is good enough? The National Standards in Foreign Language Education Project was charged with determining content standards.

References

Chamot, A. U. (1994) The teacher's voice: Action research in your classroom. *FLES News, 8,* (1) 1, 6–8.

National Standards in Foreign Language Education Project. (1996). *Standards for foreign language learning: Preparing for the 21st century.* Yonkers, NY: Author.

Phillips, J. K. (1996). Pilot sites help chart the national foreign language standards. *ERIC/CLL News Bulletin, 19* (2), pp. 1, 6–7.

Appendix

Teacher's Name _____ School _____

National Standards Project

Goal _____ Title _____

Standard _____

Language _____
Level _____
Grade _____
How Long _____

Progress Indicators (Function)	Classroom Learning Scenarios Describe in Detail (Attachments & Samples)	Assessment (Attachments & Samples)

Teacher's Name _____ School _____

National Standards Project

Goal _____ Title _____

Standard _____

Students Need to Know (not all 4 columns have to be filled in)

Language System	Culture	Communication Strategies	Learning Strategies

Springfield Massachusetts Public Schools

National Standards in Foreign Language Education Pilot Site

Teaching Moment Log

Teacher _____   School _____

Language _____   Level _____   Grade _____

Date _____

Description of Activity — What I Did:

Reaction — How It Went:

What I Learned:

Other Comments:

Reflections on National Standards

Pilot Site Process

One Year Later

Please share your thoughts about the following issues in a way that seems best to you.

1. What did you learn about *language teaching* as a result of involvement in this project?

2. What did you learn about *being a language teacher* as a result of your involvement in this project?

3. How are your language classes *different* now as a result of your involvement in this work? Please be specific in your comments.

4. What was the most significant aspect of your involvement in this project?

Name (optional) _____

Teaching Grade Level _____

Communication Goal: Meaning Making through a Whole Language Approach

Bonnie Adair-Hauck

University of Pittsburgh

Philomena Cumo-Johanssen

Carlynton School District, Pennsylvania

Where before there was a spectator, let there now be a participant.

Jerome Bruner, *Child's Talk: Learning to Use Language* (1983, p. 60)

A s we move toward the challenges of a globally-oriented 21st century, educators, school administrators, business leaders, and parents realize the critical need to prepare our students to be able to communicate in the international arena. The word "communicate" is a powerful term, one used widely in the *Standards for Foreign Language Learning: Preparing for the 21st Century* (1996); thus, it is worth reflecting on its meaning. Since the majority of our students will not be working in the specialized field of linguistics, one might choose a definition that would be relevant for the everyday layperson. Webster defines "communication" as: (1) the giving or exchanging of information or messages by talk, gestures, or writing; (2) the art of expressing ideas or feelings in speech or writing; (3) the developing of a close, sympathetic relationship. Clearly, in the past, a traditional language classroom with its emphasis on grammatical competence, did not afford learners the opportunity "to communicate" in Webster's sense of the term. Unfortunately, many of these students who had spent years learning the formal properties of the language (sound system, verb conjugations, rules of syntax, vocabulary lists, etc.) could not, in the end, exchange information, express ideas or feelings, or develop and nurture a sympathetic relationship in their second language. In other words, they could not communicate on an *interpersonal level.*

Like Webster, Cooper (1993) succinctly underscores the interpersonal nature and the universal implications of the term communication, when he states: "It is through *communication* that we are able to improve our world, to prosper and to enjoy it (p. 43)." *The Standards for Foreign Language Learning* (1996) emphasize that "communication" is at the heart of second language learning. Communicating interpersonally in Webster's or Cooper's sense of the word involves more than Chomsky's (1965) notion of linguistic or grammatical competence. Therefore, second language researchers and practitioners now espouse a much broader understanding of communicative competence which includes not only grammatical, but also sociolinguistic competence (the ability to adjust one's meaning or intention according to the situation, task or role of the participants); discourse competence (the ability to organize and combine utterances so that there is cohesion and coherence); and strategic competence (the ability to avoid a breakdown in communication by using both verbal and nonverbal strategies, such as paraphrasing, circumlocution, slower rate of speech, gestures, etc. (Canale and Swain, 1980; Canale, 1983). In lay terms, the *Standards* (1996) capture the notion of communicative competence by stressing the need to *"know how, when, and why to say what to whom"* (p.11).

The pioneering work of numerous second language researchers and practitioners has contributed to a more comprehensive understanding of the variables that influence a learner's ability to communicate in a second language. Second language classrooms that engender interpersonal communication afford students the opportunity to:

1. listen to and understand personally relevant and useful speech (Krashen and Terrell, 1983; Scarcella and Oxford, 1992);
2. read, listen, and transact with authentic texts (Glisan, 1988, Joiner, 1986; Swaffar, Arens, and Byrnes, 1991);
3. interact with the teacher and with their peers through collaborative, problem-solving activities (Long and Porter, 1985; Cohen, 1986; Pica and Doughty, 1985);

4. construct their own personal meanings and convey these personal meanings in authentic language learning experiences (Rigg and Allen, 1989; Goodman and Goodman, 1990);
5. feel safe to take risks, make approximations, make mistakes, and learn from their mistakes (Selinker, 1972; Dulay, Burt, and Krashen, 1982);
6. hypothesize about the grammar or systematicity of L2 with the assistance of the teacher (Schmidt, 1990; Long, 1991; Donato and Adair-Hauck, 1992);
7. interact with activities that connect language learning and culture (Seelye, 1994; Au, 1993);
8. learn and try to use various language learner strategies (Oxford, 1990; O'Malley and Chamot, 1990);
9. convey their ideas and feelings and share their personal histories through writing activities (Barnett, 1989; Kroll, 1990; Scott, 1992);
10. participate in activities that develop their awareness of the interconnectedness and interdependence of a community of language learners (Little and Sanders, 1989; Young, 1991; Moffit, 1996).

As exemplified in this list, *interpersonal* communication is dependent on one's ability to interpret the message heard or read and should help to develop one's ability to *present*, or express, ideas and opinions. Indeed, the communication goal, as defined in the *National Standards* (1996), is undergirded by three modes of communication: Interpersonal, Interpretive, Presentational.

Nevertheless, even those teachers committed to providing communicative and interactive language learning experiences for their students, find it a challenge to integrate grammar into their classrooms. The *Standards* stress that knowledge of the language system including grammar, emerging vocabulary, phonology, pragmatic and discourse features undergirds the *accuracy of communication*. Researchers agree that grammar or focus on form (Long, 1991) can be beneficial to second language learners for it raises the learners' consciousness concerning the differences and similarities of L1 and L2 (Rutherford and Sharwood Smith, 1988; Lightbown and Spada, 1990; Herron and Tomasello, 1992). In this respect, grammar instruction can be used as a "linguistic map" with reference points or "rules of thumb" to assist students as they explore the "topography" of the language. One needs to remember, however, that grammatical structures by themselves are rather useless. Like road signs, grammatical structures take on meaning only if they are situated in context and in connected discourse. Krashen (1982) reminds us that grammatical structures will become internalized only if the learners are placed in a situation in which *they need to use the structures for communicative purposes.* Consequently, an important role of the teacher concerning grammar instruction is to create learning situations in which the students feel a need to exploit the grammar for comprehension and communication in the target language.

Although many professionals agree on the benefits of grammar instruction, *how* to teach grammar has met with little agreement (Hammerly, 1975; McLaughlin, 1978; Omaggio, 1986; Krashen, 1985; Scott, 1989; Schaffer, 1989). In particular, the field has been divided between two opposing views: an explicit approach (Rivers, 1983; Higgs and Clifford, 1982), which advocates direct teacher explanations followed by manipulative exercises; or an implicit approach (Dulay and Burt, 1973; Terrell, 1977; and Krashen, 1985) which theorizes that with sufficient comprehensible input, learners can hypothesize and generalize about target forms on their own. (For a more thorough discussion of the explicit/implicit dichotomy, see Donato and Adair-Hauck, 1992.)

Both the explicit and implicit approaches share some notable deficiencies. Neither approach acknowledges the role of the teacher in negotiating classroom explanations; neither approach acknowledges the contributions and backgrounds that the learner brings to the classroom setting (Tharp and Gallimore, 1988; Donato and Adair-Hauck, 1992; Adair-Hauck, Donato, and Cumo, 1994). Considering these shortcomings, Donato and Adair-Hauck (1994) have proposed an alternative paradigm, called PACE, for reframing the teaching of grammar in a second language classroom. The PACE model is grounded in both Vygotskian cognitive psychology and whole language teaching. Before discussing how the PACE model can be implemented into a communicative classroom, some basic tenets of Vygotskian psychology and whole language teaching need to be addressed.

The Need to Explore Other Cognitive and Psychological Models for Guidance

Dissatisfied with the traditional lecture, teacher-directed or "recitation script" (Tharp and Gallimore's term, 1988) to learning, many cognitive and developmental psychologists are turning to the work of Vygotsky, who had the foresight to recognize that the development of consciousness is the result of prior social interaction.[1] According to Vygotsky (1978), psychological processes, such as perception, attention, and voluntary memory, which are critical components of the learning process, result from *communication* and *social interaction* with adults or more capable peers. Unlike many of his predecessors, Vygotsky emphasized the importance of *discursive interaction*. Vygotsky was less concerned about language systems per se, and more interested in how language systems are utilized in social interaction and individual cognitive functioning. In a natural setting, a child or learner develops cognitively and linguistically, by observing, participating, or interacting with adults or skilled peers in society. Through dialogue and guided participation (Rogoff's term, 1990) in whole tasks (e.g., baking a cake, packing a lunch, doing a puzzle), the adult or expert challenges, supports, and finally empowers the learner or novice to solve the task on his/her own. The expert must be sensitive to include the learner step by step in the process; all the while the expert constantly probes the learner's level of consciousness for a slightly higher challenge. Vygotsky (1978, p.86) has termed this plane the zone of proximal development (ZPD), which he defines as "the distance between the *actual developmental level* as determined by independent problem solving and the level of *potential development* as determined through problem solving under adult guidance or in collaboration with more capable peers" (emphasis added).

Vygotsky's notion of semiotic mediation serves as a tool for both the expert and the novice for co-constructing meaning in the ZPD. Through the discourse of the expert, the novice comes to share the expert's definition of the situation, because the novice is afforded the opportunity to carry out the task in the ZPD through *other-regulation* (Wertsch, 1979). As the novice's understanding of the situation changes, his or her role within the ZPD changes moving from other-regulation to *self-regulation*, or moving from the *interpersonal plane* to the *intrapersonal plane*.

Discourse, or how we as human beings use speech to communicate and interact on an interpersonal level, plays a critical role in everyday joint problem-solving or guided participation (Bakhtin, 1986; Rogoff, 1990). To illustrate this point, let's look at some discourse of an adult and child interacting through guided participation. The following protocol occurred when one of the author's sons, Spencer, took his first skiing lesson at the age of four. Anna, the expert ski instructor from Switzerland, had been giving skiing lessons for the past ten years in the United States. Note that Spencer was apprehensive and anxious about his first lesson.

Protocol A: Spencer's First Skiing Lesson

A₁   Anna   Hi, Spencer. My name is Anna. *We're* going to ski today.
A₂   Do you want to learn how to ski?
A₃   Spencer   (Barely nods in the affirmative)
A₄   Anna   Good, because *we're* going to have fun skiing.
A₅   Anna   Do you like pizza, Spencer?
A₆   Spencer   Yes (and shakes his head very positively).
A₇   Anna   Good. Because *we're* going to make pizza in the snow.
A₈   Anna   See, like this. (Anna models a "pizza" wedge or snowplow
                 in the snow.)
A₉   Anna   Ok. Spencer. *Let's both* make a pizza wedge in the snow.
                 (Expert and novice start to ski.)

Protocol A demonstrates how an expert uses speech or discourse to entice and encourage a novice to participate in the whole task. Note that the expert does not give Spencer a litany of rules on how to ski. On the contrary, even though the child's body language shows that he is hesitant, the expert entices him to participate in the activity from the very beginning of the lesson. She uses inclusive discourse strategies, such as "we're" and "let's both" in order to include the learner in the activity. Furthermore, she taps into Spencer's prior background knowledge in A₅ "Do you like pizza?" which helps him to situate the present task and relate it to prior knowledge and a familiar experience. The expert then models the activity and quickly invites Spencer to likewise snowplow or make "pizza wedges."

This protocol illustrates how human beings need to exploit or use certain types of discourse strategies in joint problem-solving tasks between experts and novices. Later, we will demonstrate how similar discourse strategies can be used to orchestrate a lesson to focus on form in an L2 classroom that stresses interpersonal communication. But first, we need to discuss some basic tenets of a whole language approach to language instruction.

A Whole Language Approach to Language Learning[2]

As early as 1976, Ken Goodman, a psycholinguist, stated that "Language is language only when it is whole" (Fountas and Hannigan,1989, p.134). According to Goodman, the whole is always viewed as being greater than the sum of its parts, and it is *the whole that gives meaning to its parts.*[3] This approach resists language differentiation, that is, reducing language to word lists, verb conjugations, discrete grammar points or isolated linguistic elements. Language differentiation results in what Goodman calls "non-language." Moreover, words, phrases, or sentences are not linguistic islands unto themselves; on the contrary, these linguistic elements only gain meaning when used in conjunction with the whole. Therefore, students need to experience "whole" contextualized language (stories, legends, poems, songs, recipes, etc.) with an emphasis on meaning-making and sense-making before focusing on form. Once students experience the whole, then they are better able to deal with the parts (Fountas and Hannigan, 1989).

Unlike transmission, or language differentiation approaches, which stress isolated skill development, a whole language approach is *transactional* in nature, in that students are viewed as *whole learners* who bring a host of background information and knowledge to the language learning experience (Cooper, 1993). Whole language learning encourages learners to transact and derive their own meanings from authentic language learning experiences situated in a rich variety of contexts (Rigg and Allen, 1989). Again, *personal meaning-making or sense-making* is at the core of whole language learning. Whole language affords the learners plenty of opportunities to share or communicate their personal meaning-making experiences with one another which in turn enables the learners to better understand one another on the interpersonal level.

Recently, second language specialists have been underscoring the importance of meaning-making, authentic contexts, and connected discourse in second language development. The integration of content-based instruction (Sternfeld, 1988; Leaver and Stryker, 1989; Met, 1991) and the call for authentic listening and reading materials (Glisan, 1988; Christensen, 1990; Bacon, 1992) stress the importance of whole, connected, or unified discourse as a starting point in second language development.

Storytelling is particularly adaptable to whole language instruction, since it is natural to tell stories orally, stressing listening and speaking skills, followed by role-playing and reading and writing skills. Oller (1983) and Bruner (1990) remind us that the episodic organization represented in stories facilitates comprehension and retention. The framework of the story provides a continuous flow of mental images which help the learners to glean eventually the meaning of the story. And finally, whole language stresses an *integrative or holistic approach* to language learning by incorporating listening, speaking, reading, writing, thinking, and culture early on in the language learning experience (Halliday, 1975; Goodman, 1986; Cooper, 1993; Adair-Hauck, Donato, and Cumo, 1994).

PACE: A Model to Focus on Meaning and Form

The following PACE model developed by Donato and Adair-Hauck (1994) is rooted in both Vygotskian psycholinguistics and a whole language approach to language learning. PACE is an acronym for the four phases of the model which are: Presentation, Attention, Co-Construction, and Extension. Unlike bottom-up processing models which fragment the language system by encouraging students to learn the grammar rules and vocabulary *before* using them to communicate, the PACE model uses language communicatively from the very beginning of the lesson. Futhermore, bottom-up processing models are traditionnally linear in nature, while the PACE model is cyclical. (See Figure.)

Presentation

During the Presentation phase of the cycle, the teacher embeds or foreshadows the grammar structure with an appropriate text. A whole "text" could be a story, poem, song, cartoon, recipe demonstration, etc. The teacher needs to be creative and use plenty of nonverbal strategies, such as visuals, props, mime, facial expressions, gestures, to negotiate the meaning of the story or whole "text." Negotiating of meaning is critical during this phase in order to provide a presentation (input) that is comprehensible for the learners. Negotiation of meaning is also addressed in the *National Standards* (1996) as characteristic of learners who are developing the capacity to communicate in the interpersonal mode. To negotiate meaning in the classroom (Long, 1983), the teacher may use verbal strategies, such as using simplified vocabulary, familiar structures, paraphasing, in order to secure mutual understanding. The presentation needs to be *interpersonal and interactive*, that is, the teacher needs to include the learners in the storytelling activity (tapping into prior or background knowledge), using signaling (thumbs up/down) to check learner comprehension, or, asking students to act out certain scenes as the teacher tells the story. During the Presentation phase the students listen as the teacher portrays or tells the story. At this point, *meaning-making or sense-making* (Cazden, 1992) is driving the lesson. Clay and Cazden (1992) remind us that most of our class time should be spent on "the road to meaningful language." Therefore, the teacher need not be apprehensive that the presentation may take a period of time, even an entire class session. (For detailed suggestions on meaning-making and storytelling activities, see Adair-Hauck, 1996.)

Attention

During the second, or the attention, phase of PACE, the teacher and students take an "instructional detour" (Clay and Cazden's term, 1992) to focus on some aspect of the language used during the Presentation activity.

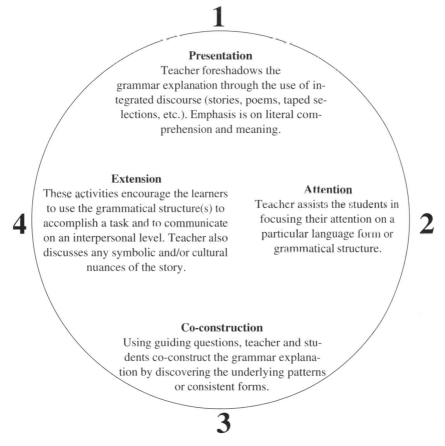

Figure. PACE: A Whole Language/Guided Participatory Approach to Language Instruction (Donato and Adair-Hauck, 1994)

Note that while the learners attend to *meaning* during the Presentation phase, now with the teacher's guidance, they turn their attention to *form* as the teacher uses the story to highlight some regularity of the target structure (e.g., first conjugation or "er" verbs in French, adjective agreement in Spanish, noun formation in Japanese). Using an overhead projector, the teacher circles or highlights the forms to be explored. Looking at the circled forms, the learners have the opportunity to attend to the sytematic nature or regularity of some aspect of the language. Unlike the Presentation or meaning-making stage, this phase of PACE should be brief.

Co-construction

During the Co-construction, or third, phase of PACE, the teacher assists the learners in raising their awareness about a selected feature or linguistic element of the target language. During this stage, the teacher guides the students in hypothesizing, predicting, guessing, and finally forming a generalization about the form in question. To do so, the teacher asks assisting questions, such as, "Do you see any repetition of words in the text?"; "Do you notice any similarities about these words?"; "Do you see a pattern to the underlined words?"; "Can you guess how the meanings of the words change when the forms change?" (Donato and Adair-Hauck, 1992). This phase again is interactive, that is, the teacher prompts and guides the learners to attend to and hypothesize and finally generalize about the selected forms of the text. The reciprocity of the dialogue encourages the learners and the teachers to co-construct and discover the underlying patterns or consistent forms. In this way, consciousness-raising during PACE is viewed as an active, collective endeavor.

Extension

Finally, the teacher completes the cycle by encouraging the learners to interact and communicate through Extension activities which encourage the learners to work cooperatively in the second language. (See Figure.) During the extension activities the learners have the opportunity to use new skills creatively and communicatively. Extension activities may include, but are certainly not limited to, information-gap activities, role-playing, simulations, paired interviews, class surveys, creative writing projects, drama activities. The Extension phase, like the Presentation phase, focuses on meaningful and interactive use of the language. The extension activities should afford the learners the opportunity to negotiate meaning and to communicate interpersonally with one another by giving and exchanging information, by sharing and expressing their feelings, and by developing a more thorough understanding of themselves and others. To be sure, the Extension phase, like the Presentation phase, will take plenty of time.

Through these *interpersonal* extension activities, the learners become more aware of the *function* of the grammatical structure. That is, they learn that they can carry out a particular task or function by using the appropriate grammatical structure. This approach is in agreement with Larsen-Freeman's (1991) suggestion that meaning, form, and function need to be "interacting dimensions" of language development. (For a more thorough discussion of the PACE model, as well as sample PACE activities, see Adair-Hauck, Donato, and Cumo, 1994.)

And finally, at some time during the PACE lesson, the teacher needs to discuss with the students any symbolic, figurative, and/or cultural nuances of the story. By using authentic texts, a whole language approach incorporates a cultural and humanities component even at the beginning levels of second language learning.

The Motivating Question: How Would This Model Actually Look in Practice?

In order to explore how the PACE model could actually be implemented in a classroom setting, Bonnie Adair-Hauck, a second language teacher trainer and researcher, and Philomena Cumo-Johanssen, a secondary-level French teacher with over twenty years in the foreign language classroom, decided to collaborate and conduct an action-based research project. Furthermore, Richard Donato, an associate professor in Foreign Language Education, frequently met with the authors to provide guidance and assistance on how to actualize the project. The three second language specialists agreed that a case-study approach telescoping two different approaches to grammar explanation — a traditional approach, or explicit explanation vs. a whole language/guided participatory explanation — would be of interest to the profession. In particular, they were interested in answering the following research questions: (1) Are there differences in the types of activities (tasks) in the whole language/guided participatory approach vs. the explicit, teacher-directed approach? (2) Are there differences in the teacher's discourse strategies in the whole language/guided participatory approach vs. an explicit, teacher-directed approach? (3) How does the teacher focus the learners' attention to form (grammar) when teaching in a whole language/guided participatory approach? To investigate these research questions, Adair-Hauck, Donato and Cumo designed three different PACE units to teach the past indefinite tense in French (first conjugation, second conjugation, and intransitive verbs). They also discussed concerns for the implementation of two versions of the lessons and designed retention tests to assess the effectiveness of the instruction. Adair-Hauck observed many of the traditional and whole language lessons, and all of the lessons were videotaped.

School Setting and Subjects

The project took place in a suburban school setting in Western Pennsylvania. The school district enrolls approximatively 1,780 students and serves a working class community with an average per capita income of approximatively $12,652. The French department is planning to buy new books; however, for this project they used a traditional textbook. The classroom teacher has attended numerous professional development programs, therefore she invigorates the curriculum by integrating real-life tasks and by encouraging the students to work cooperatively on group projects. The subjects included thirty-eight tenth-and eleventh-grade students enrolled in a French II program. Data collected from the Iowa Achievement Test scores as well as the Differential Aptitude Test scores (both scholastic and language aptitude) attested to the comparabililty of the two groups. With respect to contact time, both French classes met for approximately forty minutes per day, five days per week.

Data Collection

The data for this study were collected over a three-month period. Both groups were videotaped during three instructional grammar episodes all of which taught the past indefinite (*passé composé*) tense in French. An instructional episode has been defined by Leinhardt and Putnam (1987) as a detachable piece of material having a recognizable beginning and end point for both teacher and students. An instructional episode might last five to ten or even more class sessions. The three instructional episodes included in this study were: (1) "The Lion and the Mouse" (*Le lion et la souris)* or the past indefinite tense with first conjugation "er" verbs using "avoir" as the auxiliary, (2) "Little Red Riding Hood" *(Le petit chaperon rouge)* or the past indefinite tense with "ir" and "re" verbs using "avoir" as the auxiliary, and (3)"Magic Johnson" or the past indefinite tense of intransitive verbs which use "être" as the auxiliary. (For synopses, see Appendix; for whole language stories, see Adair-Hauck, 1993).

One French II class (non-treatment group) was taught the instructional episodes explicitly with direct teacher explanations followed by explicit textbook explanations and oral practice. The second group (treatment group) was taught the same grammatical structures using a whole language approach, which created a context for grammar through storytelling. Moreover, focus on form (Long, 1991) was conducted through group discussions with the teacher in which grammatical explanation was co-constructed in collaborative teacher-student discourse rather than explicit statements from the teacher. Both the storytelling and the grammar explanations involved the use of guided participation (Rogoff, 1990) in which the teacher scaffolded the students' involvement in the narrative and in the explanation of form. Scaffolded instruction (Wood, Bruner, and Ross, 1976) allows learners the opportunity to participate in problem-solving activities which they would be incapable of doing without assistance from an expert or more capable peer. In this case study, the teacher scaffolded the presentation of the stories by recruiting and maintaining the interests of the learners in the storytelling activity and by negotiating the meaning of the stories through the use of nonverbal strategies (pictures, props, gestures) and verbal strategies or cues (story context, familiar vocabulary/structures, comprehension checks). She also scaffolded the grammar explanation by using cognitive probes or "hints" which encouraged the students to reflect upon, hypothesize, and generalize about the language system. These cognitive probes or discourse strategies enabled the learners to *participate in the grammar explanation.* Class exercises also reflected interpersonal and interactive, storytelling activities. Bruner (1983, p. 60) cogently describes the imperative for *active participation* on the part of learners by stating: "Where before there was a spectator, let there now be a participant!"

The teacher planned her lessons so that the instructional episodes were the same length in time for each group (three days of instruction for each instructional episode). Also, during the time from the completion of an instructional episode until the students took a retention test (approximately 3 weeks), both groups received the same instruction, identical classroom material, homework assignments, etc. Finally, it should be noted that the teacher had a vested interest for *both groups* to succeed in this project. The school district has a relatively small number of foreign language students. In order to sustain a French III and IV program and maintain her teaching position, the teacher needed as many students as possible to be successful in her French II classes and to continue into advanced-level French. In other words, attrition was a serious consideration for this teacher.

Data Sources

The following qualitative data sources were used for the interpretation and completion of the project.

1. *Lesson plans.* Cumo-Johanssen's plans provided information regarding the goals and objectives for each lesson. The lesson plans served to focus Adair-Hauck's attention before observing the videotaped lessons.
2. *Videotapes.* The videotapes provided documentation on the kinds of instruction that both groups received. In addition, Adair-Hauck was able to refer to the tapes in interpreting the data.
3. *Transcripts of videotapes.* Transcripts of selected sections of the instructional episodes enabled Adair-Hauck to analyze the discourse used to orchestrate the various instructional episodes.
4. *Researcher's notes.* These notes, or memos, served as reminders of impressions or "hunches" which emerged during data collection as well as during the rounds of data interpretation.

Quantitative data sources included:

5. *Retention tests.* Approximately three weeks after the completion of each grammatical episode, both groups of learners took retention tests. The retention tests included five sections: discrete point, guided writing, listening comprehension, reading comprehension, and a metalinguistic section. (Given the focus of this chapter, the qualitative data sources will be analyzed.)
6. *Whole language student questionnaire.* All students in the treatment group took a questionnaire concerning the whole language or storytelling activities.

Analysis of the Data

After having completed all the videotaping for the three instructional episodes, we began to consider ways of analyzing the data. It became evident that certain themes or patterns were emerging for both approaches. We then transcribed numerous segments of the instructional episodes in order to capture or to illuminate the emerging themes or patterns. Our review determined that an in-depth discussion of the "Lion and the Mouse," or Episode I, would be the most appropriate in order to reveal the genesis of the learners' new and developing skills, as they began to develop competency in past tense verb formation and the function of past tense narration. We also realized that our analysis should include more than just describing *what* was happening during the instructional episode. Limiting our discussion to *what* was happening would only result in a surface-level description. On the other hand, uncovering the communicative dynamics of the instructional episode would lead to a much deeper and interesting discussion. In particular, we discovered that the teacher used different discourse strategies or semiotic mechanisms when teaching the whole language/guided participatory vs. the explicit teacher-directed episode. The following descriptions of activities and protocol analyses revealed these discourse strategies.

Types of Activities: Explicit, Teacher-Directed Approach

Table 1 illustrates the various activities for the explicit grammar instructional episode on the teaching of the past tense of first conjugation "er" verbs with "avoir." Table 1 furthermore shows the length of time for each activity as well as whether the activities were conducted in English or French. This particular instructional episode encompasses three days of instruction. Recall that Leinhardt and Putnam (1987) define an instructional episode as a detachable piece of instructional material having a recognizable beginning and end point for both teacher and student. The teacher begins the episode on Day 1, Activity #3, with a very explicit teacher explanation of past tense of "er" verbs. She ends the episode with a quiz on this grammatical structure. (Please note that the first two activities for Day 1 do not relate to the episode or to this study.)

Table 1. List of Activities, Episode I. Explicit, Teacher-Directed Approach:
Past Indefinite Tense, First-Conjugation Verbs with "Avoir"

Day 1	
Activity 1 2 min. English	Discussion relating to previous quiz—common mistakes, etc. *(not related to study).*
Activity 2 5 min. French	Using flashcards, (T) reviews vocabulary on professions *(not related to study).*
Activity 3 5 min. French	Using overhead—very explicit (T) explanation regarding formation of past tense in French for "er" verbs with "avoir." Gives numerous examples.
Activity 4 4 min. French	Oral practice. Using overhead, (T) gives subject pronoun and infinitive; (SS) must say the past tense forms.
Activity 5 3 min. English (mainly)	Using board, (T) demonstrates how to negate past-tense verbs.
Activity 6 5 min. French	Using overhead, (T) provides subject pronoun
Activity 7 2 min. English	(SS) confused about subject Pierre et vous, or second-person plural forms. (T) explains reasoning for second-person plural.
Activity 8 1 min. English	(T) directs (SS)' attention to textbook explanation on formation of past indefinite tense.
Activity 9 1 min. English	(T) emphasizes again the meaning of "passé composé."
Activity 10 5 min. French	(T) directs (SS)' attention to list of adverbs of time which indicate past tense. (T) pronounces words, (SS) repeat. (SS) practice reading sample sentences aloud.
Activity 11 1 min. English	(T) reminds (SS) to reread textbook explanation to reinforce today's lesson.
Activity 12 2 min. English	(T) gets (SS) to restate rules for forming "passé composé." Homework textbook p. 176, Ex. B–C.

Note: (T) = teacher; (S), (SS) = student(s)

Table 1 (cont'd.).	
Day 2	
Activity 1 1 min.　French	Warm-up—"ça va bien," etc.
Activity 2 1 min.　English	(T) reviews how to form past indefinite tense. (T) gets (SS) to state the rule.
Activity 3 4 min.　French	Using overhead, (T) provides "vous avez" plus infinitives. (SS) must complete sentences by providing past participle. Both individual and choral responses.
Activity 4 3 min.　French	(T) asks (SS) questions in past tense such as "J'ai étudié le français; qu'est-ce que vous avez étudié au lycée?" (SS) answer in past.
Activity 5 3 min.　French	(T) continues to use overhead—now (SS) see auxiliary negated; individual (SS) read and complete entire sentence by adding a past participle.
Activity 6 10 min.　French	(T) and (SS) correct homework. (S) gives answer. (T) shows correct answer on overhead. Ex. B, p. 176. Sentences are in past tense (SS) must change sentence by using different subject pronoun; ex. C (SS) negate same sentences used in Ex. B.
Activity 7 8 min. (3 min. French, 5 min. English)	Using overhead, (T) writes some sentences in past tense. (SS) must write and change sentence back to present tense. (SS) have trouble with this task—so teacher reviews formation of present tense "er" verbs. Explanation changes into English. (SS) pass in papers from this activity.
Activity 8 7 min.　French	*(Not related to study.)* (SS) listen to taped exercise involving vocabulary for professions.

Table 1 (cont'd.).	
Day 3	
Activity 1 1 min. English	(T) explains that (SS) will have a quiz tomorrow on past tense. They need to know how to form past tense of "er" verbs.
Activity 2 4 min. French	Warm-up—(T) asks (SS) some questions in both present and past tense.
Activity 3 2 min. English (mainly)	(T) and (SS) review rules for formation of past indefinite tense.
Activity 4 10 min. French	(T) passes out worksheet to review past tense with "er" verbs. Using overhead, (T) and (SS) together complete worksheet. Individual (SS) say the answer before (T) shows correct response.
Activity 5 3 min. French	Review vocabulary for professions using flashcards *(not related to study)*.
Activity 6 5 min. French (mainly)	Teacher discusses topic of reading "Au Poste de Police" or "At the Police Station" which incorporates the use of past tense. As a pre-reading set, (T) highlights difficult vocabulary and structures.
Activity 7 10 min. French	(SS) begin to read the reading silently to themselves and then they begin to answer questions about the reading. (T) walks around room and answers any questions. (SS) should complete assignment for homework.

A review of the activities for the explicit grammar teaching episode clearly indicates a "bottom-up" approach to grammar. The learners are engaged in a series of activities sequenced from simple to complex. Moreover, these simple tasks are mainly skill-getting (Rivers, 1983) in nature where learning the forms of the language (sound system, morphological inflections, word order, etc.) is practiced before communicative use of the language.

The activities for this episode also reveal a deductive and explicit approach to grammar instruction with teacher-directed explanations followed by related, manipulative exercises. The episode begins with a five-minute explicit teacher explanation on the formation of the past tense with "er" or first conjugation verbs. After the direct teacher explanation, the students are exposed to numerous manipulative or "skill-getting" activities (Rivers, 1983).

Protocol B is extracted from Day 1: Activity #4 of the explicit instructional episode illustrates the building block paradigm which encourages controlled, conscious processes or automatization on the part of the learners. The students have just listened to a five-minute explicit teacher explanation on how to form the past tense in French with first conjugation verbs. (A detailed description of the role of the teacher will be discussed later.) On an overhead, the teacher points to a subject pronoun and an accompanying infinitive. The learners chorally provide the past tense form.

Protocol B: Explicit/Teacher Directed Approach

B₁	T	Bon, continuez avec le verbe "danser" (pointing to second-person plural "you").
B₂	SS	Vous avez dansé.
B₃	T	Bon. Vous avez dansé. Chanter.
B₄	SS	Vous avez chanté.
B₅	T	Bon. Premièrement, quand je vous dis "chanter,"
B₆		c'est-à-dire, quand je montre le premier mot, quelles
B₇		sont les dernières lettres?
B₈	SS	"er" (English)
B₉	T	"*er*", mais quand *vous* le dites, quelle est la terminaison?
B₁₀	SS	An accent.
B₁₁	T	An accented "e." Um hum. (T repeats Ss response in English, then switches back to French.)
B₁₂		Bon, essayez un autre. (Points to first-person plural "nous" form with the infinitive "porter" [to carry].)
B₁₃	T	Um. Porter.
B₁₄	SS	Nous avons porté.
B₁₅	T	Nous avons porté. Bon. Emmener.
B₁₆	SS	Nous avons emmené.
B₁₇	T	Nous avons emmené. (This exercise continues for approximately four minutes.)

Protocol B demonstrates that the learners are involved in an activity in which the language is unnatural, decontextualized, and unauthentic. In other words, the learners are dealing with fragmented discourse such as

B_2 "Vous avez dansé" [You have danced]; B_4 "Vous avez chanté" [You have sung]; B_{14} "Nous avons porté" [We have carried]. Moreover, we could conceivably argue that the learners are oftentimes drilling at word-level rather than at sentence-level discourse. For example, B_{14} "Nous avons porté" and B_{16} "Nous avons emmené" [we have brought] in normal conversation are incomplete and require a noun phrase or complement following the rules for subcategorization in French.

Clearly, the emphasis of this activity is on *codebreaking* or understanding the *forms* of the language, rather than on *decoding* or understanding the *meaning* of the forms the students are using. At no time during this segment does the teacher verify or question for meaning. In fact, teacher questions are very sparse during this segment. The few questions provided are assessing questions rather than assisting questions. Tharp and Gallimore (1988, p. 59) explain that assessing questions "inquire to discover the level of the pupil's ability to perform without assistance." Assisting questions, on the other hand, "inquire in order to produce a mental operation that the pupil cannot or will not produce alone." Duffy and Roehler (1986) remind us that assessing questions are predominant in the culture of our schools. For example, in Protocol B the teacher asks B_{5-7} "Quand je vous dis 'chanter', c'est-à-dire, quand je montre le premier mot, quelles sont les dernières lettres?" [When I point and say "to sing" to you, what are the last two letters?] and B_9 "Mais quand *vous* le dites, quelle est la terminaison?" [But when *you* say it, it ends in what?] The teacher is *assessing* the learners' knowledge to verify that they know that the infinitive ends in "er" while the past participle ends in accented "é." These questions are evaluating the learners' metalinguistic knowledge, i.e., knowledge *about the language.* In other words, the teacher is requiring the students to display their metalinguistic knowledge in order to evaluate it rather than assisting them to perform using this new grammatical feature.

The fact that the learners can answer the two assessing questions in unison, (B_8 and B_{10}) acknowledges the uniformity and lack of variability in the lesson. This protocol highlights automated, convergent, or "cloning activities" (Goodman and Goodman, 1990) which are evident in many "bottom-up" approaches to the teaching of grammar.

As Protocol B illustrates, there is little room for linguistic creativity or risk-taking in the activities for the explicit instructional episode. Rarely are the learners asked to create in the language. In other words, the language produced by the students is either *teacher-driven* or *text-driven.*

Furthermore, the activities are highly constrained with a limited set of appropriate responses which inevitably lead to a pre-established and narrow set of verbal responses. An administrator observing this class would undoubtedly be impressed with its efficacy, smoothness and the learners' apparent "knowledge of" and "understanding of" how to form the past tense in French. In reality however, closer examination of the discourse reveals that the students are not required to attend to the meaning of the words they produce.

Types of Activities: Whole Language/Guided Participatory Approach

The whole language/guided participatory episode (see Table 2) contrasts significantly with the explicit episode. Activities in this three-day episode indicate that the teacher is using a top-down approach to instruction involving the use of meaningful texts before moving to activities that focus on form.

Table 2 shows that during the first class session the teacher spends most of the class focusing on decoding meaning (approximately twenty-six minutes) before moving to a formal analysis of the structural elements of the language. For example, first the teacher introduces the "Lion and the Mouse" story using props, visuals, and gestures. Then using the same props and visuals she retells the story while at the same time encouraging the students to participate in the storytelling event whenever possible (see Protocol C). After twelve minutes of focusing on meaning and listening comprehension, the learners see the written text for the first time. As a fourth activity, the teacher retells the story using visuals, but this time the pictures are not in chronological order. Again, she encourages the students to enter into the storytelling whenever possible. Finally as a fifth activity, the students reread the story, this time with an accompanying vocabulary list used to clarify the meaning of unknown words.

During the presentation phase of the lesson, the teacher is weaving a number of skills—listening, speaking, and reading—into the whole language activities. Clearly, at first, the emphasis is on listening comprehension. However, the learners are not just listening to short isolated sentences; on the contrary, they are exposed to whole texts and *how to listen* and *how to search for meaning* from longer stretches of discourse. Clearly, we see a strong experiential component throughout these activities. The students are experiencing, observing, and interacting with "real" language, i.e., language with a function and purpose. Cook (1991, p. 93) reminds us that "this experiential component appears to be a vital element in the development of functional second language skills."

Table 2. List of Activities —Episode I. Whole-Language/Guided Participatory Approach: Past Indefinite Tense, First Conjugation Verbs with "Avoir"	
Day 1	
Activity 1 7 min. French	Teacher tells story "Le lion et la souris" (The Lion and the Mouse) in present tense. Uses visuals, gestures, and props. (SS) do not see text.
Activity 2 4 min. French	Using pictures, (T) retells the story. (T) encourages (SS) to tell the story whenever possible. Pictures in chronological order.
Activity 3 3 min. French	(T) gives (SS) copy of text; story in present tense. (SS) have 2–3 minutes to read story to themselves.
Activity 4 4 min. French	(T) holds up visuals depicting story, but this time pictures not in chronological order. (T) encourages (SS) not to look at text.
Activity 5 3 min. French	(SS) reread the story in present tense. (T) gives (SS) a vocabulary list that they may refer to if necessary.
Activity 6 5 min. French	(T) asks (SS) to look at the story and name any "er" verbs, e.g., demander, passer, crier. (T) gives "hints" such as, "There are two more verbs that begin with the letter 'a'" whenever necessary. (T) writes a list of these infinitives on overhead transparency.
Activity 7 5 min. English	(T) switches transparency and shows (SS) sentence from text. (T) writes sentence in present and then in the past. (SS) guess the difference in meaning. After one more example (T) and (SS) co-construct grammatical rule for past tense formation.
Activity 8 4 min. French	Individual (SS) pick out a sentence from the story and put it in the past tense.
Activity 9 1 min. English	(T) asks (SS) to summarize the moral of the story.
Note: (T) = teacher; (S), (SS) = student(s)	

	Table 2 (cont'd.).
Activity 10 3 min. French	(T) reviews vocabulary for professions *(not part of the study)*. Homework: Finish making a list of "er"verbs from the story. Also make a list of ten other "er" verbs not found in the story.
Day 2	
Activity 1 1 min. French	Warmup; date, time, weather, etc.
Activity 2 6 min. French	(T) reintroduces "Le lion et la souris" story in present tense. Two student volunteers use props to act out story. (T) coaches and assists class to retell story as a group.
Activity 3 7 min. French	(SS) share list of verbs they generated for homework. (T) writes (SS)' infinitives in two columns on board. One column—verbs found in story; other column—different infinitives. (T) makes up sample sentences using infinitives on board. Then individual (SS) make up sentences in past tense. (T) writes sentences on board.
Activity 4 3 min. English	(T) calls (SS) attention to rule in book if (SS) need to review rule formation. (T) asks (SS) how one says, "What happened" in French. (T) and (SS) collectively summarize rule.
Activity 5 2 min. French	(T) directs (SS) attention to book and adverbs of time which denote past time events. (T) lets (SS) pick out and say different adverbs.
Activity 6 5 min. French	(SS) make up a sentence in past using an infinitive from their Hwk verb list. (T) writes sentences on board. (T) then shows (SS) how to make sentence negative in past.
Activity 7 3 min. French	(T) asks (SS) to write two sentences in the past tense and then to make them negative. (T) walks around room providing assistance when necessary. (T) reminds (SS) to refer back to sample sentences on board if necessary.
Activity 8 1 min. French	(T) and (SS) orally practice and conjugate verb "avoir" both in positive and negative form.

	Table 2 (cont'd.).
Activity 9 5 min. French	(T) hands (SS) photocopy of story. This time all the "er" verbs have blanks. (SS) will rewrite the story in the past by filling in the blanks with correct past tense form. At first (T) lets (SS) guess the "infinitive" that would be appropriate. Then she writes the remaining infinitives on the board. (T) collects photocopies of completed story.
Activity 10 5 min. French	Listening comprehension taped exercise *(not part of story)*. For Hwk. create 5 sentences in present tense. Then make them past tense. Make sure to negate at least 4 sentences.
Day 3	
Activity 1 3 min. English	(T) explains that (SS) will have a quiz tomorrow on the past tense. They need to know how to change the present tense to past tense for "er" verbs. (T) hands back (SS) completed "Lion and Mouse" story. Reminds them to note any corrections.
Activity 2 3 min. French	(T) writes 3 sentences on the board in present tense from "Lion and Mouse" story. At their seats, (SS) write the 3 sentences in the past. (T) walks around room helping when necessary.
Activity 3 3 min. French	Volunteers change the sentences on the board to the past tense. Then other volunteers change the sentences to the negative.
Activity 4 2 min. French	Three volunteers write examples of their homework sentences (past tense) on board. During this time (T) reviews voc. on professions with the other students.
Activity 5 5 min. French (mainly)	(T) reads aloud sentences generated from students in Activity 3 and 4. (T) notes any errors.
Activity 6 5 min. French	(T) gives (SS) infinitive such as "poser," "rater," "nager," etc. (to ask, to fail, to swim). At their seats, (SS) then write their own sentences in present using a different subject pronoun each time.

Table 2 (cont'd.).	
Activity 7 8 min. French	(SS) read sentence aloud, another (S) goes to board and writes sentence in past. If problem, (SS) help one another. (T) also ensures that various pronouns are used. Ex.: We need a sample sentence with "nous."
Activity 8 5 min. French	(SS) complete taped listening comprehension exercise on professions *(not part of study)*. Homework.: Read text pp. 177–178. Answer questions in complete sentences.

The activities listed in Table 2 indicate the judicious use of recitation. On Day 2, Activity #8, the teacher spends approximately one minute reciting the conjugation of the verb "avoir" with the students. This is the only activity that can be characterized as a recitation and controlled processing activity. The other activities, whether listening, speaking, reading, or writing, can be characterized as activities that encourage the learners to comprehend and to use language as a way to develop communicative competence.

Even when the students engaged in exercises that focus on form at the sentence level, (Day 2: Activity #3, or Day 2: Activity #6), the learners, and not the teacher or the textbook, are creating and making up the exercises. For these activities, the learners generate a list of "er" verbs for homework. Then in class the learners are asked to use their verb lists and create sentences in the past indefinite tense. These types of "generative activities" (Goodman and Goodman, 1990) encourage the learners to construct and to create with language. In other words, rather than the textbook and its authors, it is the learners who are being asked to compose and create much of the language used in the classroom (Freeman, 1992).

Let us now turn to analysis of the protocols for a more in-depth discussion of some of these whole language/guided participatory activities. Protocol C (Day 1: Activity #1) illustrates that the students are interacting in the second language through the teacher's presentation of an interesting narrative. The storytelling activity provides the learners with rich second language input that focuses the learners on the meaning of words rather than on their form. Immersing the learners in the storytelling activity with its longer stretches of discourse affords the learners the opportunity to develop comprehension skills and at the same time a tolerance for dealing with long stretches of discourse. The following protocol illustrates how the teacher begins the story by assuming that the students understand the literal meaning of the story's important vocabulary.

Protocol C: Whole Language/Guided Participatory Approach

C_1	T	Tout le monde, écoutez. Fermez vos livres et écoutez.
C_2		Aujourd'hui nous allons lire une histoire.
C_3		C'est l'histoire d'un lion et d'une souris
C_4		(points to picture). Voici le lion.
C_5		Il dort (tips head to one side).
C_6		Vous comprenez? Il dort. Qu'est-ce que le lion fait?
C_7	SS	Il dort.
C_8	T	Et voici une petite souris. Qu'est-ce que c'est?
C_9	SS	Une petite souris.
C_{10}	T	Qu'est-ce que c'est (points to lion picture)?
C_{11}	SS	Un lion.
C_{12}	T	Et qu'est-ce que le lion fait (tips head)?
C_{13}	SS	Il dort.
C_{14}	T	Et qu'est-ce que c'est?
C_{15}	SS	Une petite souris.
C_{16}	T	La petite souris commence à courir sur le lion (pointing to picture, then running fingers through the air).
C_{17}	T	Elle commence à courir sur le lion. Vous comprenez?
C_{18}		Sur le lion. Bon. Maintenant. Qu'est-ce qu'elle fait?
C_{19}		Qu'est-ce qu'elle commence à ... (running fingers through air).
C_{20}	SS	Sur
C_{21}	T	Courir
C_{22}	SS	Courir
C_{23}	T	Courir (runs fingers through air) ... sur ...
C_{24}	SS	Le lion
C_{25}	T	Le lion. O.K. Et le lion se réveille (Teacher jerks head up as if waking up).
C_{26}		Vous comprenez? Le lion dort (tips head to side),
C_{27}		il se réveille (jerks head up).
C_{28}		Et il attrape (quickly opens and closes fists in air),
C_{29}		il attrape la souris (shows picture to SS).
C_{30}		Vous voyez? Il attrape la souris.
C_{31}		Maintenant, qu'est-ce qu'il fait?
C_{32}		Il dort (tips head to side, then jerks head up) et puis il ...
C_{33}	SS	Il se réveille.

C$_{34}$	T	Oui, il se réveille. Et puis il … (T closes fist in air)
C$_{35}$	SS	Attrape
C$_{36}$	T	Il attrape …
C$_{37}$	SS	La souris.
		(Teacher continues to introduce story in this manner using props, visuals, and verbal demonstrations.)

In contrast to the activities in the explicit episode described earlier, Protocol C demonstrates that the teacher and the learners are engaged in the storytelling process and that verbal interaction is authentic, natural, and contextualized (Adair-Hauck and Donato, 1994). In addition, the text itself is authentic. Little, Devitt, and Singleton (1988, p. 23) define an authentic text as "one that is created to fulfill some social purpose in the language community in which it was produced." In this respect then, the storytelling of "The Lion and the Mouse" is an authentic, functional activity with a purpose (telling, understanding, and enjoying the story), and it is similar to the kinds of authentic tasks that one finds in real life.

Although one of the teacher's primary objectives of this lesson is to provide an explanation of the past tense in French, she initially tells the story in the present tense. When asked about this decision, she explained that introducing the story in the present tense would simplify the activity and make it more familiar and easier for the students to understand. In other words, her first concern was to develop literal comprehension of the story. Later, she planned to use the story as a context to explore the *function and form* of the past tense. (Note that for the subsequent lesson on intransitive verbs in the past indefinite, the teacher felt comfortable introducing the story in the past tense.)

Protocol C demonstrates that the learners are engaged in a more complex task than they would be capable of producing by themselves, in other words, performance before competence (Cazden, 1981). Through mediation with the use of visuals, gestures, and behavioral demonstrations, the teacher and learners are negotiating the meaning of the text.

In Protocol C the teacher does not need to frame the lesson with explicit statements of her intent (Donato and Adair-Hauck, 1992). On the contrary, she focuses the students' attention on the activity of storytelling itself. To do so, she uses an imperative. C$_{1-2}$ "Tout le monde, écoutez. Fermez vos livres et écoutez. Aujourd'hui, nous allons lire une histore." [Everyone listen. Close your books and listen. Today we are going to read a story.] In other words, she explicitly acknowledges the activity of the lesson (telling stories) rather than the content to be learned (past tense narration.)

Protocol C illuminates that the learners are engaged in an activity in which an expert is providing assistance and encouraging the learners to participate (Tharp and Gallimore, 1988; Rogoff, 1990). The teacher is scaffolding the activity (Wood, Bruner, and Ross, 1976) by first recruiting the learners' interest in the task through the use of visuals, gestures, voice intonation, and behavioral demonstrations. In Protocol C the teacher scaffolds comprehension of the story by calling attention to critical lexicon: "the lion," "the mouse," "he is sleeping," "begins to run on," "the lion wakes up," etc. Building a scaffold for the learners enables them to maintain pursuit of the goal (understanding the meaning of the story) and helps control frustration during the problem-solving process (Wood, Bruner, and Ross, 1976).

Another distinguishing characteristic of the discourse in Protocol C is the fact that turn-taking is not overtly marked. This type of discourse often predominates in the genre of schools, but is *not* reflective in everyday communicative exchanges that occur outside the classroom (Coulthard, 1977; Tharp and Gallimore, 1988). In many of the explicit episode activities, the teacher overtly marks turn-taking with comments such as "Yes," "Good," "Questions?" However, in the whole language/guided participatory activity (Protocol C) the teacher does not need to mark explicitly turn-taking, because she and the learners are engaged in a collective, participatory discursive act (Donato, 1988). The teacher and learners are participants in a very natural, human activity, storytelling. Therefore, unnatural and artificial turn-taking moves are not needed. Clearly, in Protocol C the teacher is focusing more at the discourse level and emphasizing meaning; consequently unnatural teacher-talk such as corrective feedback (*non, c'est correct?*) and evaluative comments (*très bien, bravo*) are unwarranted.

Protocol D contrasts with Protocol C, because now the students are engaged in a whole language activity that requires them to retell the whole text of the story. Protocol D occurs on Day 2: Activity #2 of the whole language/guided participatory episode. Using the same props from the preceding day's storytelling activity, the teacher asks for two students to act out the story. The teacher then assists the other students in the class to retell the story as the two students in front of the class dramatize its events. She also asks the students at their desks not to refer to their printed copy of the story.

Protocol D: Whole Language/Guided Participatory Approach

Teacher (using puppet props for lion and the mouse) asks SS not to refer to their story, if possible.

D_1	T	O.K. Tout le monde, qu'est-ce que c'est? (points to lion)
D_2	SS	Le lion.
D_3	T	Et qui est-ce?
D_4	SS	La souris.
D_5	T	Qui peut commencer l'histoire? (Teacher points to two
D_6		volunteers.) O.K., Monsieur et Mademoiselle. (Two students go to the front of the room. One student holds a lion puppet, the other a mouse.)
D_7	T	Qui peut commencer l'histoire? Qu'est-ce qui se passe? (Pause ...)
D_8	T	Qu'est-ce que le lion fait, premièrement? Il ...
D_9	SS	Dort.
D_{10}	T	Oui, il dort. (Student makes lion puppet sleep.)
D_{11}	T	Très bien. Il dort et ... ?
D_{12}	S_1	La souris "passer" (student uses infinitive form of verb).
D_{13}	T	La souris passe et ... (teacher uses two fingers to represent "to run"—student with mouse begins to run on the lion. No one says verb "courir" [to run] so teacher provides it.)
D_{14}	T	Courir classe, la souris commence à courir sur le lion et
D_{15}		qu'est-ce que le lion fait?
D_{16}	S_2	Se réveille.
D_{17}	T	Oui. Il se réveille ... Et puis qu'est-ce que le lion fait?
D_{18}	S_3	Attrape.
D_{19}	T	Attrape. Qui attrape?
D_{20}	S_3	Le lion attrape la souris. (Students with puppets act out the lion catching the mouse. Teacher and students continue to retell entire story with emphasis on verbs used in story.)

The goal of Protocol D appears to be to check the students' comprehension of the text presented the day before and to review the vocabulary used in the story. The teacher begins the activity with two assessing questions: D1 "O.K., tout le monde. qu'est-ce que c'est?" [O.K. everyone, what is this?] (points to lion) and D3 "Et qui est-ce?" [And who is this?] The teacher uses closed-ended assessing questions to evaluate whether or not the learners can remember the vocabulary from the previous day. The teacher then invigorates the activity with a very general question, D_7 "Qui peut commencer l'histoire?" [Who can begin the story?] "Qu'est-ce qui se passe?" [What is happening?] The learners' failure to respond to the teacher's general question serves as a clue or hint to the teacher that she needs to adjust her support to the learners' level of understanding. In other words, the learners need more strategic direction (Tharp and Gallimore, 1988). Therefore, the teacher reciprocates with an assisting question D_8 "Qu'est-ce que le lion fait, premièrement? Il …" [What is the lion doing first? He …] The teacher's assisting question serves to reduce the degree of freedom of the task (Wood, Bruner and Ross, 1976). The teacher's assistance enables the learners to concentrate on a very specific part of the story, in this case, one action; therefore the class responds in unison D_9 "dort" [is sleeping]. The teacher continues to facilitate the activity by providing truncated assistance with additional assisting questions such as D_{15} "qu'est-ce que le lion fait?" [what does the lion do?] and D_{17} "Et puis, qu'est-ce que le lion fait?" [And then what does the lion do?] These questions serve to guide the learners to think about the episodic structure of the story line.

The learner's partial performance in D_{18} "Attrape" [Catches] provokes the teacher to respond with another assisting question D_{19} "Attrape, qui attrape?" [Catches, who catches?] The teacher's question assists the learner to move from vertical level speech D_{18} "Attrape" to horizontal level speech (Hatch, 1978) D_{20} "Le lion attrape la souris" [The lion catches the mouse.] This type of responsive assistance contrasts sharply with the explicit conventional episode in which the teacher mainly uses questions to assess rather than to assist.

One final point regarding Protocol D concerns the need for risk-taking and the use of linguistic approximations on the part of the learners. These learners are engaged in language production *before* they have consciously mastered all the necessary sub-skills (e.g., morphology). To participate, the learners need to take risks, approximate and make errors. Notice the student error in D_{12} "La souris passer" [The mouse to pass], where the student uses the infinitive form of the verb. The teacher never asks the student to correct the error; on the contrary, she accepts the approximation and then models the correct form for the student, D_{13} "La souris passe et …" [The mouse passes and …]. This interaction underscores again the teacher's emphasis on meaning rather than form.

Both Protocols C and D highlight the mediational aspect of teaching in the zone of proximal development. The teacher's discourse strategies assist the learners to participate in a whole-task activity in which, *if un-assisted*, they would be incapable of participating (Tharp and Gallimore, 1988; Newman et al., 1989). Through responsive assistance, the teacher is challenging the learners to participate in the storytelling activity from the very beginning of the lesson.

Role of the Teacher when focusing on Form: Explicit Approach

Redefining the role of the learner requires reformulating the role of the teacher (Tharp and Gallimore, 1988). The data show that the role of the teacher, like the role of the learner, varies considerably between these two approaches. The data also show that the whole language/guided partici-patory approach clearly redefines learning to *include learner participa-tion in the grammar explanation itself*. Protocol analysis extracted from the two different instructional episodes will illuminate the differences in these teacher roles.

It is particularly interesting to note how the teacher encourages the learners to attend to form and how she presents an explanation since these instructional episodes have as their primary objective the teaching of grammar. In Protocol E, we see an explicit and direct approach to grammar instruction in which the teacher begins the instructional episode with at-tention focusing activities followed by an explicit explanation.

Protocol E: Explicit/Teacher-Directed Focus on Form

Teacher directs SS attention to overhead. One transparency has the infinitive "avoir" conjugated. Another transparency has various "er" verbs in past participle form.

E_1	T	Ecoutez, faites attention parce que nous allons apprendre
E_2	T	quelque chose de différent. (Walks in front of the
		television and says)
E_3		Maintenant je regarde la télévision.
E_4		Oui? (Points to TV). I'm watching TV. Oui?
E_5		Maintenant. Mais hier soir, mardi, c'était mardi soir,
E_6		n'est-ce pas? Hier soir, c'était mardi. Aujourd'hui
E_7		c'est mercredi. Hier soir, j'ai regardé la télévision.
E_8		Aujourd'hui, je regarde la télévision. Hier, j'ai
E_9		regardé la télévision. Qui peut me dire la différence?

E_{10}	S_1	Um. Like watching the television show or whatever, or
E_{11}		I mean just looking at it.
E_{12}	T	No. (Points to another student.)
E_{13}	S_2	The word "regarder." You said "j'ai regardé"
E_{14}		one time and you said "j'ai regarde" another
E_{15}		time. (S is mispronouncing subject pronoun).
E_{16}	T	Ah, voilà, you heard the difference. Only it's not "j'ai
E_{17}		regarde," it's "je regarde." "Je regarde," right now,
E_{18}		but yesterday, Tuesday, "j'ai regardé." What did I do?
E_{19}	S_3	Put it in the past.
E_{20}	T	Yes, right, I put it in the past tense. I'm going to tell you
E_{21}		exactly how this is done. I just want you to listen right
E_{22}		now. You notice this first transparency I have up has
E_{23}		the conjugation of the verb …
E_{24}	SS	Avoir.
E_{25}	T	Avoir. Right, the conjugation of the verb "avoir." So
E_{26}		that's the first thing you have to know. You have to
E_{27}		know the conjugation of the verb "avoir." Second thing
E_{28}		is, I put a verb that you already recognize, but I changed
E_{29}		it a little. What did I do to it? (Teacher shows past
		participle of "regarder" on transparency.)
E_{30}		What did I have to do to make that different? Jean?
E_{31}	S_4	Put an accent on it?
E_{32}	T	Yes, I put an accent, right? I put an accent on the "e" to
E_{33}		make it different. So now instead of saying, I'm
E_{34}		watching TV, I'm saying …
E_{35}	SS	I watched TV.
E_{36}	T	I watched TV. I did it yesterday.
E_{37}	S	So you mean you put an accent over the "e" to make it
E_{38}		past?
E_{39}	T	These are "er" verbs we're talking about.
E_{40}		Right, you put an accent on the "e", and that makes it
E_{41}		past. But you can't leave it alone like this. You have to
E_{42}		use it with avoir.
E_{43}		You have to use it with avoir. Look at the next one. (The
		lesson continues as the teacher directs the students'
		attention to the overhead and then they change present-
		tense sentences to the past tense.)

In Protocol E, we see a deductive approach to grammar instruction where the rules are presented first and then later applied by the learners.

The teacher is serving as a conduit of information (Reddy, 1979) as exemplified by the directness and prescriptiveness of the explanation (have to …). The teacher first frames the lesson with a metastatement to recruit the learners' attention. E_{1-2} "Ecoutez, faites attention parce que nous allons apprendre quelque chose de différent." [Listen, pay attention because we are going to learn something new.] She then provides a "context," that of watching TV today compared to watching TV yesterday. The context is rather shallow, for it does not situate or frame the content of the lesson. In other words, it does not provide contextual clues to support the learners' understanding or comprehension of the lesson (Freeman and Freeman, 1992). Furthermore, notice that the example is centered around the teacher, that is the difference between I (the teacher) am watching TV and I (the teacher) watched TV. After the learners notice the difference between the present and past tense of watching TV, the teacher uses another metastatement to orient the students' attention to the explanation proper. (E_{20-22} "I'm going to tell you exactly how this is done. I just want you to listen right now").

The explanation in Protocol E can be characterized as monologic with its heavy emphasis on teacher-talk (Donato and Adair-Hauck, 1992). The use of metastatements (E_{1-2}, E_{20-21}) "I'm going to tell you exactly how this is done" characterizes the explicitness and directness of the explanation and, in many ways, *excludes* the learners from participating in the explanation. Furthermore, the discourse in this teacher-directed explanation can be characterized as uni-directional and asymmetrical discourse. The teacher acts as a leader who transmits knowledge and information to the students or followers. Indeed, the conduit metaphor is appropriate (Reddy, 1979). In other words, the explanation can be characterized as traditional in nature with little teacher/student interaction.

Role of the Teacher when focusing on Form:
Whole Language/Guided Participatory Approach

The strategies used by the teacher to focus on form in the whole language class are different from those used in the explicit instructional approach. In her whole language class, the teacher emphasizes the meaningful use of whole texts from a top-down approach to them. Once comprehension and understanding of the "Lion and the Mouse" story is achieved, she turns the students' attention to a selected grammatical form. On the first day of this instructional sequence, after approximately twenty-six minutes of instruction, she turns the learners' attention to the language system, in this case, first conjugation or "er" verbs. The first five storytelling activities engage the learners to focus on meaning and comprehension. To do so, the teacher: (1) acts out the story in the present tense using visuals, mime, gestures, and props; (2) retells the story encouraging the learners to participate whenever possible; (3) distributes the text and gives the students time to read the story (which is still in the present tense) to themselves; (4) she retells the story, having students retell the story whenever possible; (5) the students reread the text, this time with an accompanying vocabulary list.

In Activity #6, the teacher begins to encourage the learners to call attention to some salient features of the language. She asks the students to look at the "Lion and the Mouse" story and pick out any "er" or first conjugation verbs. This activity can be characterized as problem-solving. To do so, the students need to observe, organize, and categorize particular forms or the "er" verbs. After the teacher and students spend approximately five minutes selecting the first conjugation verbs from the story, the teacher moves into Activity #7 where she is orienting the students' attention on noticing the difference between a sentence in the present and one in the past.

Protocol F: Whole Language/Guided Participatory: Attention to Form

From the story, students have just generated a list of "er" verbs which the teacher has written on an overhead. Now the teacher switches the transparency and the students see the sentence, "La petite souris commence à courir sur le lion" [The little mouse begins to run on the lion].

F_1	T	Maintenant, quelle est la différence? Quelle est la
F_2		différence entre cette phrase-ci et la phrase qui est dans
F_3		votre histoire? (Pause … no answer from SS.)
F_4	T	Si je mets le mot aujourd'hui devant cette phrase
F_5		(Teacher reads from story.) "Aujourd'hui la petite
F_6		souris commence à courir sur le lion." And if I put the
F_7		word yesterday (*hier*) in front of this sentence (points to
F_8		overhead), "Hier la petite souris a commencé à courir,"
F_9		what is the difference?
F_{10}	S_1	(??)
F_{11}	T	Hmm?
F_{12}	S_1	Yesterday

F_{13}	T	Yesterday, yes. Yesterday what happened, Jacqueline?
F_{14}	S_1	The mouse ran.
F_{15}	T	Yes, yesterday this happened. What tense is your story in?
F_{16}	SS	Present.
F_{17}	T	Present, right. The lion is sleeping, the mouse starts to run
F_{18}		on the lion. The lion wakes up. Et cetera, et cetera. It's all
F_{19}		in the present. And what is this? (Points to sentence on overhead that is in past.)
F_{20}	SS	Past.
F_{21}	T	Oui, maintenant faisons une autre phrase.
F_{22}		Um. Regardez la phrase avec la petite souris eh . . .
F_{23}		crie. (SS flipping through pages of story.)
F_{24}	T	Qui voudrait deviner comment nous pourrions changer
F_{25}		cette phrase au passé?
F_{26}	T	(Scans students for a volunteer.)
F_{27}	S_2	Hier la petite souris ... (scratches her head).
F_{28}	T	La petite souris ...
F_{29}	T	(Switches to English.) Follow the same pattern as this
F_{30}		(points to sample sentence on overhead). How do we
F_{31}		say this?
F_{32}	T	... a commen ... (Reemphasizes previous example but doesn't complete the form.)
F_{33}	S_2	A crié. (Student interrupts and completes her own sentence.)
F_{34}	T	Ah, très, très bien. La petite souris a crié. Comprenez.
F_{35}		O.K., who can explain what's happening grammatically?
F_{36}		Who can explain what's happening?
F_{37}	S_3	In those two sentences?
F_{38}	T	Yes, in those two sentences. What did we do in those two
F_{39}		sentences?
F_{40}	S_3	We changed it into the past.
		(Please note that we will see the continuation of this explanation in Protocol G.)

Protocol F is strikingly different from the teacher's explanation in the explicit episode. First, the whole language/guided participation explanation is *contextualized* and grounded in the *in the context of the story*. That is, examples are taken from the story. Notice also that throughout this protocol the teacher simultaneously focuses student attention on meaning and form. To do so, the teacher writes a sentence from the story in the present tense on an overhead transparency and then she writes the same sentence in the past tense. She begins to focus student attention on form with a question requiring comparison between two sentences. F_{1-3} "Maintenant, quelle est la différence? Quelle est la différence entre cette phrase-ci et la phrase qui est dans votre histoire?" [Now then, what is the difference? What's the difference between this sentence and the sentence in your story?] The learners do not respond, which indicates to the teacher that indeed they have not attended to the structure of the verbs in the story, and that they need more assistance or strategic direction (Tharp and Gallimore, 1988). The teacher then adjusts her level of support by responding with a semantic, not syntactic, clue. (She writes "Aujourd'hui" [Today] in front of the present tense sentence and "Hier" [Yesterday] in French in front of the past tense sentence.) She is scaffolding her assistance by reducing the degrees of freedom involved in the task (Wood, Bruner and Ross, 1976). Her guidance assists the learners to focus on meaning before form. Again, in the whole language/guided participatory episode, we see a clear emphasis on meaning. Recall however, that in the previous protocol analysis of the explicit explanation on form that the opposite occurred; that is, form, not meaning was emphasized.

After the semantic clue is provided, a student responds F_{12} "Yesterday," and the teacher follows up F_{13} "Yesterday, yes. Yesterday, what happened, Jacqueline?" And then, the student responds correctly, F_{14} "The mouse ran."

This protocol exemplifies teaching as a means of assisting performance in the zone of proximal development. We see how it is possible for people with unequal expertise to work together to jointly solve the task (Tharp and Gallimore, 1988). The teacher scaffolds the problem-solving process by holding the task constant and at the same time, she encourages learner participation through graduated and responsive assistance (Tharp and Gallimore, 1988; Rogoff, 1990). This protocol reveals that through scaffolding, the teacher is able to guide and assist the learners through the problem-solving process. Notice that the *student*, not the teacher, solves the problem. In this sense, the teacher's responsive assistance is *mediating* the learning, not controlling or intervening in it (Goodman and Goodman, 1990).

Unlike the explicit episode, the discourse of this protocol is reciprocal, supportive, and collaborative. For example, in this protocol, the teacher is directing the learners to put a sentence from the story into the past, but she softens the direction by including herself F_{21} "Oui, maintenant faisons une autre" (Yes, now let's do one more). The use of the first-person plural imperative form "let us" connotes a supportive guiding and assisting expert/novice relationship as well as a collective orientation to problem-solving. Recall that in Protocol A the ski instructor (expert) used this same discourse strategy. Furthermore, the teacher uses indirect directives, i.e., question directives or hints (Ervin-Tripp, 1976, 1977) to encourage the learners to participate in the problem-solving process: F_{24} "Qui voudrait deviner comment nous pourrions changer cette phrase au passé?" [Who would like to guess how we would change this sentence to the past?] The use of the conditional tense in F_{24} with "Qui voudrait" [Who would like] and "comment nous pourrions" [how we would] are powerful invitational gestures that encourage participation in the activity (Schiffrin, 1987). These interactional features help to create an "openness" or dialogical space in which students are encouraged to reflect about and, at the same time, *participate in the activity*. Unlike the direct directives in Protocols B and E where the teacher makes use of imperatives and the second-person plural pronoun (you), this protocol illustrates the collaborative nature of developing metalinguistic competence.

The teacher does not limit herself to indirect directives. She judiciously uses explicit speech and direct directives in the whole language/guided participatory episode. For example, in F_{22-23} the teacher uses a direct directive to orient the learners' attention, "Regardez la phrase avec la petite souris eh . . . crie." [Look at the sentence that has the mouse um ... shouts.] She is also very explicit in F_{29-30} when she says, "Follow the same pattern as this (points to sample sentence on overhead)." However, unlike the explicit episode which is replete with direct directives the discourse strategies in the whole language/guided participatory episode include some direct directives, but also numerous indirect directives. At times, the teacher restricts or narrows the dialogical space by using a direct directive. For example, when the teacher states, F_{22-23} "Regardez la phrase avec la petite souris eh . . . crie.", she is narrowing the students' orientation to the task. However, immediately afterwards, she expands the dialogical space with an indirect directive, F_{24} "Qui voudrait deviner comment nous pourrions changer cette phrase au passée?" [Who would like to guess how we would change that one to the past.] This dynamic balance of discourse strategies allows for a "looseness" or "fluidity" when working in the zone of proximal development. Newman, Griffin, and Cole (1989) remind us that this "looseness" or "fluidity" in the zone of proximal development (ZPD) allows "minds to meet" as the expert/novice cooperate together in attending to form.

Unlike the explicit explanation, Protocol F provides an interesting example of linguistic performance before metalinguistic understanding has been established. For example, the teacher invites the learners to change a sentence from the story into the past tense *before the students have been given the rule.* The teacher begins with an indirect directive, F_{24-25}, "Qui voudrait deviner comment nous pourrions changer cette phrase au passé?" A student starts the sentence, but hesitates, F_{27}, "Hier, la petite souris ..." (student scratches her head—which serves as a gesture that she needs assistance). The teacher responds and assists the learner by instructing her to look at the sample past tense sentence taken from the story which is written on the overhead (F_{29-31}). The teacher then starts to reread the sample sentence. However, the learner interrupts the teacher in order to complete the sentence on her own, F_{33} ... a crié [yelled]. Through guided participation, in this case reminding the student to attend to a similar target structure, the student is able to solve the problem on her own before any explicit explanation of the rule is provided. Again, when working in the ZPD, one observes *performance before competence* (Rogoff, 1990).

Finally this protocol is illustrative of the importance of instructional mediation when an expert and novices collaborate in the ZPD. The teacher's discourse strategies guide the learners through the problem-solving process. Vygotsky (1978, p. 28) reminds us that "just as a mold gives shape to a substance, words can shape an activity into a structure." In other words, the dialogue within the zone of proximal development, can be characterized as having critical "coordinates" or discourse strategies which shape the activity and assist in the negotiation of meaning between expert and novice. Consequently, the learners are able to participate in activites which would be impossible to do alone (Tharp and Gallimore, 1988).

As the data indicate, during this phase, the task of attending to form is critical for establishing joint problem-solving (Wertsch, 1979). The teacher spends a lot of time focusing the learners' attention on form before she moves into the explanation (F_{8-20} and F_{24-33}). Once the teacher and learners attend to form, then they are ready to co-construct the explanation and achieve a higher level of generalizations. Protocol G builds on Protocol F and demonstrates co-construction of the grammar explanation.

Protocol G: WL/GP: Co-constructing an Explanation of the Form

The teacher now moves to co-constructing an explicit explanation of the procedures for forming the past tense in French. She has just finished guiding the students to attend to the difference between two sentences— one in present and one in past tense. Since this was the first time for both the teacher and the students to co-construct an explanation, the teacher felt more comfortable co-constructing in English. As the teacher became more familiar with a whole language/guided participatory approach, she felt more comfortable using the target language to co-construct.

G_1	T	Who can explain what's happening grammatically? Who
G_2		can explain what's happening?
G_3	S_1	In those two sentences?
G_4	T	Yes, in those two sentences. What did we do in those
G_5		two sentences?
G_6	S_1	We changed it to the past tense.
G_7	T	We changed it to the past tense. How did we change it to
G_8		the past tense?
G_9	S_2	We added a word, yesterday.
G_{10}	T	We added a word, yesterday, yeah. That's one thing we did.
G_{11}		We added a word, yesterday and that's going to be our
G_{12}		clue word.
G_{13}	S_3	We added a participle.
G_{14}	T	A participle! Who knows what a participle is?
G_{15}	S_3	Um … in English you use it to make it past tense.
G_{16}	T	To make it past tense. Right. Now let's use the verb "to
G_{17}		dance."
G_{18}		Let's use the verb to dance. How do I put that in the past?
G_{19}	S_4	Add "ed."
G_{20}	T	Add "ed." That's what we do in English. Add "ed."
G_{21}		What do we do in French?
G_{22}	S_2	Add [e] (pronounces [e] ending in French).
G_{23}	T	Add a what?
G_{24}	S_2	Add "e" with an accent mark.
G_{25}	T	Did we do anything else to these two sentences? Try to com-
G_{26}		pare these two sentences you have in front of you, Julie?
G_{27}	S_5	You add an "a."
G_{28}	T	You did. Where does "a" come from? A verb you already
G_{29}		know. (Long pause)
G_{30}	T	Something you already know. (SS look at one another.)
G_{31}		François?
G_{32}	S_6	C'est le verbe "être"?

G$_{33}$ T   C'est le verbe "être" classe? Non, ce n'est pas "être."
G$_{34}$ (T conjugates entire verb "avoir" on overhead but doesn't
                     write the infinitive—"avoir" (to have) which is the
                     answer she is searching for.)
G$_{35}$ T   Qu'est-ce que c'est?
G$_{36}$ SS   Avoir. (Activity continues as T asks SS to select sentences
                     from story and then to change them to the past.)

The discourse in Protocol G reveals that a whole language/guided participatory explanation is a collaborative process. The predominant use of the inclusive second-person pronoun "we" throughout the co-constructed explanation indicates a collective orientation to explanation. In contrast, the explanation for the explicit approach (Protocol E) reveals that the first-person pronoun "I" or the teacher's orientation is emphasized.

This protocol demonstrates a problem-solving approach to grammar explanation, for the teacher is encouraging the learners to search for an answer or to solve the "mystery" of how to construct a verb in the past tense. To do so, she begins with a question, G$_{1-2}$, "Who can explain what's happening grammatically? Who can explain what's happening?" She then uses a number of assisting questions to help the students tease out the important characteristics of past tense formation: G$_{4-5}$, "What did we do in those two sentences"; G$_{7-8}$, "How did we change it to the past tense?"; G$_{18}$, "How do I put that (referring to English verb "to dance") in the past?"; G$_{21}$, "What do we do in French?"; G$_{25}$, "Did we do anything else to these two sentences?" These assisting questions serve to encourage the students to think about the procedures of the past tense formation. These questions assist rather than assess learning, for the students have not yet been given the rules for past tense formation in French. The teacher is not *evaluating* their knowledge; on the contrary, she is using questions to keep their attention, to focus on the grammatical problem, and to help them articulate their generalizations. In other words, the teacher is guiding and supporting the learners as they accomplish the task of explaining past tense formation.

Protocol G demonstrates that the learners are capable of co-constructing the explanation. First, the students remark about the function of the form, G$_6$, "We changed it to the past tense." Then they notice a semantic difference with the use of adverbs of time: G$_9$, "We added a word, yesterday." They notice morphological differences such as the acute accent to form the past participle: G$_{24}$, "Add 'e' with an accent mark." They notice the use of the auxiliary verb: G_{27}, "You add an 'a'." At the end of the protocol, the students have difficulty naming the infinitive form of the helping verb "avoir." In a sense, they have successfully noted the four principal characteristics of past tense "er" verb formations when using them in the third-person singular form. However, they are unable to recognize that the auxiliary verb "a" comes from the infinitive "avoir." The teacher tries to help them discover the infinitive form of the auxiliary verb in order to achieve a generalization about the rule for past tense formation. To do so, the teacher asks, G_{28-29}, "Where does 'a' come from? A verb you already know." When her truncated assistance fails, the teacher provides a visual clue by writing the conjugation on the overhead, yet she does not write the infinitive form which is the answer to the problem. All these clues help the learners to remember that the word "a" comes from "avoir."

After co-constructing the grammar explanation, the teacher encourages the learners to retell the story in the past by picking out sentences from the story and changing them to the past tense.

Completing the Cycle of PACE

In the PACE model, Donato and Adair-Hauck (1992) propose a four-phase cyclical approach for situating grammar instruction in a whole language lesson. During the first or *Presentation* phase, the teacher presents a whole text, for example a story, and the emphasis is on literal comprehension. During the second or *Attention* phase, the teacher guides the learners to attend to a target form used in the Presentation phase. As the data indicate, the discourse for this phase reveals the use of both verbal and non-verbal (underlining, highlighting, pointing) directives. Once the learners have attended to form, then they are better prepared to move into the third or *Co-construction* phase in which the teacher uses guiding questions in order to assist the learners to achieve higher level generalizations. Through the teacher's responsive assistance, the learners are encouraged to reflect upon and to participate in the explanation. In this way, consciousness-raising is viewed as an active and collective endeavor. During the final phase, the students engage in *Extension* activities which encourage the learners to go beyond the text as presented and to use the particular target form in a new task. At this time the teachers and learners could also discuss any symbolic, figurative, or cultural nuances of the story. Before turning our attention to an in-depth discussion of the extension activities, we need to acknowledge some of the other instructional strategies which the teacher incorporates during the first three phases of PACE.

A Dynamic Web of Interrelated Events

One important objective of this case study was to reveal how a teacher implements the PACE model within the constraints of a foreign language classroom environment. In order to narrow the focus of this project, one of the three instructional episodes on the teaching of the past indefinite tense has been described in detail. The previous discussion concerned the first episode or the teaching of the past tense of first conjugation "er" verbs since we were interested in discovering the genesis of new and developing skills and in uncovering the communicative dynamics of two approaches to the teaching of this lesson. However, careful examination of all three of the videotaped episodes revealed that these are indeed a dynamic web of interrelated events. The three episodes, all of which are driven by the function of "past narration," evolve into an interconnected, integrated, and "whole" instructional event. In other words, the three different episodes with the three different stories can be viewed as sub-parts or "mini-episodes" of one principal instructional event—the teaching of the past narration or past events. Therefore, in an attempt to provide a rich and complete description of this whole language/guided participatory approach, we will examine some of the larger patterns and evolving strategies that the teacher incorporates as the "whole instructional event" unfolds. The process of focusing on form in a meaningful context is a cyclical process characterized by the whole language philosophy of moving from whole to part to whole (Freeman and Freeman, 1992).

a. Strategies for Presentation Phase

The teacher's storytelling strategies across the three episodes illustrate how they evolve as both the teacher and learners become more familiar with a whole language approach. In Episode I (The Lion and the Mouse), the teacher uses visuals, props, and gestures to present the story. She recycles the story a number of times using these same devices to assist the students in comprehending the story. In Episode II, when first presenting "Le Petit Chaperon Rouge" (Little Red Riding Hood), the teacher does not use visuals or props. She removes these mediational "tools," so that the learners must listen carefully to the story for meaning making. The teacher does provide a few guiding questions to assist the learners' comprehension.

In Episode III, the teacher embeds the explanation with a story which is unknown to the students. The story is a revised version of the text "L'Autographe Spéciale" from *Deuxième Livre*, published by Amsco. The story centers around "Magic Johnson" (see Adair-Hauck, 1993, for text). Although not an authentic text, this story does embed the target structure in a context that is of interest to high school students. In contrast to the previous episodes, the teacher presents the "Magic Johnson" story in the past tense even though many of the verbs are intransitive and require "être" for the auxiliary verb (an untaught structure). Episode III is also different, for the teacher takes a much less active role in presenting this story. The teacher stands on the sidelines and reads the text, the students listen (no copy provided) and volunteers act out the episodic actions using props. In other words, in Episode III, the students, and not the teacher, act out the story.

As these storytelling strategies evolve and as these episodes unfold, the teacher transfers more of the responsibility for the learning to the students, and teacher-control evolves into student initiative (Stevick, 1980; Freeman, 1992). As both the teacher and the learners become more familiar with the whole language/guided participatory approach, the teacher's role in presenting the stories decreases and concurrently, student participation and initiative increase.

b. Strategies for Attention on Form and Co-constructing Explanation

As with the previous section, we will describe briefly how the teacher's strategies for focusing on form develop as the episodes progress. The protocol analysis of Episode I showed that the teacher focuses on form after the first five activities which stress meaning and comprehension. However, in Episode II with the "Little Red Riding Hood" story, she encourages the students to listen to the story for meaning, but at the same time she wants them to notice any "er" or first-conjugation verbs. For the "Little Red Riding Hood" story she is encouraging them to attend to meaning, to comprehend, and to pay attention to a particular verb form at the same time. When we queried the teacher about this decision, she mentioned that the learners were familiar with the "Red Riding Hood" story in their native language and that they had already practiced attending to "er" verb forms in Episode I; therefore she was reinforcing this strategy from the beginning of Episode II.

Another strategy that the teacher uses to focus attention on form in Episode II is that she encourages the students to highlight graphically the different classes of "ir" and "re" verbs. For one of the homework assignments the students reread the story which is in the present tense and then circle any "ir" verbs and box any "re" verbs. The students can then use these graphics or "clues" when they rewrite the story in the past tense.

In Episode III, the teacher selects a very different approach to attend to form as well as the co-construction of the explanation. The first three activities engage the learners to focus on the meaning of the "Magic Johnson" story. Then in Activity #4, approximately twenty minutes into Episode III, the teacher divides the learners into groups of four. The students have the "Magic Johnson" story with the past indefinite forms with "être" underlined. In this case getting students to attend to a particular form is done by the teacher. The learners' task is to act as detectives with the mission of trying to figure out how the underlined words are used in French. The learners need to collaborate and work together to: (1) figure out what clues they need to look for when exploring how the underlined words are used in French; (2) write down their understanding of how the underlined words are used in French; (3) make a list of other words or expressions in the text that serve as clues to solve the mystery of the underlined words or phrases; and finally (4) using the underlined words as models, they need to create three of their own sentences. Note that the first three questions may be answered in English; the last answer must be in French.

The groups then work together on this activity for approximately ten minutes. Using the questions as guides, the learners collaborate on an explanation and answer the questions. In so doing, the learners are co-constructing the explanation. The teacher walks around the room providing help when necessary. After the learners have co-constructed the explanation in teams, then the teacher calls the class back together as a whole and the teacher and learners engage in a collective summary of explanation. It is interesting to note that this time the *co-construction* of the explanation is in French whereas in the previous episodes it was in English.

Again, the theme of teacher-control transforming into student-initiative emerges as the episodes evolve (Stevick, 1980, Freeman, 1992). As noted above in Episode III, it is the students who act out the story. Likewise, in Episode III, the students collaborate with one another to co-construct the explanation. This case study clearly demonstrates that as both the teacher and learners become more familiar with a whole language/guided participatory approach, the teacher affords the learners with more opportunities to be initiators in the learning process.

Phase IV: Extension Activities

As mentioned earlier, the PACE model incorporates a four-phased, cyclical approach to grammar instruction. The Extension phase indeed is exceptionally critical with respect to the *Communication Goal and the Interpersonal and Presentational Standards*. Extension activities afford the learners the opportunity to use new skills creatively and interpersonally. Meaning-making is at the heart of extension activities. This phase encourages the learners to negotiate meaning, and simultaneously, to express their ideas, feelings, and opinions. In other words, these activities emphasize self-expression and self-realization on the part of the learners.

For example, in the "Lion and the Mouse," the teacher asks the students to create their own sentences in the past tense as a homework assignment. The following day's lesson is then centered around the learners' own words. Consequently, the language used in class is more learner-driven than teacher-or text-driven, as the learners are encouraged to be generators and producers of language (Goodman and Goodman, 1990). This generative approach promotes interactions that stress meaning-making or sense-making. Concurrently, the extension activities encourage the learners to hypothesize about the correct use of target forms and use them to ensure that communication is realized.

To assist the students' attempts to negotiate meaning during the extension activities, the teacher covered one wall with discourse facilitators such as, "Répétez, s'il vous plaît"; "Comment? Je n'ai pas saisi ça"; [Pardon me. I didn't catch that] or "Comment dit-on _____ en français?" [How do you say _____ in French?]. In this way, the teacher signaled to the students the importance of using these discourse facilitators to negotiate meaning and at the same time decorated her walls with the "curriculum."

The types of extension activities used in the case study evolve considerably as the teacher and learners become more familiar with a whole language approach. For example, for the first episode the activities involve sentence-level discourse on the part of the learners. However, in Episode II (Red Riding Hood), the extension activities become more challenging and integrative. On Day 3 (Act. #1), the students work in groups to describe pictures from the stories. They can describe the story as they wish, or they may add to or change the story line. As they move from sentence-level to paragraph-level discourse, the learners are developing literacy skills (reading and writing) along with listening and speaking.

In Episode III, the teacher integrates more extension activities that involve cooperative learning. For example, on Day 2, the class is divided into two teams with the goal of recreating "Human Sentences." Students are given cards with different parts of speech; as the teacher reads a sentence in the past tense, the teams must listen carefully in order to construct correctly a "Human Sentence." On the same day, in teams, students recreate the "Magic Johnson" story changing it from the present tense to the past tense using graphic organizers. On the third and final day of the instructional episode, student volunteers act out a poem "Déjeuner du matin" by Jacques Prévert. The students work in teams to create their own poems which must be written in the past tense. Later on, the learners read their poems to the other members of the class. This activity incorporates listening, speaking, reading, writing, thinking, and culture skills. This final project completes the cycle as the activity moves back to the "whole." The teacher explained that she believed that the learners were ready for this type of "whole language activity" by the end of the final instruction episode.

In Phase IV, as with the previous phases, we see the emerging theme of teacher-control evolving into student initiative. As the episodes develop and unfold, the teacher integrates more meaning-making activities that encourage the learners to cooperate with each other in order to convey their ideas and negotiate meaning in the target language on an interpersonal level. Through these meaningful language learning activities, the students observe and begin to understand the utility of the target language system. These socially-based, interactive activites underscore some basic tenets (Cooper, 1993, p. 10) on how learners acquire language for communicative purposes:

1. When they have a need that is meaningful and real;
2. Through interactions with adults and peers;
3. By making approximations of real language;
4. At varying rates and in various stages even though they all go through similar phases of development.

Summary of Qualitative Analyses

The purpose of this case study was to add to the experience and to increase an understanding of one particular area of foreign language pedagogy, the teaching of grammatical structure in a meaningful whole language context. To do so, we designed and implemented two theoretically motivated instructional episodes (whole language/guided participatory vs. an explicit teacher-directed approach to the teaching of the past indefinite tense in French) in order to observe the interactive processes of teaching and learning within these two varying instructional contexts. More specifically, we have tried to describe the learners' behaviors, the teacher's behaviors, and the social interactions within these instructional contexts. We have attempted to elucidate not only what was happening during these instructional episodes, but also how the activities were carried out within these two varying contexts, and in particular, how the communicative dynamics varied between these different contexts.

The renewed interest in understanding the social contexts in which meanings are negotiated has encouraged educational researchers to examine "real" activities of "real people" within the school setting, which is indeed a social context (Newman, Griffin, and Cole, 1989). Furthermore, sociolinguistic research is now interested in classroom discourse as a medium for changing thinking (Tharp and Gallimore, 1988; Newman et al., 1989; Duffy and Roehler, 1986). According to these theorists, classroom discourse analysis serves as a window for observing and describing the process of cognitive change. Newman et al. (1989, p. 74) remind us that this type of classroom discourse analysis provides a useful understanding of a teacher's work: "Unlike Piaget's approach, Vygotsky emphasized the origin of knowledge in the *social interactions* the child engages in. This makes his theory interesting for us because it gives *an important role to the teacher and helps to account for the variability in the process and its outcomes*" (emphasis added).

As mentioned earlier, the role of speech serves as a cornerstone to Vygotskian psycholinguistics. Speech or discourse is viewed as a mediating and regulatory system as well as a psychological tool that serves to organize higher psychological processes such as perception, attention, and memory (Vygotsky, 1978). Throughout his research, Vygotsky consistently reminds us that "speech accompanies activity and plays an important role in carrying it out" (p. 25), and he further explains that "The more complex the action demanded by the situation, and the less direct its solution, the greater the importance played by speech in the operation as a whole (pp. 25–26)."

Within the domain of this project, we have observed and discussed the critical role of speech when teaching within a whole language/guided participatory vs. explicit, teacher-directed context. More specifically, the data have revealed some essential discourse strategies or semiotic mechanisms that promote or engender interactions within these varying contexts. Through protocol analysis, we have shown that the teacher clearly exploits different discourse strategies when interacting with learners within the contours of these different settings. In the explicit, teacher-directed episode, we see an asymmetrical and monologic "exchange" which serves to promote, favor, and crystallize the teacher's ideas and perceptions. Discourse strategies, such as the use of the first-person singular subject pronoun "I," direct directives (imperatives and desire statements), and closed-ended or assessing questions dominate the discourse. Metastatements about the explanation (i.e., explanations about the explanations) (Donato and Adair-Hauck, 1992) and overt turn-taking signals with evaluative feedback dominate and direct the classroom interaction. As a result, classroom discourse can be characterized as explicit and monologic speech (Donato and Adair-Hauck, 1992). The discourse reveals that within this context, it is the teacher who is responsible for the explanation. The discourse strategies that coordinate the explanation limit the involvement of the learners. Therefore, the learners are assigned a passive role.

In contrast, when we observe the teacher within a whole language/guided participatory context, different discourse strategies or semiotic mechanisms emerge from the data. A whole language/guided participatory approach is facilitated by discourse strategies that stand in contradistinction to the discourse features used in conventional, teacher-directed approaches to learning. These discourse strategies help to coordinate the learners' actions as they participate in activities which would be impossible to do alone (Vygotsky, 1978; Bakhtin, 1981). When a teacher invites the learners to participate in the explanation, critical discourse strategies such as the use of the first-person collective subject pronoun "we," the use of the conditional verb tense, and indirect directives (question directives or hints) (Ervin-Tripp, 1976, 1977) followed by complimentary assisting questions support both the expert and novices as they try to establish a shared definition of the task. These discourse strategies serve to coordinate and to mediate the activity.

The data from the whole language/guided participatory episode also revealed that when a teacher offers responsive assistance she uses metastatements about the function of the task or activity and fewer evaluative remarks. These discourse strategies serve to shape or mold the classroom discourse and to be more reflective of natural discourse that occurs in everyday real life situations (Coulthard, 1977). Consequently, classroom discussion on the teaching of grammar becomes dialogic, responsive, and reciprocal. (See Table 3 for chart highlighting these different discourse strategies.)

Table 3. Characteristics of Discourse Strategies in the Explanation of Grammar.	
Whole Language/Guided Participatory Approach	*Explicit, Teacher-Directed Approach*
Dialogic or symmetrical exchange combination of teacher and student talk. Both (T) and (SS) responsible for explanation.	Monologic or asymmetrical exchange —more teacher talk. (T) responsible for explanation.
Use of first-person plural or collective pronoun "we."	Use of first-person singular pronoun "I."
Indirect directives mixed with some direct directives.	Direct directives emphasized.
Use of conditional tense as well as some imperative forms.	Use of imperatives or commands.
Questions that assist as well as assess.	Mainly questions that assess.
Turn-taking less clearly marked.	Overt turn-taking signals.
Metastatements that frame the task or activity.	Metastatements that frame the explanation (explanation about the explanation).
Fewer evaluative remarks or feedback.	Evaluative remarks or feedback clearly marked.
Note: (T) = teacher; (SS) = student	

These findings again support the research of Wells and Montgomery (1981) who argue that in first language development an adult or caretaker with a supportive style frequently adjusts speech in negotiating meaning in order to secure mutual understanding. Within a supportive context, the caretaker uses discourse features such as open-ended questions that assist rather than assess the child's knowledge and fewer overt evaluative remarks in order to help move the conversation along. In this sense, speech is a dynamic tool which coordinates and facilitates the explanation and, concurrently, speech challenges the learners to participate in activities which would be impossible for them to do alone.

Reflection on the Goal

This project has highlighted the PACE model or a whole language/guided participatory approach to grammar instruction in order to assist learners to communicate on an interpersonal level in a second language. Second language researchers now stress the importance of developing communicative competence which includes not only grammatical, but also discourse, sociolinguistic, and strategic competence. The PACE model affords the learners the opportunity to plant the seeds for communicative competence early in the foreign language learning sequence. Through storytelling, learners are exposed to extended-level discourse, not just word-level or sentential speech (discourse competence). Through the use of authentic texts, students are exposed to various levels of sociolinguistic appropriateness (sociolinguistic competence). Through joint problem-solving between expert and novices, the students become aware of the salient features of the language (grammatical competence). And finally, through collaborative and cooperative extension activities, the students have the opportunity to develop strategies for language learning, e.g., social, cognitive, metacognitive, and compensation strategies (strategic competence).

A whole language/guided participatory approach is a *socially-con structed approach* for communicative development in a second language classroom. By contrasting the interactive environments (Hall, 1996) of an explicit, teacher-directed approach vs. a whole language/guided participatory approach, this action-based research project revealed their opposing discursive frameworks. Hall and Brooks (in preparation) remind us of the critical role that interactive environments play in language development by stating: "The development of a significant part of our ability to competently and creatively interact with other community members is inextricably tied to the interactive environments to which we are exposed and given extended guidance and assistance" (p.8).

Finally, the whole language/guided participatory approach acknowledges the complementary nature of cognitive, linguistic, social, *and af-*

fective development. Whether focusing on *meaning* (through stories), on *form and function* (through guided participation) or on skills in new directions (interpersonal and meaning-making extension activities), the learners are consistently listening to, using, or thinking about language via semiotic mediation and social interaction with adults/experts or with peers. The videotapings, discourse analyses, and the students' questionnaire attest that the PACE model can engender positive, affective interpersonal relationships in a second language classroom. Hall and Brooks remind us of the benefits of developing positive, prosocial relationships in communicative development:

> These positive relationships in turn engender an active interest in learning, and a high degree of self-confidence and positive emotional energy. It is upon prosocial behaviors (Hinde, 1987; Hinde and Groebel, 1991) that individuals base their development of more complexly realized social, linguistic and cognitive action (p.12)

For this particular action-based research project, one needs to underscore that this case study is just one teacher's attempt at implementing a whole language/guided participatory approach to grammar instruction. This investigation has telescoped one teacher's efforts to incorporate the PACE model into the real world of classroom teaching. In no way can one extrapolate these findings and generalize that all teachers would indeed integrate the approach in exactly the same way. One can say, however, that this is how one teacher in collaboration with second language researchers, incorporated the PACE model in her classroom.

Furthermore, we need to underscore that the PACE model *is not prescriptive* in nature, that is, it does not delineate a well defined set of procedures or "scripts" for second language learning/teaching. On the contrary, the PACE model is constructive, interactive, and reciprocal in nature. A Vygotskian or sociocultural approach to teaching/learning affirms that second language teachers need to be encouraged to predict, hypothesize about, and create interpersonal language learning experiences for their students. As these instructional events unfold, the teachers need to reflect upon and to evaluate critically which kinds of language learning experiences best meet the *personal needs of their students in their particular instructional/social contexts.* Indeed, no single strategy, procedure, or methodology will be appropriate for all students (Cooper, 1993).

Personal Voice of the Teacher

Having learned a foreign language in the very traditional grammar-translation way and having believed it to be the very best way, I resisted the thought of change in my classroom after twenty years of relative success with grammar-driven lessons. My students, however, found native speakers to be practically incomprehensible. As I attended more conferences, seminars, workshops, and weeks of methods training, where a myriad of second language learning approaches were presented, I incorporated into my lessons the methods I thought would benefit my students.

When Bonnie Adair-Hauck asked me to participate in this study using whole language, I was ready! However, I wasn't ready for the overwhelming acceptance of this change on the part of my students and the remarkable increase in their eagerness and their ability to sustain interpersonal communication, even with native speakers. I found myself working longer and harder than I ever had and enjoying it more. When using the PACE model, it is imperative that the teacher prepare a variety of meaning-making activities, so that the use of time and energy in the classroom targets the desired goal. The more activities I prepared, the more quickly new ideas came for more interesting ways for my students to learn. All the while I was still attending conferences and workshops; only now I was concentrating on presentations dealing with interpersonal communication. I resolved to plan at least five activities for each class period to maximize the use of time. After my initial presentation of a text (story, song, video, etc.), most students seemed to grasp enough meaning of the text to arouse their attention. Once this happened, it became easy to assist them to think critically about how we can use language to express our interpersonal needs. Then they were eager to see if they could participate in interactive learning activities and express their ideas, thoughts, and feelings in the second language. I tried to impress upon them Goodman's idea that just as each person's thumbprint is different, each person's language (whether a first or second language) will have its own personal voice or style. I encouraged my students to take risks and express their personal needs, ideas, thoughts, and feelings through cooperative learning activities. These interpersonal, communicative experiences helped my students see the connection between the language system (grammar) and communication on an interpersonal level. Furthermore, the PACE model helped us to develop a true sense of community. My role as a teacher changed from one who directs to one who guides and supports second language learning. Likewise, the students started to see how they needed to support and assist one another as they tried to share their needs, thoughts, and feelings.

And finally, from this research project, I felt much more comfortable taking other curricular risks. For example, I tried to make connections with other communities (Goal 5) by creating projects where my students had to go out into the community to interview native French speakers (both in person and on the phone). And I felt more confident in making interdisciplinary connections (Goal 3) with faculty in the arts, home economics, and music. Once my students and myself had the opportunity to see the "whole picture" of how whole language can work, it became much easier to make these connections.

As a result of our participation in this study, both my students and I have a renewed love of learning a foreign language. And that's the main goal for teaching a foreign language, *n'est-ce pas*?

Personal Voice of the Researcher

I enjoyed this project immensely, because I had the opportunity to work in tandem with a classroom-based teacher and her students. From classroom observations and from hours of videotaped footage, I was able to really get to know Philomena and her students. I was thoroughly amazed at the eagerness and willingness of the students to participate in an approach that was totally "foreign" or new to them. The project also made me cognizant that I had to give Philomena the flexibility to implement the PACE model according to her own judgments and intuitions. For example, on the first day when Philomena presented "The Lion and the Mouse" story, I thought that we had agreed that she would tell the story in the past tense. (Theoretically, I wanted her to foreshadow the grammatical structure, the past indefinite tense, by telling the story in the past.) Later on, Philomena explained that she did not feel comfortable doing that; therefore she decided that her students should hear the story in the present tense first. As Philomena and her students became more comfortable with the PACE model, she felt more at ease with foreshadowing a grammatical structure during the Presentation phase. As a result of the project, I became more aware that a teacher, just like her students, needs *time* to become familiar with new techniques and methodologies. In other words, teacher training and retraining is not an instantaneous event; on the contrary, teacher development is a gradual and progressive process.

I was also intrigued with how well the students learned and retained the grammatical structures using the PACE model. Since I had spent long hours watching videotapes of the non-treatment group who received very explicit teacher instructions with a lot of drilling of the target forms, I thought that perhaps the non-treatment group would outperform the whole language group, especially on the discrete point sections of the retention tests. However, the retention tests showed that as the whole language learners became more familiar with this approach, they performed as well as the non-treatment group and actually outperformed the non-treatment group in metalinguistic competence (For results on retention tests, see Adair-Hauck, 1993). These results can be explained by the fact that PACE encourages the learners to develop metalinguistic awareness or how the language system functions by participating in meaningful, co-constructed explanations that enhance language awareness and by participating in co-operative learning activities that allow the learners to use the language system in interpersonal and functional ways.

Voices of the Students

Before concluding, one should acknowledge the thoughts and opinions of the learners regarding whole language activities for second language learners. In order to provide multiple perspectives on this case study, and to shed light on the data collected from the other instruments, the students in the whole language (treatment group) took a questionnaire concerning the whole language/guided participatory activities. The students' responses concerning the whole language activities were overwhelmingly positive.

For example, when asked, "Was it easier to learn French by listening to the stories?", 90 percent of the students answered "yes"; one student responded negatively and one student said, "yes and no." The students' qualitative responses to the question, "What did you like most about the storytelling activities?" were particularly enlightening. One perceptive student commented, "I liked learning with pictures and props. That way, if there was something I didn't understand, then I knew what it was." Another student responded, "I liked the storytelling activities because they had a good effect. You seem to remember things if you have to do something with the words you're learning." And finally, one student made this comment regarding a positive, affective climate, "I liked the fact that it gets the class into the story, and it makes it more fun. I think I learn better when I enjoy the class."

Future Concerns

This action-based research project underscores a number of needs and concerns for our profession. First, the data reveal an important psycholinguistic implication which challenges the present explicit/implicit controversy. Through protocol analysis in this case study, it has been shown that inductive reasoning in a foreign language is a socially derived process. Through co-construction and guided participation of the grammar explanation, the teacher assists the students to think inductively about the foreign language. In this sense, co-construction allows "thinking" to be made public and later internalized for independent problem-solving (Donato and Adair-Hauck, 1992). As a result, the students learn strategies for hypothesizing, predicting, and generalizing about the language. A longitudinal study may show that co-construction of grammar explanations will eventually lead to the students' ability to internalize and think inductively on their own. Over an extended period of time, the students may be able to pick out the salient features of the language without assistance from the teacher.

Additionally, we discovered that the students enjoyed learning French in a whole language/guided participatory manner. In particular, they mentioned that they appreciated the break from tedious grammar exercises. The new *Standards for Foreign Language Learning* (1996) advocate an extended and longer sequence of foreign language instruction. Numerous school districts are also considering the advantages of longer sequences of study in foreign language. As a result, curricular specialists and teachers will have to find ways to capture the students' interest and keep learners involved in meaningful classroom activities for an extended period of time. The learners in this study showed a clear preference for the whole language/guided participatory approach. This philosophy may be instrumental in promoting student interest in foreign languages over an extended period of time. Most importantly, it is an approach appropriate for younger learners as well.

Designing appropriate whole language/guided participatory curricular materials will require language and literature faculties to share their expertise. A whole language/guided participatory approach is a literature-based method that would benefit from collaborations between language and literature faculties. For example, literature experts can assist in the selection of linguistically accessible texts or effective models of literary texts with natural redundancies and repetitions. The literature specialists can point out the themes and the figurative, symbolic, and cultural nuances of the texts. In turn, the language specialists can offer their expertise by suggesting interesting ways to present the texts and by designing cooperative learning and extensive activities that relate to the texts. In other words, literature and language specialists will need to collaborate on how to integrate literature with language arts into activities that assist the learners to develop linguistic competence.

Teachers also need to be trained in mediating texts and ways to encourage learners to attend to form and to co-construct explanations. This study illustrated that a whole language/guided participatory approach requires the use of discourse strategies that stand in contradistinction to the discourse strategies used in a conventional approach. Teachers need to be made aware of these powerful semiotic mechanisms which enable the teacher to assist the learners within their zones of proximal development.

The final implication of this case study relates to the issue of teacher education. The *Standards for Foreign Language Learning* (1996) emphasize that communication is at the heart of language learning. Students learn how to communicate by transacting and deriving their own meanings from authentic language learning experiences situated in a rich variety of contexts (Rigg and Allen, 1989). Most preservice and inservice teachers have never experienced a whole language or transactional approach to language development. Unlike transmission approaches, transactional approaches require a high level of expertise on the part of the teacher (Cooper, 1993). When teachers are negotiating the meaning of the stories, or when they are focusing on parts and co-constructing explanations in the target language, they need to be thinking about how to scaffold the tasks in order to include the learners in the activities. To do so, teachers need at least an advanced level of oral proficiency in the target language.

This case study revealed that teacher training and retraining takes time. At the beginning of the study, the teacher was hesitant to use texts that embed target structures which were unknown to the students. However, by the end of the study, she felt comfortable using this technique. Also, with time, the teacher became more comfortable in co-constructing the explanation in French and with providing the learners with more extension activities that included cooperative learning and problem-solving activities. We saw a clear pattern of change from teacher control to more student initiative (Stevick, 1976; Freeman, 1992). The change was not instantaneous; on the contrary, it was a gradual and progressive process.

Dissemination of the Project

This project will most likely intrigue teacher trainers, preservice and inservice teachers, as well as curricular specialists. Furthermore, second-language research specialists might want to continue to explore a number of research questions stemming from this project, such as, "Over an extended period of time, does whole language/guided participatory learning improve listening or reading comprehension?"; "Are whole language/guided participatory learners more capable of communicating and discussing their ideas in the target language?"; or "Over an extended period of time, does whole language/guided participatory learning increase student motivation?" Whichever research paths one might decide to explore, one fact remains certain: improvement in second language learning/development necessitates collaborative action-based research projects within the social contexts of the schools.

Notes

[1]All work in this area is to a greater or lesser degree rooted in the research of activity theorists such as Vygotsky and Leontiev. For examples of recent research see Lave (1977); Cole (1985); Newman, Griffin, and Cole (1989); and Rogoff (1990).

[2]Please note that although we support many of the ideas concerning a whole language philosophy as espoused by Goodman (1991) and Freeman (1992), much of their research focuses on whole language for first language learners or for second language learners who have the continued support and reinforcement from the target language environment. Unlike the authors cited above, our research is primarily geared for foreign language learners who have very little daily contact (around 45 minutes) with the target language. In other words, we are espousing a whole language/guided participatory approach that is compatible with the limitations of the foreign language classroom and that which is feasible considering the demands of teaching grammar within this context.

[3]As early as the first quarter of this century, Vygotsky and Piaget, both constructionists, stressed that the whole is always greater than and gives meaning to its parts. However, unlike Piaget, Vygotsky stressed that social interaction and semiotic mediation lead to cognitive development.

References

Adair-Hauck, B. (1993). *A descriptive analysis of whole language/guided participatory versus explicit teaching strategies in foreign language instruction.* Unpublished doctoral dissertation, University of Pittsburgh.

Adair-Hauck, B. (1996). Practical whole language strategies for secondary and university level FL students. *Foreign Language Annals, 29,* 253–270.

Adair-Hauck, B., Donato, R., & Cumo, P. (1994). Using a whole language approach to teach grammar. In J. Shrum & E. Glisan (Eds.), *Contextualized foreign language instruction K–12* (pp.90–111). Boston: Heinle and Heinle.

Adair-Hauck, B., & Donato, R. (1994). Foreign language explanation within the zone of proximal development. *Canadian Modern Language Review, 50,* 532–557.

Au, K. (1993). *Literacy instruction in multicultural settings.* Austin: Harcourt Brace.

Bacon, S. (1992). Phases of listening to authentic input in Spanish: A descriptive study. *Foreign Language Annals, 25,* 317–333.

Bakhtin, M. (1981). *The dialogical imagination.* Austin: University of Texas Press.

Bakhtin, M. (1986). *Speech genres and late essays.* Austin: University of Texas Press.

Barnett, M. (1989). Writing as a process. *French Review, 63,* 39–41.

Bruner, J. (1983). *Child's talk. Learning to use language.* New York: Norton.

Bruner, J. (1990). *Acts of meaning.* Cambridge, MA: Harvard University Press.

Canale, M. (1983). Communicative competence to communicative language pedagogy. In J. Richards & R. Schmidt (Eds.), *Language and communication* (pp. 41–56). London: Longman.

Canale, M., & Swain, M. (1980). Theoretical bases of communicative approaches to second language teaching and testing. *Applied Linguistics, 1,* 1–47.

Cazden, C. (1992). *Whole language plus.* New York: Teachers College Press.

Chomsky, N. (1965). *Aspects of the theory of syntax.* Cambridge, MA: MIT Press.

Christensen, B. (1990). Teenage novels of adventure as a source of authentic material. *Foreign Language Annals, 23,* 531–537.

Clay, M., & Cazden, C. (1992). A Vygotskian Interpretation of Reading Recovery. In C. Cazden (Ed.), *Whole language plus* (pp. 114–135). New York: Teachers' College Press.

Cohen, E. (1986). *Designing group work: Strategies for the heterogenous classroom.* New York: Teachers College Press.

Cole, M. (1985). The zone of proximal development: Where culture and cognition create each other. In J. V. Wertsch (Ed.), *Culture, communication and cognition* (pp. 146–161). New York: Cambridge University Press.

Cook, V. (1991). *Second language learning and language teaching.* London: Edward Arnold.

Cooper, D. (1993). *Literacy: Helping children construct meaning.* Boston: Houghton Mifflin Company.

Coulthard, M. (1977). *An Introduction to discourse analysis.* White Plains, NY: Longman.

Cummins, J. (1984). *Bilingualism and special education: Issues in assessment and pedagogy.* San Diego: College-Hill.

Donato, R., & Adair-Hauck, B. (1992). Discourse perspectives. *Language Awareness, 1*(2), 73–89.

Donato, R., & Adair-Hauck, B. (1994, November). *PACE: A model for integrating form into a whole language lesson.* Paper presented at the American Council on the Teaching of Foreign Languages Annual Conference. San Antonio, TX.

Duffy, G., & Roehler, L. (1986, April). The subtleties of instructional mediation. *Educational Leadership, 43,* 23–27.

Dulay, H., Burt, M., & Krashen, S. (1982). *Language Two.* New York: Oxford University Press.

Dulay, H., & Burt, M. (1973). Should we teach syntax? *Language Learning, 23*, 245–258.

Ervin-Tripp, S. (1976). Is Sybil there? The structure of some American English directives. *Language in Society, 5*, 25–66.

Ervin-Tripp, S. (1977). Wait for me roller skate! In Ervin-Tripp and Mitchell-Kernan (Eds.), *Child Discourse* (pp. 165–188). New York: Academic Press.

Fountas, I., & Hannigan, I. (1989). Making sense of whole language: The pursuit of informed teaching. *Childhood Education, 65*(3), 133–137.

Freeman, D. (1992). Collaboration: Constructing shared understandings in a second language classroom. In D. Nunan (Ed.), *Collaborative language learning and teaching* (pp. 56–80). New York: Cambridge University Press.

Freeman, Y., & Freeman, D. (1992). *Whole language for second language learners.* Portsmouth, NH: Heinemann Educational Books, Inc.

Glisan, E. (1988). A plan for teaching listening comprehension: Adaptation of an instructional reading model. *Foreign Language Annals, 21*, 9–16.

Goodman, K. (1986). *What's whole in whole language?* Portsmouth, NH: Heinemann Educational Books, Inc.

Goodman, Y., & Goodman, K. (1990). Vygotsky in a whole language perspective. In L. Moll (Ed.), *Instructional implications and applications of sociohistorical psychology* (pp. 223–250). New York: Cambridge University Press.

Hall, J. K. (1996). "Aw, man, where we goin?": Classroom interaction and the development of L2 interactional competence. *Applied Linguistics, 6*(2), 37–62.

Hall, J. K., & Brooks, F. (manuscript in preparation). An integrative framework linking classroom interaction, interactive practices and the development of interactional competence.

Halliday, M. (1975). *Learning how to mean.* New York: Elsevier North Holland.

Hammerly, H. (1975). The deductive/inductive controversy. *The Modern Language Journal, 59*, 15–18.

Hatch, E. (1978). Discourse analysis and second language acquisition. In E. Hatch (Ed.), *Second language acquisition: A book of readings* (pp. 401–435). Rowley, MA: Newbury House.

Herron, C., & Tomasello, M. (1992). Acquiring grammatical structures by guided induction. *French Review, 65*, 708–717.

Higgs, T., & Clifford, R. (1982). The push toward communication. In T. Higgs (Ed.), *Curriculum competence and the foreign language teacher* (pp. 57–79). Skokie, IL: National Textbook Company.

Hinde, R. (1987). *Individuals, relationships and culture.* Cambridge: Cambridge University Press.

Hinde, R., & Groebel, J. (1991). *Cooperation and prosocial behavior.* Cambridge: Cambridge University Press.

Joiner, E. (1986). Listening in the foreign language. In H. S. Lepke, *Listening, reading, writing: Analysis and application.* (pp. 43–70). Middlebury, VT: Northeast Conference on the Teaching of Foreign Languages.

Krashen, S. (1982). *Principles and practice in second language acquisition.* Oxford, England: Pergamon Press.

Krashen, S. (1985). *The input hypothesis.* New York: Longman Group Ltd.

Krashen, S., & Terrell, T. (1983). *The natural approach.* Hayward, CA: Alemany Press.

Kroll, B. (1990). *Second language writing: Research insights from the classroom.* Cambridge: Cambridge University Press.

Larsen-Freeman, D. (1991). Teaching grammar. In M. Celce-Murcia (Ed.), *Teaching English as a second or foreign language* (pp. 279–95). Boston: Heinle and Heinle Publishers, Inc.

Lave, J. (1977). Cognitive consequences of traditional apprenticeship training in West Africa. *Anthropology and Education Quarterly, 8*, 177–180.

Leaver, B., & Stryker, S. (1989). Content-based instruction for the foreign language classrooms. *Foreign Language Annals, 22,* 269–275.

Leinhardt, G., & Putnam, R. (1987). The skill of learning from classroom lessons. *American Educational Research Journal, 24,* 557–587.

Lightbown, P., & Spada, N. (1990). Focus on form and corrective feedback in communicative language teaching: Effects on second language learning. *Studies in Second Language Acquisition, 12,* 429–448.

Little, D., Devitt, S., & Singleton, D. (1988). Authentic texts in foreign language teaching. *Theory into practice.* Dublin: Authentik.

Little, G., & Sanders, S. (1989). Classroom community: A prerequisite for communication. *Foreign Language Annals, 22,* 277–286.

Long, M. (1991). The least a second language acquisition theory needs to explain. *L Quarterly, 24,* 649–666.

Long, M., & Porter, P. (1985). Group work, interlanguage talk and second language acquisition. *TESOL Quarterly, 19,* 207–228.

McLaughlin, B. (1978). The monitor model: Some methodological considerations. *Language Learning, 28,* 309–332.

Met, M. (1991). Learning content through language. *Foreign Language Annals, 24,* 281–295.

Moffit, G. (1996). Addressing the affective needs of students. In E. Spinelli (Ed.), *Creating opportunities for excellence through language* (pp. 152–166). Lincolnwood, IL: National Textbook Company.

National Standards in Foreign Language Education Project. (1996). *Standards for foreign language learning: Preparing for the 21st century.* Yonkers, NY: Author.

Newman, D., Griffin, P. & Cole, M. (1989). *The construction zone: Working for cognitive change in school.* New York: Cambridge University Press.

Oller, Jr., J. (1983). Some working ideas for language teaching. In J. Oller, Jr. & Richard-Amato (Eds.), *Methods that work* (pp. 3–37). Rowley, MA: Newbury House.

Omaggio, A. (1986). The proficiency-oriented classroom. In T. V. Higgs (Ed.), *Teaching for proficiency: The organizing principle* (pp. 43–84). Lincolnwood, IL: National Textbook Company.

O'Malley, J. M., & Chamot, A. (1990). *Learner strategies in second language acquisition.* Cambridge: Cambridge University Press.

Oxford, R. (1990). *Language learning strategies: What every teacher should know.* New York: Newbury House/Harper Row.

Pica, T., & Doughty, C. (1985). The role of group work in classroom second language acquisition. *Studies in Second Language Acquisition, 7,* 233–249.

Reddy, M. (1979). The conduit metaphor—a case of frame conflict in our language about language. In A. Ortony (Ed.), *Metaphor and thought* (pp. 284–324). Cambridge: Cambridge University Press.

Rigg, P., & Allen, V. (1989). *When they don't all speak English.* Urbana, IL: National Council of Teachers of English.

Rivers, W. (1983). *Communicating naturally in a second language.* Chicago: University of Chicago Press.

Rogoff, B. (1990). *Apprenticeship in thinking.* New York: Oxford University Press.

Rutherford, W., & Sharwood Smith, M. (1988). *Grammar and second language teaching.* New York: Harper and Row Publishers.

Scarcella, R., & Oxford, R. (1992). *The tapestry of language learning.* Boston: Heinle and Heinle Publishers.

Schiffrin, D. (1987). *Discourse Markers.* Cambridge: Cambridge University Press.

Schmidt, R. (1990). The role of consciousness in second language learning. *Applied Linguistics, 11*(2), 129–158.

Scott, V. (1989). An empirical study of explicit and implicit teaching strategies in French. *The Modern Language Journal 73*, 14–22.

Scott, V. (1992). Write from the start: A task-oriented developmental writing program for foreign language students. In R. Terry (Ed.), *Dimensions: Language* (pp. 1–15). Southern Conference on Language Teaching.

Seelye, H. (1994). *Teaching culture: Strategies for intercultural communication*. Lincolnwood, IL: National Textbook Company.

Selinker, L. (1972). Interlanguage. *IRAL, 10*, 209–230.

Shaffer, C. (1989). A comparison of inductive and deductive approaches to teaching foreign languages. *The Modern Language Journal 73*, 395–403.

Sternfeld, S. (1988). The applicability of the immersion approach to college foreign language instruction. *Foreign Language Annals, 21*, 221–226.

Stevick, E. (1980). *Teaching language: A way and ways*. Rowley, MA: Newbury House.

Swaffar, J., Arens, K., & Byrnes, H. (1991). *Reading for meaning*. Englewood Cliffs: Prentice-Hall.

Terrell, T. (1977). A natural approach to second language acquisition and learning. *The Modern Language Journal 61*, 325–337.

Tharp, R., & Gallimore, R. (1988). *Rousing minds to life: Teaching, learning and schooling in social context*. Cambridge: Cambridge University Press.

Vygotsky, L. (1978). *Mind in society: The development of higher psychological processes*. Cambridge, MA: Harvard University Press.

Wells, G., & Montgomery, M. (1981). Adult-child interaction at home and at school. In P. French & M. MacLure (Eds.), *Adult-Child Conversation* (pp. 121–134). New York: St. Martin's Press.

Wertsch, J. (1979). From social interaction to higher psychological processes: A clarification and application of Vygotsky's theory. *Human Development, 22*, 3–22.

Wood, D., Bruner, J., & Ross, G. (1976). The role of tutoring in problem-solving. *Journal of Child Psychology and Psychiatry, 17*, 89–100.

Young, D. (1991). Creating a low-anxiety classroom environment: What does language anxiety research suggest? *The Modern Language Journal, 74*, 426–439.

Appendix
Synopses of the Stories

Le lion et la souris (The Lion and the Mouse)

This well known fable by Lafontaine describes the problem of a little mouse who wakes up a lion and, consequently, is captured by him. The mouse convinces the lion to let him go, so that, maybe in the future, the mouse can return the favor. The lion listens to the mouse and sets her free. Later on, the lion is captured by some hunters. The little mouse sets the lion free by gnawing at the rope, which the hunters had tied around the lion. This time, the little mouse gives the lion his freedom.

Moral: Little friends can become big friends.

Le petit chaperon rouge (Little Red Riding Hood)

This is the famous fairy tale about Little Red Riding Hood, who is going to grandma's house with a basket of goodies. Most of the students in this study were not familiar with the French version of this tale which is much more graphic than some American versions. The French version depicts the wolf swallowing the grandmother whole, as well as Red Riding Hood. Later on, a hunter, who had heard the cries of Red Riding Hood, goes to the cottage and sees the fat and tired wolf sitting in grandma's chair and shoots him in the head. Using his knife, the hunter cuts open the wolf's stomach, and both the grandmother and Red Riding Hood are saved.

Moral: Listen to the advice of your elders.

L'Autographe spéciale de Magic Johnson
(The Special Autograph of Magic Johnson)

Cumo and Adair-Hauck adapted this story from *Deuxième Livre* by Amsco (the original story concerns an opera star). The new version centers around the famous basketball player, "Magic" Johnson. Although not an authentic text, the story embeds the target structure in a context that is of interest to high school students. (The school district participating in this study had just won the state basketball championship.) One of the boys, Nicolas, excuses himself to go to the bathroom. Upon leaving the bathroom, Nicolas bumps into "Magic" Johnson. Nicolas asks "Magic" to write his autograph on his napkin. "Magic" tries to tell the excited student that he is not "Magic," but Nicolas will not listen; he just wants the autograph. The exuberant student rushes back to the dinner table to share his good news. However, then another student reads the autograph aloud: "Je ne suis pas Magic Johnson. Je suis Lean LeBlanc" [I'm not Magic Johnson. I'm Jean LeBlanc]. Indeed, Nicolas is disappointed. However, his friends try to cheer him up by saying that at least he has an autograph by Jean LeBlanc, a normal, regular person.

Moral: Listen and don't jump to conclusions.

Addressing the Culture
Goal with Authentic Video

Ana María Schwartz

University of Maryland–Baltimore County

Mark S. Kavanaugh

Urbana High School, Frederick, Maryland

You realize that your culture means more than you think it does. It's not just, like, a different part of your life that you go to sometime. It is your life, you know, your background.

Shey, 9th Grade, Spanish III.

To Collaborate: To Work Together
in a Joint Intellectual Effort

On February 1996, Mark Kavanaugh, high school Spanish teacher, and Ana María Schwartz, university professor of Spanish and teacher education, met for the first time and began planning the collaborative action research project described in this chapter. Their challenge was to bring the National Standards in Foreign Language Education Project's (1996) Cultures Goal to life by designing and implementing a language and culture unit with authentic video as its principal focus. And a challenge it was. Over the next three months they met and exchanged views, ideas, and materials; they faxed and negotiated; they became frustrated; they talked on the telephone; they made decisions. Ultimately, the team taught a unit on immigration through the study of conditions in Guatemala, using various video materials, including the film *El Norte.* They shared perspectives as the project took shape: Ana María offering Mark the opportunity to explore a wider view of *culture* and new ways of working with video. Mark shared with Ana María the constraints and possibilities of teaching ninth-grade students as well as the opportunity to see a master teacher in action.

Overview of the Chapter

What follows is an account of both process and product. In order to place the project in its theoretical context, the chapter begins with a discussion of the culture standards and how they relate to the unit. This is followed by a brief review of the four phases which guided the action research. Described within those phases are the instructional issues we wanted to address in teaching culture, the instructional strategies and materials used, and the student data gathered. Finally, an analysis of the student data, and an evaluation of the project as a whole, as well as reflections on the process by both the classroom teacher and the university faculty member are presented. The chapter closes with suggestions for further action in the implementation and dissemination of projects such as this, and of the National Standards.

The Cultures Goal

Language and culture are inseparably connected. Culture encompasses the totality of a group's thought and experience: for example, the group's values, beliefs, and traditions; its political and social systems; its foods and clothing; its language. Language, then, is both an element of the culture and the primary vehicle through which the culture is transmitted.

This inseparability of language and culture has long been a basic assumption of second language teaching, yet culture is often taught as "an expendable fifth skill, tacked on, so to speak, to the teaching of speaking, listening, reading, and writing" (Kramsch, 1993, p. 1). In this case, the language becomes not the vehicle of culture, but the vehicle of information about culture—the caption under the picture, the recipe for making soufflé.

The *Standards for Foreign Language Learning* (1996) are standards for the teaching of language *and* culture; whether the goal is Communication, Connections, Comparisons, or Communities, Cultures are the recurring subtext. In fact, the *Standards* state that, "students cannot truly master the language until they have also mastered the cultural contexts in which the language occurs" (p. 27). It is only through the process of acquiring a second language that the learner will experience the interdependence of language and culture.

The Standards adopt an anthropological view of culture, one that explains culture in terms of three closely interrelated components: perspectives, practices, and products.

- **Perspectives** are the underlying beliefs, values, traditional ideas, and attitudes of a particular group or society. Perspectives are handed down through generations and help make sense of the world for the individuals in the society.
- Behavioral **practices** refer to patterns of socially-agreed behavior. Practices represent the knowledge of *what to do, when, and where* in that society.
- The **products** of a culture may be tangible, such as artifacts, crafts, or works of art; or intangible, such as laws, or a system of government, or music.

As illustrated by the diagram below, each component arises or is derived from another, forming a closely interrelated whole.

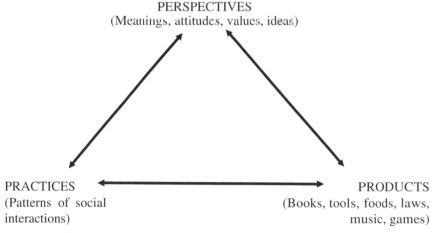

PERSPECTIVES
(Meanings, attitudes, values, ideas)

PRACTICES
(Patterns of social interactions)

PRODUCTS
(Books, tools, foods, laws, music, games)

Standards for Foreign Language Learning (1996, p. 43)

The Cultures Goal includes two standards:

Standard 2.1   Students demonstrate an understanding of the rela-
                    tionship between the *practices* and *perspectives* of
                    the cultures studied, and
Standard 2.2   Students demonstrate an understanding of the rela-
                    tionship between the *products* and *perspectives* of the
                    cultures studied.

Each standard focuses on one of two components of culture (practices or products) while at the same time relating it to the other and to the underlying
perspectives of the culture.

For example, in Standard 2.1 a teacher may focus on the *quinceañera*
celebration—an adolescent female rite of passage practiced in many Latin
American countries—(a practice) and explore not only the underlying
perspectives which have given rise to the tradition, but also how and why
it may be evolving. For Standard 2.2 a class may analyze the painting
Guérnica (a tangible product), and research the forces and conditions (the
perspectives) which inspired Picasso.

Teaching Culture with the Standards

The objectives of our immigration unit relate most directly to Standard
2.2. The unit explored the ideas, attitudes, and values of Guatemalan immigrants to the U.S., and of our students (their perspectives), through the
study of the social, economic, and political institutions in Guatemala and
in the U.S. (intangible products of the cultures).

We had to address several issues as we planned the unit. The first issue
to be decided was one of content focus. Given, as we believe, that culture
is everything, we had to decide which of many themes to address. Traditionally, two approaches have guided the selection of the culture content
included in U.S. foreign language curricula: the "Big C" or formal culture
approach (e.g., the formal social, political, economic institutions; the fine
arts; literature); or the "small c," sociological or anthropological approach, an exploration of the daily-life aspects of culture (e.g., food, clothing, patterns of behavior).

Omaggio Hadley (1993) observes that the systematic study of culture
is not regularly included in many language courses. She suggests several
reasons for this omission, one being the difficulty in deciding which as-

pects of culture to teach. This lack of clear direction also leads to unarticulated, idiosyncratic culture curricula. Galloway (in Omaggio Hadley, 1993) describes four all-too-easily identified "common approaches to teaching culture":

1. The Frankenstein Approach: A taco from here, a flamenco dancer from there, a gaucho from here, a bullfight from there.
2. The 4-F Approach: Folk dances, festivals, fairs, and food.
3. The Tour Guide Approach: The identification of monuments, rivers, and cities.
4. The "By the Way" Approach: Sporadic lectures or bits of behavior selected indiscriminately to emphasize sharp differences (p. 360).

The content of this collaborative unit focused on the "Big C" and the "little c" aspects of culture in an integrated whole, as we attempted to show the relationship between the social, political, and economic institutions of Guatemala and the U.S. as well as the daily life of these immigrants, in Guatemala and in the U.S.

The cultural themes we chose to explore in our unit required us to address issues that went beyond content. Omaggio Hadley (1993) suggests that language teachers may avoid presenting all but the most superficial culture content out of a concern with having to deal with student attitudes, specifically negative attitudes such as ethnocentrism, prejudice, and cultural stereotyping. People interpret other cultures through the prism of their own culture. "Ethnocentrism leads to a *subjective* [our emphasis] evaluation of how another culture conducts its daily business" (Porter and Samovar, 1994, p. 13). It is, therefore, imperative that we explore our own perspectives in the process of exploring those of others. We must provide many opportunities for a variety of interaction with the target culture and create activities which develop students' observation and crosscultural-analysis skills. It is through this level of contact that there is any hope of uncovering and rejecting stereotypes. This is a tall order, but if we endorse the concept of the interdependence of language and culture, the only way we can avoid dealing with these issues is by ceasing to be language teachers.

Teachers are not the only ones who disregard "hot" topics; language textbooks also tend toward the less controversial. In an examination of the kinds of cultural content presented as subject matter in secondary Spanish language textbooks, Ramírez and Kelly Hall (1990) found that information on topics dealing with politics, law and justice, poverty, or political strife were not presented at all. The major cultural themes presented in these texts were themes such as leisure, eating and shopping, and literature, music, and arts. The social classes most commonly depicted were the middle and upper-middle classes, and the social places featured were those attended by the educated or well-to-do, e.g., museums, sports resorts, very modern shops, and universities.

Planning the Immigration Unit

We chose to base all unit activities on two authentic texts, the film *El Norte*, and a video segment from Spanish-TV Magazine,[1] *La Voz Indígena: Rigoberta Menchú*, a documentary interview with the Guatemalan Nobel Peace Prize winner. The decision to use videos as primary texts made complete sense to us: in no other way could we convey the complexity of the issues to students at this proficiency level. Additionally, the medium would provide our students with a crosscultural perspective that we could not have duplicated. Finally, through the video we were able to introduce easily a topic of a somewhat controversial nature.

Each of the videotexts we used was produced for a different language community and with a different perspective: *El Norte*'s primary audience was an American (perhaps bilingual) community; the Rigoberta Menchú documentary was produced for television news in Spain. Opportunities to explore still other perspectives were provided by interviewing a Guatemalan immigrant who lives in the community and by viewing two short documentaries, in English, on the Guatemalan political refugee problem. These documentaries were produced by an American "peace" organization.

As we developed the unit activities, we naturally wove in other goal areas and curricular elements from the *Standards*. The students worked in all three modes of the Communication Goal. In the *interpretive* mode they worked with the videos to develop their listening comprehension skills. Comprehension of the language was not only of paramount importance if our culture objectives were to be realized, but comprehension and language development were in and of themselves objectives for the unit. Teacher-directed viewing strategies such as skimming, scanning, making hypotheses and inferences, and paraphrasing and summarizing, greatly enhanced the degree of interaction between the students and the videotext and facilitated comprehension. Careful preparation and execution of viewing plans and activities ensured that students achieved comprehension of the segments that were deemed to be key to achieving our cultural objectives.

The face-to-face interview with the Guatemalan immigrant and the many oral activities, including the role plays and the debate, enabled students to work in the *interpersonal* mode, that is, in direct oral communication. The writing exercises, in particular the culminating essay, engaged students in productive communication in the *presentational* mode.

Students made interdisciplinary connections by acquiring information and reinforcing their knowledge of current affairs and geography. In order to develop background knowledge, students researched various topics related to Guatemala prior to viewing any of the videos. The research was conducted in English to allow the students to gain full understanding of the issues involved. Through a collaboration with one of the English teachers, students also worked on their composition skills before writing their final essays. They also made connections within their own community, as they shared perspectives with the Guatemalan immigrant. Finally, the Comparisons Goal was central to our unit, as we and our students, worked to perceive and appreciate perspectives, practices, and products that were similar and different from those of our own cultures.

Action Research: A Reflective Cycle

Reflective practice refers to the careful consideration of the relationship between an educational process (one's teaching) and educational outcomes (student learning). The aim of reflective practice is to "choose a course of action in a particular set of circumstances" (Elliott, 1991). Action research can be seen, then, as formalized reflective practice.

Nunan (1992) states that an action research project functions as an ongoing cycle "in which the teacher reflects on, returns to, and extends the initial inquiry" (p. 18). The action research cycle begins with a question posed by the teacher, a question which arises from a concrete classroom problem which needs to be addressed. The research may be collaborative (often between the teacher and a university-based researcher) but may also involve teaching colleagues. As mentioned above, the impetus for conducting action research is to improve practice, to act on the previously identified problem or situation.

The research framework followed in this project is an adaptation of Elliott's (1991) model of the action research process. The cycle consists of four activities, or phases:

Phase One: Identifying and clarifying the problem
Phase Two: Describing and explaining the context
Phase Three: Constructing and implementing the plan of action
Phase Four: Evaluating the project

Each phase is described below in the context of the research project, that is, of the conceptualization, development, implementation, and evaluation of the immigration unit.

Phase One: Identifying and Clarifying the Problem

In this phase, the *general idea*, problem, or research question is formulated and then clarified through a process of reflection. The general idea must be something the teacher would like to change or improve. It must also be a situation which is within the teacher's sphere of influence, that is, something the teacher can do something about (Elliott, 1991).

In general, our project focused on the problems associated with teaching culture. More specifically, we were concerned with applying the overall objectives of second language study articulated by the National Foreign Language Standards. In order to clarify what we meant by teaching culture and to more coherently define it in terms of goals for the project, the classroom teacher reflected on his own experiences as a Spanish high school teacher teaching culture. In doing so, he tried to identify what he felt hindered him in fulfilling both the letter and the spirit of the Cultures Goal and of the Standards in general.

The university professor participated in this reflective process only as a "sounding board" and did not contribute directly to the teacher's reflection. The interplay between practitioner and academic in the context of action research, is most clearly articulated by Elliott (1991):

> Action research ... constitutes a resolution to the theory-practice issue as it is perceived by teachers. Within this form of educational inquiry, theoretical abstraction plays a subordinate role in the development of a practical wisdom grounded in reflective experiences of concrete cases. ... Comparisons with past cases illuminate practically relevant features of the present situation. Inasmuch as such comparisons prove insufficient in furnishing a practically relevant understanding of a situation, some explicit theoretical analysis will be appropriate. ... This ... [is] an important task for academic educationalists to perform, but it is one which is parasitic on teachers' attempts reflectively to change their curricular and pedagogical practices in schools (p. 53).

Earlier in this chapter the university professor provided the theoretical frame for the issues relevant to our research. Now the teacher reflects on the culture standards and on his practice/teaching of culture. His comments are presented below.

Mark Kavanaugh:

I have encountered three major problems in the teaching of culture in high school Spanish classrooms. First, there is no set culture curriculum. Other than the issues which happen to come up in the textbook, I have not found scope and sequences nor specific district expectations in any of the four school districts in which I have worked. I feel that the school systems have taken for granted that as a Spanish teacher who has studied and worked in Mexico and in Latino communities in the U.S., I could and would teach culture. But that expectation has never been defined to me. No one has ever told me exactly what to teach, or how to teach it, or how to assess what I have taught (or exposed students to) in terms of culture.

I find that given a lack of curriculum, the teaching of culture becomes incidental, or accidental; it is added whenever it can be fitted in. Culture is what I am least intentional about teaching. I am never too sure what my role is as a teacher or what I am trying to accomplish in the culture area other than simply exposing students to culture. When we have time left over from communicative activities, I try to expose students to interesting aspects of foreign culture or sensitize them to important cultural issues which I think they should know. If we are ahead of where we should be in the curriculum and I have time, I may show a film or direct the students in a research project. If our semester is shortened due to snow, or if I am moving slowly through the curriculum with a particular class, the cultural aspects that I had intended to teach are the first to go. I have my "old favorites" I like to teach, but I know that this "unintentional" approach lessens the impact on the students.

The third issue that most concerns me with regards to teaching culture is probably the most important: my students do not seem to be impacted by the cultural information being presented. They are not able to identify with the cultural information because although it may be interesting, it is not relevant for them, and what cultural information they do learn seems to simply come off as trivial knowledge that has little effect on them or their lives. Either due to methodology or content, I have little success in helping students become aware of and make connections between themselves and their culture and the people and cultures of other countries.

Many of my students do not seem to see a need to understand a foreign culture except to the extent that that knowledge can entertain them. For example, the fact that sixteen year olds are allowed to drink alcohol in Spain, yet they cannot drive a car until they are twenty-one, would only be seen by many of my students as a reason to vacation in Spain instead of an opportunity to compare and contrast some real differences in the cultures. At different times, and throughout my courses (Introduction to Spanish through AP Spanish), I have attempted to expose students to issues of Latin American politics, living situations, family relationships, religion, classism, racism, exploitation, human rights, relations with the U.S., and emigration and immigration to the U.S. I have attempted to get students to look at their own culture and that of our new Hispanic residents from a different perspective and with some new understanding. Yet I do not feel as though many students are fully appreciating what they have learned, nor are they being helped to develop awareness or sensitivity for another culture.

Although I use videos to expose students to cultural information, I am concerned about the materials, viewing methods, and video activities I currently use when showing a video. The materials that I have adapted and now use are geared toward listening comprehension and story line. I have created worksheets that practice certain grammar points or the vocabulary we may be studying at the time of the film's showing. I have developed analytical writing assignments for students that highlight important, historical, political, or cultural information. Yet, I vacillate on whether to show films with or without subtitles, and I am interested in experimenting and learning about different video viewing materials and activities that will allow the cultural information to have a greater impact on my students.

To sum up, I would like to examine ways to teach culture in my high school classroom that will help my students gain a greater appreciation of both their own and another culture and which will help them digest the information as important and relevant for them, instead of as seemingly distant, unconnected facts that have no relationship or intrinsic value to them.

Research Questions

The following research questions grew out of the above discussion.

These questions also constituted the goals for the project.

- How can I teach culture in a way that will have a greater impact on my students:
  - so they will become aware of and appreciate the connections between themselves and their lives and the people and lives of others in another culture?
  - so that the information and activities will be presented in an organized, unified, intentional way that will be relevant and make sense to them?
  - so that it can be done in the context of communicative language practice of the four skills in the L2?

Phase Two: Describing and Explaining the Context

A full description of the context in which the action research project takes place is necessary in order to better understand the questions posed, the data generated by the research, and the conclusions reached. This section describes the school setting: the school and the school district, the students involved in the project, and the school's foreign language curriculum.

The Setting

The School

Urbana High School (UHS) is the newest high school in rapidly-growing Frederick County, Maryland. Urbana is approximately 30 minutes north of Washington, D.C. and 45 minutes to the west of Baltimore. While there are still many rural families in the community most of the population is white collar, relatively affluent, and of high socioeconomic status. The majority of the community members are professionals who travel to Washington, D.C., Baltimore, or the surrounding areas to work. The school population is mostly white.

UHS opened in March 1996 with one class of ninth graders. One class will be added each year until it is operating at full capacity in 1998. Courses at UHS are taught on a 90-minute block schedule: four periods per day with full year courses being taught on a semester schedule. Each student takes eight classes per year.

The school is organized into three integrated clusters. The Humanities

Cluster houses English, Social Studies, and Foreign Language. Math, Science, and Technology classes are huddled into one cluster and Physical Education, Visual and Performing Arts, and Life Skills into a third cluster. The twenty-five UHS teachers are encouraged to collaborate and develop integrated instructional units within their clusters.

The Students

The students in this project were in a ninth-grade Spanish III class of ten students. All of them started their Spanish studies in the middle school and had completed Spanish II with Mr. Kavanaugh the previous semester (Fall 1995) on the block schedule. All of the students were generally good students and highly motivated learners, although not all were extremely proficient in Spanish. During the semester, students' grades ranged from B– to A but were consistently above a 3.0. Eight of the ten students intend to study Spanish IV and A.P. Spanish in the 1996–97 school year. There were eight girls and two boys in the class.

The Foreign Language Curriculum

Currently, Introduction to Spanish through Spanish III and French I and II are taught at UHS. German and Latin, as well as upper level Spanish and French, will be added in 1996–97. The 90-minute block schedule allows for younger students to take upper levels of foreign language earlier in their high school careers. Since some students complete Level V AP by the end of their sophomore year, teachers are currently in the process of developing advanced studies and literature courses for students interested in continuing language study beyond Level V.

Phase Three: Constructing and Implementing the General Plan

In this phase the general plan of action for the research is laid out, and the action steps outlined in the general plan are implemented. The general plan of action includes the unit objectives as well as the resources needed (e.g., videos, equipment, use of the media center and the computer lab), the proposed assessments for the activities, and the actual day-to-day unit plans. It is essential that a project be closely monitored for unintended effects that may dictate a change in the general plan or which may need to be documented in the final evaluation of the project (Elliott, 1991).

A description of the general plan of action, including an overview of the unit, a description of the collaboration, a timeline, and the unit plans follow.

Overview of the Unit

The unit was broadly based on the social/political situation of poor and indigenous people in Guatemala and the resultant effect of that situation on the United States: the influx of legal and illegal immigrants from Guatemala (a large number of whom live in the Washington, D.C.-Baltimore area). Two videos were used in the unit, the movie *El Norte* and *La Voz Indígena: Rigoberta Menchú,* a documentary-interview with the Guatemalan 1992 Nobel Peace Prize winner, from Spanish-TV Magazine. Intensive listening comprehension work was done in the classroom with *El Norte* and with the Rigoberta Menchú video. Other instructional activities included library research and presentation of the research to the class, role plays, an interview with an immigrant from Guatemala, a debate, two written essays (one in English and one in Spanish) and comprehension and language practice worksheets based on *El Norte.* The unit lasted fourteen mostly consecutive days for fourteen 90-minute periods.

The Collaboration

The classroom teacher, Mark, and the university faculty member, Ana María, collaborated fully in all aspects of the design, planning, and execution of the unit. Ana María designed all of the video lesson plans and worksheets and conducted the final student interviews. Mark designed the initial research activity, the role play, the debate, and the written essay activities and their assessment. He also arranged the visit and interview of the Guatemalan immigrant. Ana María taught all of the video lessons, except for the second part of the Rigoberta Menchú lesson, which Mark taught using Ana María's plan. Mark either taught or directed the rest of the unit activities. Ana María was present in the classroom all but two of the fourteen days of the unit. The data were examined and analyzed independently by Mark and by Ana María.

The Unit Objectives

The objectives of the unit were as follows:
1. Gain knowledge of the perspectives and products of Guatemala and its people.
2. Develop observation skills (through the video work) focusing on both differences and similarities in their perspectives, practices, and products.
3. Compare others' expectations of "the good life" with the "American Dream."
4. Explore issues of emigration and immigration: understand why people emigrate and uncover their own attitudes, values, ideas about immigrants to the U.S.
5. Language objectives: preterite/imperfect; narration in the past; introduction to present subjunctive with *querer, dudar, no creer*; composition skills, oral discussion, interviewing.

Timeline

The planning, design, implementation, and evaluation of the unit took place from February to June 1996:

February– March 1996	Identifying and clarifying the problem (initial discussions, reading of the literature, review of video materials)
April 1996	Constructing the plan of action (identifying unit goals and writing unit plans)
May 9–May 30	Implementing the action steps (teaching the unit, assessment of activities)
June 13	Student exit interviews

Unit Plans

Day 1:
    Introduce the unit:
    Present Dr. Schwartz to the class (informal Q/A by students).
    Introduce the project and our expectations of ourselves and of the students [English].

Divide students into three groups and have them brainstorm (to activate background knowledge) on these topics [English]:

Guatemala, immigration, emigration, the Nobel Peace Prize;

Come together and share information, put on butcher paper.

Divide students into four groups and assign the library research and the oral presentation, model the oral presentation.

Assign English essay: *Your understandings and feelings about immigration to the U.S.*

Assign students to write five questions in Spanish that they would like to ask a person who has recently come from Guatemala.

Day 2:

Library group research on Guatemala [English]; four groups and their topics: Geography, history and politics, people and population, Rigoberta Menchú Students use print materials and search the WWW.

Day 3:

Tie up loose ends on research and oral presentation and look over rough drafts of presentations.

Review and practice use of imperfect/preterite together. Incorporate presentation vocabulary into grammar practice.

Day 4:

Oral group presentations, each group:

Distributes vocabulary lists to be used as reference during the presentation;

Organizes the presentation with note cards;

Develops a worksheet to be used by the members of the class as a guide to the presentation (the worksheet is to include ten comprehension questions based on the presentation);

Each group asks the comprehension questions after the presentation.

Take-home essay test on information from the oral presentations.

Day 5:

Video activities for *El Norte*, Part I (listening comprehension activities, work with skimming, scanning, making hypotheses, making inferences based on the images, and other viewing activities).

Homework worksheet, practice preterite/imperfect using content from Part I.

Day 6:
>   Finish viewing activities for Part I.
>   Review homework.
>   Practice narrative in the past: in a circle, retell the plot in Part I.

Day 7:
>   Role play: act out Part I.
>   Predict what will happen in Part II.
>   Discuss what each character should do (considering their predicament) and what *they* would do if they were in Guatemala (use teacher-prepared questions to focus the discussion).
>   Introduce subjunctive with things that are unknown, tie-in to Part I.

Day 8:
>   Video activities for Part II (as in Part I).
>   Grammar worksheet for homework, subjunctive/indicative, tied to Part II.

Day 9:
>   Introduce vocabulary for Rigoberta Menchú video.
>   Begin *La Voz Indígena: Rigoberta Menchú* viewing activities (preparation for viewing activities, building up background knowledge, compare and contrast with *El Norte*, discuss differences in accents—Spanish, Guatemalan, Mexican, Indigenous dialect).
>   Assign reading of several current newspaper articles dealing with the "American Dream" and immigration issues [English] for homework.

Day 10:
>   Continue viewing activities for Rigoberta Menchú segment. Discussion in English and Spanish on the "American Dream" vs. Rigoberta Menchú's "Guatemalan Dream" (from the video).
>   Review subjunctive/indicative worksheet.
>   Computer lab practice of subjunctive.
>   Subjective worksheet, tied-in to *La Voz Indígena*.

Day 11:
>   Video activities for *El Norte*, Part III (as in Part I).
>   Discuss culture shock, acculturation [English/Spanish]. Assign final essay.
>   Assign preparation of interview questions for Guatemalan visitor.

Day 12:

Interview of Guatemalan immigrant, entire period.

Day 13:

View documentary films about Guatemala's political situation and refugee problem, *If the Mango Tree Could Speak* and *The Long Road Home* [English]. (Teachers not present, handled by substitute; no discussion or viewing activities).
Prepare for debate: *Should immigration to the USA be permitted or limited?*, two groups.

Day 14:

Conduct debate:
Students are given 15 minutes to organize their points;
Class divided into the two teams, formal debate conducted with opening statements, and statements and rebuttals.
After debate students tell their real feelings on the issue. Entire debate conducted in Spanish.
Re-play the last 10 minutes of *El Norte*.
Assign Spanish essay: *Your understandings and feelings about immigration to the U.S.*

[Day 15]:

[Individual student exit interviews, out of class.]

Phase Four: Evaluating the Project

Two types of evaluation were conducted as part of the unit project: students were assessed by the teacher for purposes of grading, and data were collected and analyzed to determine what impact, if any, the unit had on the student's depth of awareness of the situations presented and on their ability to express themselves in Spanish on those issues. The students were assigned points for their performance in the library research and on their presentations, for their English and their Spanish essays, for quizzes based on the information presented in class, for the Guatemalan visitor's interview questions, and for the debate. These points were the basis of their grade for the unit activities.

In his discussion of the various methods and techniques available to gather evidence in action research, Elliott (1991) recommends a multi-technique approach which brings together a variety of angles or perspectives for comparison and contrast. Accordingly, the project was examined from the students', the teacher's, and the university faculty member's perspectives, as well as from the standpoint of the the students' written work. Four types of data were collected and analyzed to evaluate the impact of the unit activities: (1) the students' pre- and post-unit work (the interview questions for the Guatemalan visitor and the English and Spanish essays), (2) the individual student interviews conducted after the completion of the unit, (3) the classroom teacher's observations of the project and its activities, and (4) the university faculty member's observations of the project and its activities. These data are presented below.

Student Data

Pre-Unit and Post-Unit Interview Questions

Each student was given the following task at the beginning of the unit and at the end:

Preguntas (Questions) — You have recently met a person from Guatemala who speaks no English. You would like to learn why he or she decided to leave Guatemala and come to the United States, how he or she arrived, and how he or she feels about life in the US as an immigrant. Write the five best questions that you would ask him or her in order to ascertain this information.

The pre-unit questions (Day 1) were written in class, collected, and not returned until after the interview, so that the students would not just copy them for the post-unit assignment (Day 11). They were given 15–20 minutes to formulate seven questions, choose the best five, and write them in Spanish. The post-unit questions were assigned for homework later in the project and were due the day of the interview of the Guatemalan immigrant. The questions were compared for grammar and for the ideas presented.

There was no improvement from pre- to post-unit questions as far as grammatical correctness, although most students demonstrated a good command of the present and preterite (past) tenses in both sets of questions. If anything, the post-unit questions were less grammatically correct, as the students tried to ask more complex questions, for example [equivalent question from the same student]:

Pre: *¿Qué le parace el EE.UU.?* [What do you think of the U.S?]
Post: *¿Ud. quiere la vida en el EEUU mejor que la vida en su país viejo?*
         [Do you like life in the U.S. better than life in your old country?]

The greatest differences between the pre- and post-unit questions were in terms of content. Overall, the pre-unit questions seemed more superficial, while the post-unit questions in many cases reflected the knowledge and interest generated by the unit activities. For example, several post-unit questions reflected student understanding of the difficulty of immigrating to a foreign country and the challenges of assimilating into a new culture:

- When you had just arrived how did the USA seem to you?
- Was it a difficult trip?
- How did you feel when you arrived?
- What problems did you have [when you came]?

There were also more compare and contrast questions in the post interview and more questions about preferences:

- What is a similarity between the USA and Guatemala?
- Which country do you like better and why?
- Is this country very different from your country?
- Did you have a good life in Guatemala?

Some questions invited Guatemalan opinion and insight into our country, beliefs, laws, and customs or reflected knowledge and interest in the political conditions in Guatemala:

- How do you feel about the USA?
- What do you think the USA should do about immigration?
- Do you like the customs of the USA?
- Did you want to come to the USA?
- Did you have problems with the army in Guatemala?
- Are you from a country without a good government?

More of the post-unit questions probed the feelings of Guatemalan immigrants in the USA and considered the possibility of their wanting to return to their homeland:

- What is life like for an immigrant?
- How do you feel living in the USA?
- Are you going to return to Guatemala some day?
- If you can return do you want to?

Rather than improvement in form, i.e., correctness, the pre-to post-questions demonstrated that the unit activities seem to have impacted the content of the questions asked in the post-unit. In comparison with the pre-unit, the post-unit questions demonstrated a greater interest by the students in Guatemala and Guatemalans. Some of the questions suggested a broadening of the students' perspectives, an understanding that Guatemalans may feel as patriotic about aspects of their country as we do about ours. None of the pre-unit questions reflected this cultural sensitivity, curiosity, and openness.

Written Essays

Students were asked to write essays on the topic of immigration at the beginning and at the end of the unit. The first essay was written in English and the second in Spanish. The directions for the English essay were as follows:

Un Ensayo [An Essay] — Organize and write a 200-word English composition on your understandings and feelings about immigration to the United States. Make sure that your thoughts are well developed and supported by reasons and examples. Within your compositions you must answer the following questions:

- How would you define the type of person that immigrates to the United States?
- What are your personal feelings about those who immigrate to the USA?
- What things have you read or heard that have made you feel this way?
- Have you had any personal experiences with immigrants that have made you feel this way?
- Why do you believe that immigrants choose to come to the United States as opposed to other counties?
- Do you think that immigration should be restricted? Why or why not?

The directions for the Spanish essay were the same except for the addition of the question, "Do you think differently now than you thought before this unit?"

The English essay was assigned on Day 1 (a Friday) and was due the following Monday. The purpose of having the students write in English was to to allow them to express whatever knowledge, feelings, ideas, or experiences they had on the topic without the constraints of their incomplete command of the second language. These essays would then serve as baseline to assess the impact of the information gained and the opinions formed through the unit activities. For purposes of grading, the English essays were corrected by an English teacher colleague of the classroom teacher. This teacher also spoke to the class about the mechanics of essay writing prior to their writing in Spanish. The Spanish essay was assigned on Day 11 and due two weeks later, a week after the final activity of the unit.

The English and Spanish essays were compared for content, as organized by the questions the students were asked to address. Although grammatical accuracy was part of the criteria for the students' grade, for this comparison the essays were primarily judged in terms of communication: Did the student get his or her point across in a comprehensible way?

The Spanish Essays

In all instances the Spanish essays were longer and more complex. These essays were 22% longer than the English essays. They ranged in length from 264 words to 604 words, with an average length of 417 words. Overall, students presented approximately 30% more distinct ideas or arguments in the Spanish essays than in the English essays.

Most of the Spanish essays were much stronger thematically: they were better organized, contained more examples and supporting facts, and better addressed the topic. Students used a wide variety of vocabulary and attempted, and many times succeeded in mastering, complex sentence constructions.[2]

The students described immigrants in positive terms: courageous (*una persona que inmigra cualquier sitio es muy valiente ... esta dispuesto sale su pais nativo y empieza con nada*), strong (*para un inmigrante a sucede [tener éxito] en EE.UU. el/ella tiene que ser un/a persona muy fuerte*), optimistic (*generalmente una persona que inmigra a los EE.UU. tiene que estar optimista que la vida aquí es mejor como la vida allá*). They gave many reasons for people wanting to come to the U.S. One student stated that many think that people immigrate to get rich, but that there are many other reasons (*mucha gente cree que personas inmigrar por dinero y hacerse rico, pero hay muchas razones*). Where in the English essay "quality of life" was often given as a reason to come to the U.S. in the Spanish essay students gave more specific reasons, among them: freedom of religion and speech, educational opportunities, medical care, personal safety, and stable government.

The information shared and discussed in the unit seems to have caused students to rethink, dissect, and struggle with issues about which they had certainly heard, but with which they were marginally familiar. It was apparent that immigration was not something they had spent a lot of time thinking about. In the end, students took very definite postions on the issues surrounding immigration and were able to elaborate on their reasons for taking those positions. In comparing the first and the second essay it was found that students had double the number of supporting ideas when they wrote the Spanish essay!

Of the ten students in the class, eight stated that immigration should be restricted and two students thought that it should not. Students mostly addressed themselves to illegal immigration, one student writing that those who broke the law to come to the U.S. would break other laws once here (*personas que no tengan respeto para las reglas de inmigración no va a tener respeto para otros reglas*). Another student suggested that the U.S. government should make it easier to obtain a green card [residency permit], that way fewer people would come illegally.

The students supporting restricted immigration cited reasons such as: lack of jobs (*nosotros debemos cuidarse para los trabajos de los ciudadanos antes de los trabajos de los inmigrantes*); overpopulation (*no hay tanto espacio para mas personas*); immigrants don't speak English (*comunicación es un problema grande de los inmigrantes, no podemos hablar con ellos porque ellos no hablan ínglés*); immigrants get social benefits and citizens pay for them with their taxes (*yo comprendo porque los inmigrantes venen a los EE.UU. pero nosotros tenemos no suficiente cosas para gente que no paga los impustos*); and that the government should take care of its poor first (*los EE.UU. no pueden ayudarlos si no pueden cuidar de su propia gente. Hay mucha pobreza y una falta de comida, casas, y trabajos*).

Arguments supporting immigration included, that immigrants help the economy (*los americanos dicen que los inmigrantes deben volver a sus países pero sin los inmigrantes no hay nadie para el trabajo dificil. Los americanos no piensan en eso*); that immigrants provide cultural diversity (*me siento que personas que inmigra aquí prove [proporciona] diversidad cultural...es posible que prejuicio puede decrecimiento*); and that everyone should have the same opportunities as our ancestors (*nosotros inmi-*

gramos aquí, por qué los inmigrantes no pueden ahora?).

Whether in favor or against restricting immigration, students saw the issue from more than one perspective. One student said she was ambivalent about the people who immigrate. She understood why people risked their life to come for a better life, but, she added, "I also think it is possible that an immigrant may take my father's or my mother's job" (*tambien considero que es posible que un inmigrante toma el trabajo de mi padre o mi madre*). Several students stated that if people were in danger for their lives they should be allowed to come (*si la gente va a morir, entonces los EE.UU. debe permitir los inmigrantes vene aquí.*). But, another added, where do you draw the line? How can you tell one person they can come because their life is in danger and tell another person who doesn't have a job or a house that they can't come? (*¿como dice una persona puede venir porque su vida es en peligro, y dice que una otra persona que no tiene trabajo o una casa no puede venir?*)

Six students addressed the question of whether they saw the immigration issue differently after having participated in the unit activities. All six wrote that their thinking had been affected. Some said that before they had no opinion or didn't consider the issue important but that now they felt more strongly because they knew more. Others mentioned that their opinion had not changed, but that they understood the issue better. Three students seem to capture the impact of the experience for the class as a whole:

- I didn't know what the life of the immigrant was like. I thought they shouldn't come, now I think they have a right to live here as well as me.
- Before I didn't have an exact opinion, now I do, and I think we should restrict immigration, even if I feel sad for them.
- After seeing the movie my opinion of immigration changed a bit, but it was my opinion of the U.S. that changed. I think that the U.S. government is not perfect but that people in the U.S. have a good life if they have opportunities. I think that there are a lot of people already in the U.S. that don't have opportunities. After we find the solution for the problems in the U.S. we can let more immigrants come to the U.S.

To summarize, the Spanish essays were, overall, longer and better organized, and with more supporting ideas, more specific information, and more complex arguments than were the English ones. They evidenced greater insights and a broader knowledge base of the issues. The impact of the unit activities was evident in the students' ability to look at many more sides of the issue than before, to look at the issues more critically, and to make more connections between what they learned in class with personal experiences. Most important, many students began to look at their own culture from the perspective of another and vice versa, and to put themselves into another's shoes as they considered what immigration would be like it they were the ones forced to immigrate.

Student Exit Interviews

Almost two weeks after the final unit activity, the university faculty member conducted and recorded individual student interviews while the class reviewed for the final exam. She asked a series of five questions. Some results from the student interviews are presented below.

1. Of all of the activities we did during the unit on Guatemala:
a. which did you like best and why?

Student responses to this question were mixed. No one activity stood out as the favorite, and four students mentioned liking more than one activity. The debate, the video, and the role plays emerged as the students' favorite unit activities: they were each mentioned first by three students. One student said she liked library research best and another two mentioned the research and the presentation as a preferred activity. The students explained their choices in these ways:

- I liked a lot of things about the whole unit because it gave us a lot of cultural awareness, especially about Guatemala. The thing I liked best was the debate...because then it gave us a lot of chance to talk and you had to listen to and hear what the other team was saying.
- I guess watching the video, because it was not like a documentary, but it relayed a lot of what it was like in Guatemala and it was all in Spanish, so you got to learn Spanish, but also got to learn a lot about their culture.
- I liked the role plays, definitely the role plays. I just enjoy acting. It was interesting you did not have to know...you had to get the feel of what the language was saying...you didn't have to know very little word. I liked the role play because then you can put it in your own words.

b. [of all the unit activities] which did you like least and why?

The responses to this question were also mixed. Three students did not like the grammar/comprehension worksheets assigned for homework. They thought the worksheets were busy work, or they seemed to be contrived to fit the materials and were not well integrated to the rest of the work, or were difficult to understand. One student remarked, "a lot of it was for practicing verbs. I know it was useful and you need to know that, but it wasn't enjoyable, that's all." Another three students did not like doing the initial library research on Guatemala. They thought it was too much like work in other classes!

Students disliked most the frequent stopping of the video to conduct viewing activities, but they found value in this as well as in all of the other unit activities. One student put it this way, "with the video, I didn't like how we kept stopping it, but then once we'd watch it and then we'd stop it and go over it, and then we'd watch it again, I understood a lot better what they were saying...and I could hear them talking! It was weird how I could understand, like, how they were talking. Once I found out what they were saying, it jumps out at you!"

2. Of all the video activities,
a. which did you like best and why?

There was no consensus here either. Three students mentioned enjoying the cloze worksheets where they focused on missing words in a conversation and filled in the blanks as the sections of the film were replayed several times. Again, students commented on how helpful it was hearing the same bit of dialogue several times, "when you go back and play it over and over again, I like that because you get the gist of it the first time, and then you can hear exactly what they are saying the second and third time."

There was much discussion about whether they preferred viewing the video with or without subtitles. With the exception of two students, they preferred and found more value in viewing without subtitles first and then showing the sections over with subtitles as a way of checking and verifying their guesses. Each student seems to have gone at this process of comprehension in slightly different ways. One student observed, "it was nice to go through first and try to see if you could hear anything, which a lot of times was not much, but it gave us that experience." Another student explained, "watching without the subtitles was kind of interesting because it really made you listen for what you knew and how to translate it. I just listened for anything that I knew or could comprehend quickly and then if I didn't know, then I didn't bother with it." A couple of students said that viewing with subtitles confused them, as they could not take their attention away from the subtitles. The greatest testimony to viewing without subtitles was this, "I liked it with the subtitles because I could understand it, but I liked it without because when you finally realized what they were saying, it was like... Wow! I know this! You kind of pay more attention to what they are saying when there aren't subtitles...you want to know what they're saying."

b.   which [video activity] did you like least and why?

Two students did not find the cloze exercises helpful ("nit picky little things"). The subtitles versus no subtitles debate spilled over to this question. Two students mentioned that if the subtitles were blocked they could "kind of use [their] other senses...listening and watching to figure out what is going on", but that having the subtitles confused them. Again, the students objected to interrupting the film to conduct video activities. They felt that stopping the video made it harder to understand what was going on and confused them as to where the previous sequence had left off. They found it very annoying to have the video stopped on an interesting spot.

3.   What was the most important thing (to you) that you learned during the unit?

It is interesting to see that all of the students gave focused and succinct answers to what, arguably, was the most open-ended question of the interview: it became obvious that the students had a very clear idea of what they were taking away from the unit. The responses to this question may be the most significant in the context of this project, as they correlate closely to the objectives we set out to accomplish. For example, several students commented on how they now realized what a complex issue immigration was and how they had personally connected with these issues.

- I never knew the personal side of immigration. I always knew that people wanted to come to America because of the opportunities. I never knew they were coming because they had to come. I think that was a very important thing to learn, and to realize that people don't just come here because they want to, but because they have to.
- [We learned] the other side of the story...like in America you learn that immigrants are bad people and they come here to live, and you don't understand why they are coming here, and you just think they are... and we learned the other side.

- With immigration there's not always a right and wrong. Because there's [sic] always so many situations that everyone needs to be treated separately, and that is kind of hard to do and draw the line, because...there are so many things involved.
- I learned an overall lesson about everything, and no matter how you try to fix something...in our debates...like whether they should limit immigration or not, and if you do limit it there is still going to be another problem. So no matter what you do there is always going to be another problem. Somewhere it will come out.

Another two students commented that the most important thing they had learned was how much they could understand in Spanish.

- I found out that I could actually understand it [Spanish]. The whole experience made me speak in Spanish more and helped me to understand it a little bit more.
- That I can understand Spanish. I didn't think I could understand Spanish but I understood more than I thought I had. It's a confidence booster in a lot of cases.

Finally, another student articulated what, at bottom, this project sought to accomplish.

- I learned a lot about the culture. A lot of stuff I didn't know about. We take the language, but we really don't see things from their point of view and what their countries are like.

4. Do you feel any different about your ability to understand/speak/write Spanish as a result of this work?

All the students indicated that they felt more confident and believed that their Spanish had improved. Most felt that their greatest gains had been in comprehension and felt proud to be able to understand non-classroom Spanish, or as one student put it, "just general Spanish spoken by native speakers". The class was exposed to several accents during this project: their teacher's, who is not a native speaker; the university faculty member's, who is Cuban-American; and the Guatemalan, Mexican, and Mexican-American accents in the film and of the Guatemalan immigrant they interviewed. Several students mentioned that "it was neat to hear their accents and how they talked" and one student noted that "just like people from the north and south [of the U.S.] talk different, Spanish is different all over."

One student felt that he could write "I guess a little better," and another student thought that it was now easier for her to talk. Two students mentioned having the experience of unconsciously producing Spanish, said one student (referring to the role play), "it's better to be active, like when we acted it out, that ... you don't even realize you're speaking Spanish, then you just ... it just goes." The following exchange occurred as the other student was asked to elaborate a point she had made:

Inteviewer: Did you get to any point where you were short-circuiting English, or were you always going through English to get to the Spanish?

Student: I had to think my way through it...there were times when thoughts would come to me in Spanish so I wouldn't have to go through English to think about it.

Interviewer: Did you realize that when it was happening?

Student: Yeah, afterwards...like after I said it, I would realize it.

Interviewer: Did you feel good?

Student: Yeah!

5. Do you think that we (Mr. Kavanaugh and I) attained our goals for this project?

The students had known that they were involved in a special project and it that involved teaching and learning using "different" techniques and materials, but they did not know exactly what the project had set out to accomplish. Since we wanted the students to respond to the goals directly, they were given a copy of the goal statements to read and asked to respond to the first two goals. They were not asked to respond to the third goal, "so that [the teaching of the culture content] can be done in the context of communicative language practice of the four skills in the L2" as it was not really applicable.

a. so they will become aware of and appreciate the connections between themselves and their lives and the people and lives of others in another culture.

Some students asked the interviewer to clarify this statement. She paraphrased it this way for one student, "if you feel that you are more aware [of the issues presented] and that you can see yourself in connection to these people, in a better light." All of the students agreed that the goals had been reached. It is difficult to summarize the responses, as each student's response reflects his or her own interpretation and perspective. Some of the responses were very revealing; it may be best to let the students speak for themselves:

- I think we did [accomplish the goal], because you realize that your culture means more than you think it does. It's not just, like, a different part of your life that you go to sometime. It is your life, you know, your background.

- Yeah, I think that when you look at that situation [in Guatemala] you understand that...why they are doing what they are doing...and they are trying to save themselves...and you get the other side of it. So not more sympathy, but you understand it, what is going on. You're more aware.

- I think that we did it pretty good.... I also saw the connections between family life and everyday life, like, excluding the government, everybody are people and they have their worries.

- I think with [goal] A it happened to some extent. I didn't realize it before we watched the videos that people in Spanish-speaking countries thought of us in different ways too. Just seeing them sitting around the dinner table talking about us Americans was kind of interesting.... It was just interesting to see what they thought of us.

- Yeah, I think you accomplished the majority of these goals. By doing the video and the research we did find out about different cultures and how and why people immigrated, the culture down there that causes them to immigrate. We learned what their connection with us was through immigration, and why they wanted to come here. And we also learned the similarities and differences between the two cultures.

b. so that the information and activities will be presented in an organized, unified, intentional way that will be relevant and make sense to them.

Students felt that this goal had also been attained, although several students again voiced their reservations about the interruptions of the film. A student observed that, "it pretty much flowed together except for all the breaking points of the video". Several students mentioned that the initial research on Guatemala was helpful in putting the rest of the work — the film, the interview, the debate — in context, she remarked, "I think the research in the library and listening when we presented [the group presentation on different topics]...I think that really helped me. I'm glad we did that before because when we watched the video I really understood what their position was...it hit me half-way through the movie that this really does happen, and it's not fiction."

The question remains on how to integrate such video/culture units into the established curriculum so that they are not simply an add-on component, but rather integral to the course. One student called attention to our failure to do this adequately:

- One thing I didn't like...I think if it is going to be taught...it needs to be really planned in there, because for us, it got me out of thinking of all the lessons we had been doing. And so just yesterday...we have the final exam [for the course] tomorrow, and just two days ago we were covering new stuff. So it was kind of frustrating in that aspect.

At the same time, the value of what was attempted in this project comes through loud and clear from this student:

Interviewer: So you think that, overall, when you think of how you have read or discussed cultural things [in the past], that this may have made a little bit more sense to you?
Student: Yeah, definitely. Because [in] Spanish I we had the cultural discovery projects, but we never really did anything. We just picked something that had to do with a Spanish culture, like make a mask or some art in Spanish, but this talked about everyday life in general.
Interviewer: So, more real-people type of thing?
Student: Right, yeah!

The exit interview data indicate that the project was well-received by the students. Their responses to the questions about the unit and video activities showed no consensus on which activity was best or least liked. Students unanimously expressed that it would have helped their comprehension to present longer parts of the film without interruption before doing intensive viewing exercises. Most students felt that they would have rather viewed without subtitles first in order to get the gist of what they were viewing.

All the students felt that the unit activities and the video built their language confidence and led to a higher comfort level with native-speaker-Spanish. The students indicated that they gained a different perspective on "culture" and that they became more aware of the complexities of the issues presented. Many students felt that the video and other activities had caused them to see people, including themselves, from a more universal perspective: all people joined by the everyday struggles of getting ahead in life. Finally, most students remarked on how important it had been to have background knowledge of Guatemala and its people before viewing the video and in engaging in the other unit activities. One student mentioned the need to better integrate this type of work into the course curriculum.

Classroom Teacher's Observations of Project and Activities

Use of the Target Language

I had anticipated a high level of student anxiety with Ana María conducting many of the activities, but the students felt very comfortable with her presence throughout the project. They were impressed with their own ability to understand a native Spanish speaker. They also felt that this was a glimpse of what college would be like, since she was a university teacher. Only two students missed a day of the project.

The students were surprised at how long they could remain in the target language. They were active in the language (both speaking and listening) for longer uninterrupted periods of time than in any of my Spanish III classes. They generally did not feel overwhelmed, yet they did feel some frustration at times at being forced to speak in Spanish when they had opinions, confusions, or ideas that they enthusiastically wanted to express but did not have the words in the target language.

Unit Activities

There were many different types of activities and this allowed students of different abilities and interests to participate in different things. While not all students participated equally in every activity, each student dominated or at least took a larger role in at least one activity: we seemed to hit upon all the different learning styles and levels of comfort ability. Even the least enthusiastic member of the class said that the debate "where we got to talk all in Spanish ... [with a] lot of feedback from going back and forth in arguments" was "kind of exciting"!

Students loved the role-plays, especially acting-out Part I of *El Norte*. Almost all commented that they liked these activities and would like to repeat them in the future. I found the role plays particularly interesting as you can watch students thinking on their feet and struggling to put things in their own words.

I was surprised by the success of one video activity that Ana María conducted. I was initially concerned about my students' ability to comprehend and be successful in the activities she had planned, as the students had not learned some of the vocabulary that the characters used and some of the phrases were in verb tenses that my students have not yet learned. For this activity, the students viewed a conversation between two characters with the subtitles covered. Then the class was divided into two groups and the conversation was replayed two more times with each group concentrating on a different characters' lines in the dialogue. After this group listening/decoding, each group elected one member to represent their group and act out the dialogue in front of the class. Both actors correctly paraphrased the lines of the movie in expressions they had already learned. This experience made me realize that when working with video one does not have to be overly concerned that students know all tenses and vocabulary used. When video is properly shown and materials are appropriately adapted, students are able to make connections and construct meaning even if they are not familiar with all the elements of the language.

Most students would have preferred to watch longer sections of the video in order to capture the story and then return to conduct the activities that we had planned. They did not like the constant stopping of the film. Still, they enthusiastically went along with all the activities even though the project became extended. Only one student became overwhelmed early on in the project because of her inability to comprehend. Later she caught on and felt less anxious. Most students were enthused and encouraged about their ability to understand. They liked using and figuring out what was going on in authentic, as opposed to classroom, Spanish.

The Spanish essays that were turned in were the best writing samples I have ever seen by a Spanish III class. They were probably the most extensive work I have ever assigned to students and the student work was well done. The essays integrated many of the language skills we had learned throughout the course. Two solid B students (not the strongest in the class) turned in two of the strongest essays. They were strong in terms of organization, incorporation of examples, facts and thoughts, and use of the target language. The student mentioned above, who had felt extremely overwhelmed at times, worked very hard and produced a well thought-out and insightful essay: her first A work of the semester.

The debate was a culminating activity. The students worked cooperatively, giving each other vocabulary as they formed arguments in Spanish. Most students were engaged the entire time, as they had to listen actively to the other side in order to refute points. I did not provide any facts during the debate, but only acted as last resort for vocabulary, or as facilitator, or to clarify a point, or to encourage. The students prepared and came up with their own debating points, incorporating much of what they been exposed to throughout the unit.

The students have improved with practice. This is the third debate we have had and it was much better than the first two. When asked to express their real opinions and feelings about immigration, several students expressed the exact opposite side, demonstrating their ability to express what they believe as well as issues with which they do not agree. Students do more practicing of the language when activities like the role play and the debate allow them to freely struggle, collaborate and come up with new (their own) manipulations of the language.

The frustration and confusion with some of the worksheets and take home assignments were apparent, as some were not completed on time. Of all the activities that we conducted the worksheets were the most rushed to fit into the unit and I had less time to explain them. In many cases I was passing worksheets out at the end of the period without enough time to give a thorough explanation. Still, in most cases, the students understood and admitted the value of these language practice activities.

University Faculty Member's Observations of Project and Activities

I was present in the classroom for nine of the fourteen days of the unit and conducted the video activities on five of those days. Although I participated in the class activities when we didn't work with the video, Mark was the primary instructor on those days. I found the students to be attentive and polite and with excellent language skills. The class welcomed me, but to the end there was a distance, a reserve, that I felt I was not able to bridge. I had to remind myself of my own forewarning to student teachers who begin their assignments mid-year: how hard one must work to become part of that already established classroom community.

I felt the students' intense concentration as they followed a new accent, a faster rate of speech, and new methodologies with new materials. Sometimes I thought they were in another world, but they always volunteered answers which showed that they were right with me. I was impressed with their maturity and willingness to participate, and felt that they approached the project with an open and curious mind, even if they seemed a bit overwhelmed at times.

The openness of the students in the exit interviews was gratifying. They were positive, knowledgeable, and thoughtful in their feedback and were able to easily reflect on their learning and articulate the processes they followed. I truly believe that what they have taken away from their work in this unit will continue to have an impact on their perceptions of the issues discussed.

Since the video was my primary instructional responsibility, this was the area in which I had the most interaction with the students. The approach used was to give a general overview of the action by previewing without sound or by fast forwarding through a scene, then keying in on scenes and conversations which advanced the action and were thus crucial to the overall comprehension of the plot. The individual and group cloze activities were designed for this intensive listening. The other more extensive techniques used were observing and describing the images, question-answer, posing "leading" questions, predicting and hypothesizing, and summarizing. These techniques were used to get the gist, as comprehension checks, and to cue in on similarities or differences, or make explicit points which were culturally relevant. The viewing techniques positioned the teacher as the facilitator or the mediator between the students and the video.

The students became very involved in the film. As we viewed, we would often refer to geographical, political, or social information that the students had uncovered in their initial research. The students always seemed pleased when they discovered these connections. On the other hand, they were not as interested in the Rigoberta Menchú video. This video, a documentary segment presented with the same types of viewing techniques and activities used with the film, was shown between Parts Two and Three of *El Norte*. This turned out to be a poor choice of time for *La Voz Indígena: Rigoberta Menchú*; it left a gap of two days between the second and last parts of the film, which disappointed the students and did not leave them well-disposed to the segment. No one mentioned the Menchú segment during the exit interviews, although some of the vocabulary and political/social concepts explored in the segment were reflected in some of the students' essays. The students also did not mention the two short documentaries about Guatemalan refugees (in English) which were shown by a substitute the day that Mark was absent to receive the Frederick County Teacher of the Year award.

Time became a major factor in this project, but then, time is always factor when working with video, and especially with a full-length film. *El Norte* is divided into three distinct parts, making it easier to manipulate instructionally; yet, students were insistent in the exit interview that the movie not be "chopped up." If theatrical releases such as *El Norte* are going to be used for instructional purposes, compromises must be reached between its entertainment value and its instructional value. The teacher must set specific objectives, carefully planning ahead and selectively deciding what portions to use for listening comprehension, what portions to use for its cultural content, and what portions to use for good ol' entertainment. As teachers we have the tendency to want to "instruct" every aspect of a content-rich source such as this film. In this instance, we perhaps tried to bite off more than we could chew in the allotted time. In retrospect, I would be more selective in the number of sections to exploit to meet our listening and culture objectives and show more scenes with subtitles, while all along predicting and making inferences based on what they were viewing.

Although the worksheets used for homework assignments could have been better integrated into the unit, they were nevertheless valuable. These assignments provided students with the opportunity to review and synthesize the information they had gained in class. I believe that being able to practice articulating these ideas in Spanish, in writing, with ample time to monitor their production, notice patterns, and develop ideas, ultimately paid off in an expanded knowledge base of vocabulary and structures which later enabled the students to express themselves extemporaneously. This familiarity with the vocabulary and ideas was evident in all of the speaking activities.

Mrs. M., the Guatemalan visitor, presented the students with a view of immigrants different from that of the video. She provided her own perspective, as a naturalized citizen of many years who still has strong family ties in her native Guatemala and who is very proud of her heritage. The fact that Mr. M. lives in the county, speaks excellent English, and has children the students' age, made her very accessible to the students. Yet, I think that the interview went on too long. The students were polite and intent, but I felt that many were often lost. In my experience, native speaker informants, even language teachers, tend to give very long answers or to digress, loosing students in the process. It may be best to speak to invited guests prior to the interview, alerting them to the students' comprehension needs and asking them to monitor themselves so that they give short and succinct answers, check for students' comprehension, insert pauses while they speak, and make the interview as interactive as possible. As with the Rigoberta Menchú video segment, the students did not mention Mrs. M.'s interview in the exit interviews, although snatches of the interview were again reflected in the essays.

Teacher's Reflection on the Collaboration

The process of collaborating on such a large project is something I had never done before. As excited as I was, I must admit some initial nervousness. First, I would be working with a university professor and a native speaker. Second, I would be working with video, not necessarily one of my strengths. Third, while I have a generally strong ego and am open to learning and critique, opening my classroom to another set of eyes was potentially threatening. I did not find cause for worry. Ana María's contributions were enlightening, helpful, insightful, and not threatening in any way. The observations below reflect a few of the insights which resulted from our joint venture.

- I was concerned about Ana María's ability to bridge age and maturity differences and be able to relate to 13- to 15-year olds. Could she reach the ninth grader after so many years at the university level? Yes! Good teachers can teach at different levels. After this experience I am convinced that collaborations between all levels of foreign language instruction are possible. We have a tendency to blame teachers at lower levels for sending us unprepared students. We need to experience the teaching environments from which students come and to which they are going in order to create more effective foreign language programs. It occurs to me now that not only do I need to collaborate with the university, but also with the middle school. It is only through these types of collaborations, and the articulation that happens as an outgrowth, that we can build strong regional programs.
- The teaming component was very valuable for us and for the students. The unit video activities were developed separately by Ana María, as this is her field of expertise. While she handled the bulk of the viewing activities, I chimed in with different issues that I wanted to highlight. At the same time, she focused student attention to areas that I would not have. Our combined perspectives amplified the breadth of cultural instruction.
- I have shown the film *El Norte* to my Spanish classes for the last seven years. Many things happened this time that helped students be more impacted by the issues of the film. For example, I had not anticipated that the way we used *El Norte* and *La Voz Indígena: Rigoberta Menchú* would have contributed so much to my students' confidence in the language. Watching students go from complete

confusion and non-comprehension of a video clip to mastery of a particular scene in the film was very gratifying not only for them but for me as well. At this level of foreign language learning student confidence is a critical factor. The video activities helped them attain that self-confidence and motivated student learning.

- I was also pleased with the types of questions that were raised by students, as well as by their engagement and participation, in Spanish, throughout the entire unit. It occurred to me early on that beginning the unit with the library research was critical to the success of the entire project. Through this exercise students uncovered the vocabulary they needed and learned enough about the topics so that they had a basis or an entry into the discussions that would ensue. I have been unhappy in the past with the students' level of participation and interest in some of the cultural information I have presented. It occurs to me now they may have been interested in but did not possess enough prior information nor vocabulary to participate fully in discussions at the level I had hoped nor do some of the higher level thinking activities I would have wanted them to do. I need to take more time to get students ready to learn. Student readiness is a key to making the information relevant and to having it make a greater impact.

- Through our initial discussions and planning I was able to focus on the cultural learning that was to take place. In the past I have tried to expose students to too large a topic such as, "The history, political ramification, and causes and effects of immigration and emigration in the U.S. and Latin America." This overambitious, amorphous theme is too immense to conceptualize! I believe that this lack of focus has contributed to my prior disappointments. In this unit we worked just with Guatemala. Narrowing the scope of the project allowed me and my students to better concentrate on a few issues, and helped us uncover better resources for the students to learn from. I even met a member from our school feeder pattern who had immigrated from Guatemala who came and spoke to the class during the project. I believe that this sharper focus was integral to the units' success. From that smaller focus students were able to generalize to other countries. This had always been my intent but until this project I had missed the mark.

- I feel that the most valuable activities we used were the role playing activities and the debate. In each case the students were able to move away from book work and worksheets and rework and practice the linguistic content and cultural information in their own words and from their own perspectives. Once a student was able to act out the role of a Guatemalan mother, or role play a conversation at a Guatemalan dinner table, he or she can more easily make the cultural connections we had in mind. Once students were forced to debate the issues from perspectives with which they did not agree, they were able to have more insight. Traditional worksheets and question and answer materials limit the impact that teaching culture might have.

- In the past I may have defined "making an impact on the students" in rather illogical, unattainable, and impractical ways. I may have wanted all students to change their opinion with regards to immigration as my litmus test for cultural impact—and I was always disappointed. What I realize now is that how they took in the information we presented and re-thought about it in their own lives was much more impacting than us spoon feeding them some belief system or philosophy and having them regurgitate it back to us on the assessments.

What Did I Learn about Myself as a Teacher/Researcher?

Maybe nothing earth shattering. Perhaps the continued need for planning before the unit. This unit was more effective than others I have taught in the past because it was better planned and focused, and the goals of the unit were clear. Perhaps also that enthusiasm is contagious. Since I saw this project as something new and was enthusiastic about it, my students also felt it was something special and got into it. I guess I also felt some of the same confidence as a teacher that my students felt as students. Watching their final projects and video clips was gratifying.

Students do good work on what they understand or on what they perceive as valuable and relevant. They do the bare minimum on what they do no perceive as such. For that reason the students' work on worksheets and grammar practice was not exemplary. I believe that teaching is much more like coaching an athlete in a skill than a purely academic endeavor. I have to give some instruction and theory, but the art of my teaching revolves around the good relationship I can develop with my students and around the creation of good practice activities (i.e., debates, role plays, interactive dialogues) where they can develop their skills.

Finally, research, and especially action research, is not something I still understand very well. Even after this project I do not see myself as a researcher, but rather as a teacher who is not always happy with his work and student progress and wants to see it improve. Perhaps this is the definition of an action researcher?

What Did I Learn about Myself as an Innovator?

I was willing to be creative and innovative and try new things around my areas of interest. Some of the topics we considered during our initial discussions did not interest me at all. It would have been difficult for me to be very innovative about an issue that I was not interested in. Once we touched upon an area of my interest I was able to get excited, make connections, think of possibilities, and get somewhat innovative.

I also discovered that I am a creature of habit. While I did make some adjustments to my curriculum and to the final assessments, I was initially reluctant to do so. Instead of having an in-class essay on the final day of class, I allowed students 1 ½ weeks to prepare the final essay on this unit. I was much happier with the results. I also adapted the final oral exam for this class and had each student find a native Spanish-speaking person from the community to interview. All the students had to show me was the list of the questions they asked and a sheet filled out by the interviewee that provided feedback to the student. I then took some time in class for students to debrief their experiences. This turned out to be a great performance assessment, and while it happened outside of my sphere of influence, I could tell that it was much more beneficial for them.

However, innovation and change would not have happened in a vacuum. The collaborative nature of this project was an impetus for some of the innovation that occurred. I guess in somewhat conceited hindsight, I was impressed and very pleased and proud of some of the activities that Ana María and I came up with.

What Changes Will I Make in My Practice as a Result of This Project?

I plan to adapt one cultural unit (if possible linked to a particular film or related video materials) to each course that I teach, as I found this type of activity to be extremely valuable. I am beginning to consider a unit in Spanish II related to bullfighting, and adding some of the *Spanish-TV Magazine* materials that we previewed into Spanish IV.

I will add to my repertoire several of the cloze activities and dialogue exercises/role plays that I learned from Ana María. I simply did not know how to use the video in these ways before I watched her. I now realize that the showing of films must be accompanied by instruction and viewing activities. Being able to watch her was very valuable to me as a teacher.

I will develop more communicative activities such as the acting out of scenes from the video, as they really pay off in terms of student enthusiasm and facilitate better student performance. Additionally, working with video exposes students to real Spanish (as opposed to classroom Spanish), adding to students' feeling of mastery and confidence and complementing the non-native speaking teacher. I can say that my students were much more orally proficient at this point than any other Spanish III students I have taught.

How can we better integrate such activities into the present curriculum? It took fourteen instructional days to teach the unit. I am confident that when I teach this unit again I will be better able to streamline, leave out the unnecessary in order to keep within a better time frame. Yet, we must concede that we spent more time on this unit that I had ever spent on any one thing, and we got results.

Conclusions

Our purpose in taking on this project was to plan, implement, and evaluate a more holistic way of integrating language instruction and the teaching of culture. We approached our work through the larger themes of perspectives, practices, and products set forth by the Cultures Goal of the National Foreign Language Standards. Our project focused on *products* and *perspectives*. We focused on the perspectives of the people being studied (Guatemalan immigrants) and of the students studying them (Frederick County 9th grade students). The products targeted were the social, economic, and political institutions in Guatemala and the U.S., institutions which are so intricately bound in the Central America/Mexico-U.S. immigration issue. The catalyst for language and ideas (and the "hook" into these issues) was film, principally the film *El Norte.*

We attempted, as the standards state, to help students understand the relationship among products, practices, and perspectives, to make connections, to go beyond their centeredness in their own language and culture. Our stated goal was "to teach culture in a way that will have greater impact on [our] students." As the cliché goes, we wanted to "go out and touch someone." Our challenge was that that someone, the students, had to know they had been "touched," intellectually and linguistically. In the end, we believe we accomplished our goal. Glimmers of the connections the students were beginning to make can be seen in these quotes from the student exit interviews.

- I never knew the personal side of immigration...I think that was a very important thing to learn.
- I learned an overall lesson about everything, and no matter how you try to fix

something...no matter what you do, there is always going to be another problem.

- I also saw the connections between family life and everyday life...everybody are [*sic*] people and they have their worries.
- I didn't realize that people in Spanish-speaking countries thought of us in different ways too.
- It hit me half-way through the movie that this really does happen, and it's not fiction.

To have helped students reach those insights is very gratifying. To have seen students attempt and often succeed in communicating their insights in Spanish was incredibly rewarding for us as language teachers.

In the midst of our enthusiasm, a few caveats should be inserted. It must be remembered that, by its very nature, action research is not generalizable, but very particular to the setting in which it is conducted. In our case, we were fortunate to be working with a small class of bright, motivated students, who had a solid language foundation. Our work was also facilitated by a brand-new, up-to-date, and supportive school and foreign language supervisor that encouraged this type of experimentation. Finally, in our favor was the 90-minute block schedule. Without it we could not have completed many of our activities as coherently, as the activities would have had to be broken up over a series of days.

The theme-based approach we used in the immigration unit lent itself perfectly to what we were trying to accomplish and followed closely the recommendations of all of the National Standards' goal areas. It allowed students to experience authentic language as an integrated whole, and allowed them to engage in meaningful and purposeful use of the language through interesting and relevant content. It shifted the focus of instruction to meaning rather than form, while at the same time not neglecting grammar, but rather presenting it as an enabler of communication, and thus necessary for the content being discussed. We were, perhaps, least successful in achieving this form-content integration, as some students felt that we had sort of taken a break from language instruction to do the unit. This perception of not "working on the lessons" may not only have been due to our not having integrated the form-focused activities better, but also due to the students not understanding the "novel" experience of viewing form in the context of real language and communication.

Where Do We Go from Here?

Our experience in this collaboration has already had an impact beyond what happened in the Urbana High School Spanish III classroom in the Spring 1996. In the Fall of the 1996–97 school year, the authors conducted an inservice for all Frederick County Foreign Language teachers on using video to teach culture and to practice listening comprehension skills. As a result of that inservice, Mark is spearheading an effort to create a bank of integrated units, such as the one we developed, by having groups of teachers each develop a content unit at a particular language level. The units will be shared with the other teachers in the county, thus lessening the amount of work for individual teachers. He is also recommending that decisions be made at the district level to define articulated broad-based goals of culture study for each level of language instruction. These goals would more specifically define the content of the Cultures Standards' progress indicators and could consist of, for example, working with similarities and differences between the native and target language cultures in Level I or studying products and practices through target language art and literature in Level IV.

Working in this project has also had a significant impact for Ana María in her university setting. As she has become more and more familiar with the National Standards she has seen a number of possibilities for integrating them in her work. As a result, she has begun infusing the Standards into her teacher education activities, beginning to use the five goal areas as a framework in the second language methods course. Areas of discussion she has already incorporated include, teaching language through content; working with and initiating interdisciplinary collaborations; developing and assessing interpersonal, interpretive, and presentational communication activities; seeing the community as a resource; teaching perspectives, practices, and products as content, and in an integrated manner; and teaching in block schedules.

The collaboration put Ana María in a high school classroom not as an observer, but as a participant. It enabled her to experiment with various techniques for working with video with a secondary audience, an experience she has carried over to her development of instructional materials for Spanish-TV Magazine. The collaboration has also brought her closer to issues of articulation between the secondary and post-secondary levels and is leading to departmental discussions on the impact of the Standards on the curricula; the integration of technology in courses; and the impact of block scheduling on the department's course offerings, including the availability of content-based courses for incoming students who, as Mark's students, will have a higher-than-usual degree of language proficiency by the time they enter university. Finally, she has "borrowed" more than one of Mark's teaching and assessment techniques for her own Spanish courses!

In *Action research for educational change*, John Elliott (1991) states that action research "integrates teaching and teacher development, curriculum development and evaluation, [and] research and philosophical reflection" (p. 54). We feel that we have at least lived up to Elliott's conception. The collaboration has created bridges between levels and opportunities for cross over; it has created friendships. Beyond the hard and at times frustrating work, the collaboration was a success, one we both hope to continue.

Notes

[1] Spanish-TV Magazine is a series of four yearly 60-minute programs composed of short thematic segments that reflect both the richness and diversity of contemporary Hispanic life. The segments are selected from the archives of Radiotelevisión Española. The accompanying Video Teaching Guide is produced at the University of Maryland Baltimore County (UMBC). The program is broadcast monthly by PBS.

[2] Students' writing samples in Spanish have not been edited.

References

Elliott, J. (1991). *Action research for educational change.* Philadelphia, PA: Open University Press.

Kramsch, C. (1993). *Context and culture in language teaching.* Oxford: Oxford University Press.

National Standards in Foreign Language Education Project. (1996). *Standards for foreign language learning: Preparing for the 21st century.* Yonkers, NY: Author.

Nava, G. (Director). (1983). *El Norte* [Film]. Cinecom International Films.

Nunan, D. (1992). *Research methods in language learning.* Cambridge: Cambridge University Press.

Omaggio Hadley, A. (1993). *Teaching language in context.* Boston: Heinle & Heinle.

Porter, R. E., & Samovar, L. A. (1994). An introduction to intercultural communication. In L. A. Samovar & R. E. Porter (Eds.) *Intercultural communication: A reader* (7th ed., pp. 4–26.). Belmont, CA: Wadsworth Publishing.

Ramírez, A. G., & Kelly Hall, J. (1990). Language and culture in secondary level Spanish textbooks. *The Modern Language Journal, 74*, 48–65.

Connections: A K–8/ University Collaboration to Promote Interdisciplinary Teaching

Eileen B. Lorenz

Montgomery County Public Schools, Maryland

Pierre Verdaguer

University of Maryland

Foreign language teachers must examine what students are learning in other classes, decide which areas are relevant to learning to use a second language and which areas connect in meaningful and interesting ways to language and cultures.

Connections Goal: Introduction

Communication, Cultures, Connections, Comparisons, and Communities—the five Cs of foreign language study identified in the National Standards Project (1996)—organize the many components that go into foreign language classrooms at all levels and for all age groups. The Connections Goal looks outward, beyond the foreign language classroom, to other disciplines and experiences that are an integral part of students' daily lives and focuses on two areas that may have been absent in the past from curricula and teachers' frames of reference. First, the Connections

Goal seeks to capitalize on and integrate the knowledge that students gain in other disciplines as well as general background knowledge that they bring to foreign language learning. Teachers then provide support so students can use and increase this knowledge and experience in second-language tasks. While this is most easily achieved through immersion programs, a widening of perspectives in other program models may lead to more opportunities for students to integrate and communicate what they are learning from other disciplines in foreign language classrooms. Second, the Connections Goal promotes awareness and use of unique perspectives for gaining new information and new cultural knowledge that may be available only through study of a foreign language. Specifically, the two Connections Goals are:

3.1 Students reinforce and further their knowledge of other disciplines through the foreign language.
3.2 Students acquire information and recognize the distinctive viewpoints that are only available though the foreign language and its cultures.

The project described in this paper, *Teaching Culture in Foreign Language Programs in Grades K–8,* was developed by Montgomery County Public School (MCPS), Rockville, Maryland, and funded by the National Endowment for the Humanities from 1991 through 1994; implementation is a continuous process. Participants were experienced kindergarten through grade 8 teachers of French and Spanish (FLES, immersion, and middle school teachers), MCPS central office foreign language staff, and staff from the Departments of French and Italian and of Spanish and Portuguese at the University of Maryland, College Park. This chapter will describe the process and results of the collaboration to develop lessons that integrate the teaching of language, culture(s), and other disciplines. This project resulted in a K–8 scope and sequence of objectives for teaching culture and activities in French and Spanish to teach culture in kindergarten through grade 8 classrooms.

Rationale for Project

Teaching Culture in Foreign Language Programs in Grades K–8 was developed to address a local and national need for a model for teaching culture in Kindergarten through grade 8 classrooms. While in general the teaching of culture has been widely explored in a number of documents (Byram, 1989; Lafayette, 1988; Seeyle, 1993), little guidance has been readily available to K–8 teachers. Frameworks or guidelines for teaching culture exist at the grades 9–12 level (North Carolina Competency-Based Curriculum, 1985; Indiana Department of Education, 1986); however, before this project, none existed at the K–8 level. Rhodes and Oxford (1988) conducted a survey which demonstrated that a substantial number of elementary schools with foreign language programs had no curriculum or program guidelines for teaching cultures.

Challenges of Teaching Culture in K–8 Foreign Language Classrooms

K–8 foreign language teachers have had few resources that provide guidance about *what* cultural information to teach, *when* to teach it, *how* it might best be taught, and *with what* instructional materials. *What, when, how*, and *with what* were key questions throughout the three-year project. Let us examine the role that each of these questions plays in the challenges of teaching cultures faced by K–8 foreign language teachers.

"What Culture to Teach?" and "When to Teach It ?"

These two questions go hand in hand as teachers face the task of identifying developmentally appropriate topics for teaching cultures. How do foreign language teachers decide what cultural topics should be taught? And, when is the best time to teach the wide range of topics that are part of the many definitions of culture? At what age and grade levels are students most receptive to learning about various aspects of target cultures? How can we be sure that we are promoting understanding of cultural phenomena that differ from cultures in the U.S.? The dilemma of "What to teach?" and "When to teach it ?" was summed up by one respondent to a preproject survey who wrote, " Since we have no scope and sequence and since most culture is taught in a casual way, I really do not have any idea of what students should know (and what they could know given each level's curriculum.)." A major thrust of this project in suggesting answers to the *what* and *when* questions was to examine the K–8 curricula in reading and language arts, social studies, mathematics, and science. Learning from and making connections with concepts and objectives taught in the other academic disciplines was an invaluable strategy used to identify developmentally appropriate concepts and topics to teach culture. The process of looking outward, toward what students are able and expected to do in other disciplines, and making connections with language and culture was used to develop the K–8 Scope and Sequence for teaching culture. Teachers used the K–8 Scope and Sequence during the project as a point of departure to develop activities and instructional materials that built upon and integrated what students learn outside of the foreign language class.

The question "When to teach it?" addresses the challenge of too little time during the school day to accomplish the objectives that most foreign language programs outline. At the K–5/6 level, elementary foreign language immersion teachers are charged with teaching all or at least half of the reading and language arts, social studies, math, and science objectives in a second language. Most immersion teachers will tell you that there is little or no "extra" time for teaching culture as a separate subject. In Foreign Language in the Elementary School Programs (FLES), teachers teach the second language from two to five times a week during twenty-to-forty minute periods. FLES teachers must follow the objectives outlined by their local district's program or, in cases where no objectives exist, develop them. Finally, middle school teachers (grades 6–8) also feel the pressures to teach adequately the prescribed program of studies so that students are well prepared with sound linguistic and cultural knowledge. Teaching culture as an "add-on" in any of these three program models is almost a guarantee that it will not be taught because of other program demands.

"How to Teach Culture?" and "With What?"

Once teachers have identified the areas of culture that they will teach, they must decide upon instructional strategies and materials that will engage students most effectively. Where can instructional materials be obtained? What materials work best with certain age groups? What do developmentally appropriate, authentic materials look like? How can they be used most effectively? Unfortunately, there are few clear cut answers to these questions. To complicate the issue, many teachers have had neither opportunities for adequate preparation in how to teach culture nor opportunities to update their knowledge about the cultures of the language they teach. In a preproject survey, 12 out of 28 respondents answered the question: *What concerns do you have about teaching culture?* by targeting the difficulty of remaining current and having access to up-to-date cultural information. In general, both native and non-native teachers emphasized that when travel to a country is not possible, opportunities to renew cultural knowledge are limited, at least to this particular group of respondents. Non-native teachers tended to focus on the need to update or acquire accurate cultural information. Native speakers expressed other concerns, such as those of one participant who reflected that much of her information was based on childhood memories because opportunities to update herself first hand were not possible.

In summary, *Teaching Culture in Foreign Language Programs in Grades K–8* set out to find answers to the what, when, how, and with what questions about teaching culture. Project staff worked to provide opportunities for collaboration between public/private school K–8 foreign language teachers and university faculty to explore the teaching of culture by making connections with other academic disciplines. University faculty brought academic expertise in French and Spanish language and cultures. Teachers brought pedagogical expertise from their experiences in the field of foreign language, and in the case of immersion teachers, expertise teaching the K–5 elementary school curriculum.

Interdisciplinary Approaches to Teaching Cultures

No foreign language teacher would argue with the statement that culture and language are inseparable and therefore, teaching culture should be an integral part of every classroom, as frequently as possible, if not on a daily basis. However, the challenges to effective teaching of culture, as outlined above, cannot be ignored. They are real and merit serious consideration if progress is to be made in this area. Given the lack of clear curricular guidelines, culture is frequently taught in an unplanned, casual way, in large part because many teachers have never been trained how to teach culture and are themselves self taught.

Teachers frequently approach the teaching of culture in one of four ways described by Galloway (1985):

1. The Frankenstein Approach: A taco from here, a flamenco dancer from there, a gaucho from here, a bullfight from there.
2. The 4-F Approach: Folk dances, festivals, fairs, and food.
3. The Tour Guide Approach: The identification of monuments, rivers, and cities.
4. The "By-the-Way" Approach: Sporadic lectures or bits of behavior selected indiscriminately to emphasize sharp differences.

While amusing at first glance, these descriptions may bring to mind visions of daily practices in some classes.

This project sought to develop tools to enable K–8 teachers to incorporate the systematic teaching of culture into classroom routines by aligning and connecting language, culture, and content objectives in classroom activities. University professors, serving as facilitators and subject matter experts, worked with project staff and teachers to provide current knowledge or to assist teachers in researching information and identifying authentic documents so that they could in turn design age-appropriate activities. All project participants —staff, teachers and university professors—were encouraged to broaden their mind-set to seek innovative ways to include culture objectives, language objectives, and content objectives from other disciplines into daily classroom routines, thereby expanding students' knowledge of products, practices, and daily life from target cultures.

By linking the teaching of culture to other areas of the K–8 curriculum, project participants sought resources that provided broader cultural learning perspectives for themselves and served to develop integrated activities for students. The focus outward to make connections with other disciplines resulted in a wide range of topics for cultural learning that in some cases had never before been considered. For immersion teachers, it is almost the only conceivable approach, given the demanding requirements for teaching the elementary school curriculum. For FLES teachers, this approach leads to connections with objectives being taught in the elementary classroom. Middle school teachers, often members of a team, are encouraged to explore social studies, math, science, and reading/language arts objectives.

Throughout the project, increased attention to students' background knowledge and interests served as a powerful tool in planning lessons. Participants focused on determining ways to identify the information students brought to a learning experience (such as K-W-L charts with which students identify: what we Know; what we Want to know; and what we Learned.) and to use this knowledge to adjust the content of the lesson and make sure that the context was one that helped students link new information to what they already knew.

Challenges of Interdisciplinary Teaching

Interdisciplinary teaching challenges one to go beyond the routine use of a single text or program of study. Foreign language teachers must examine what students are learning in other classes, decide which areas are relevant to learning and using a second language, and select areas that connect in meaningful and interesting ways to language and cultures. The end result should be daily lessons in which language, concepts, and information are more understandable and easier to remember, as well as highly motivating for students. In selecting concepts from other areas of the curriculum to integrate in the foreign language class, teachers should consider:

- Program goals and outcomes
- Students' prior and concurrent learning in other disciplines
- Time allocated to foreign language learning
- Availability of appropriate materials
- Teacher and student interests

In the past, interdisciplinary teaching in foreign language classes has most often occurred in K–5 classes because younger learners require a closer match between language learning and other areas of the curriculum. For example, learning outcomes for students in kindergarten and grade 1 routinely include identifying, naming, and describing shapes (triangle, circle, square, and rectangle) as a part of the math curriculum. It is therefore cognitively engaging for K–1 students to learn this and related concepts in a foreign language. In contrast, middle school students learn more advanced mathematical concepts which are more difficult to include in foreign language classrooms. In learning about the structure of a circle, grade 6 students identify and discuss the circumference, diameter, radius, center, and chord; they explore the relationships among the radius, diameter, and circumference of a circle. Foreign language teachers could conceivably integrate these math concepts in a lesson about Romanesque and Gothic architecture. However, one must ask the question, do these outcomes advance students learning in the foreign language in a meaningful way? Is the language required to explore these math concepts in a meaningful way too advanced for students? And finally, how often will students use this language after this interdisciplinary unit? The match between the language required for students to understand and talk about this mathematical concept may not play an important role in the advancement of their ability to communicate in the foreign language. Other important factors in evaluating the benefits of an integral approach are students' and teachers' interest in a theme or topic and increased motivation. Effective interdisciplinary teaching requires foreign language teachers to identify areas of the curriculum that are cognitively engaging for students but include language that is not so specialized that it is rarely generalizable to other situations.

Connections beyond the Standards for Foreign Language Learning

Central to the planning, development, and implementation of this project were:

1. Connections among language, culture, and K–8 curricular objectives in other academic disciplines
2. Connections among project staff, K–8 public and private school teachers, and university subject-matter facilitators

Description of the Project

The proposal for *Teaching Culture in Foreign Language Programs in Grades K–8* was planned and developed in collaboration with university professors who later participated in the project. The three-year project was divided into five phases:

I. Review of the literature on the teaching of culture and development of a draft Kindergarten through Grade 8 Scope and Sequence of Objectives for Teaching Culture
II. Introductory weekend seminar and 4-week Materials Development Seminar focusing on the teaching of the cultures of France and Spain
III. Weekend seminars on the cultures of France and Spain and field testing and revisions of lessons developed to teach the cultures of France and Spain
IV. 4-week Materials Development Seminar on the cultures of Francophone West Africa and Latin America
V. Field testing and revisions of lessons developed to teach the cultures of Francophone West Africa and Latin America
VI. Review, editing, and publication of selected lessons.

The Materials Development Seminar activities were organized around an academic component during which teachers explored the linguistic, ethnic, and cultural diversity of the Francophone and Spanish-speaking worlds. The first seminar focused on the cultures of France and Spain setting the stage for expanded understanding of the relationships of these two countries with the cultures of other French- and Spanish-speaking countries. The second seminar was designed to build upon year one and to explore the connections and unique characteristics of the language and cultures of Francophone Africa and the Spanish-speaking countries of Latin America.

Prior to each four-week materials development seminar, university professors were invited to visit K–8 program models in which participants taught. These visits were intended to give core faculty a glimpse of the day-to-day functioning, curricula, and instructional strategies considered "best practices" in the K–8 foreign language classroom. In most cases, core faculty members were unfamiliar with daily practices at the K–8 level, either because they had not been schooled in the U.S. or because they had not observed foreign language instruction in these settings.

Project staff and university professors worked closely to ensure that the materials development seminars included subject matter experts with specialized knowledge and differing perspectives on the teaching culture. Guest speakers met with project staff to plan presentations in order to ensure that the content of the presentations was aligned with seminar goals and that presenters used an interactive rather than lecture format. For example, a guest speaker was invited to the Materials Development Seminar on the Cultures of France to discuss the current role of the "Beurs" and their literature in French society. During the seminar on Latin America, a musicologist facilitated a discussion and activities on the role of music and musical instruments in different regions of Spanish-speaking Latin American countries. Representatives of the Embassies of France and Spain generously offered personnel and authentic materials to the seminars. Visits to sites such as the Cultural Institute of Mexico, the National Gallery of Art, and other museums in Washington D.C. added to the breadth and depth of the experiential nature of the seminars that participants valued highly.

All activities conducted in language groups, including off-site visits, were in either French or Spanish, because one of the objectives of the seminars was to offer participants many opportunities to enrich and expand their language proficiency in content areas. French- and Spanish-speaking docents were identified at the National Gallery of Art. Project staff and university professors worked together to identify French- and Spanish-speaking specialists in story telling and children's literature, and games.

An important characteristic of the seminars was the give-and-take between university professors and classroom teachers as they worked collaboratively to strike a balance between information about the cultures that teachers, as adult learners, needed and wanted to understand about new and evolving cultural phenomena, and information teachers needed and wanted to identify to incorporate into instructional materials for K–8 classes. This "tug of war" was a positive characteristic of seminar activities and was maintained throughout. It was not easy for teachers to sort through the adult-level cultural knowledge explored and discussed during the academic components and to decide what information and concepts to keep, what was beyond students' level of cognitive development, and how best to present an accurate, meaningful picture of target cultures for K–8 students.

At the same time, university professors worked toward a better understanding of application of cultural concepts in the classroom and identification of authentic materials to meet the needs of the teacher audience. Such materials included various books (Kimmel, 1992; Mermet, n.d.; and Michaud and Kimmel, 1990) or videos (*L'histoire immédiate*) that offer an overview of present-day France or provide a better understanding of key historical periods (*La mort monumentale*, on World War I, or *De Gaulle*). Studies with a crosscultural focus (Carroll, 1987; Wylie, 1981) were also used. Autobiographical works exemplifying specific cultural attitudes such as the perception of social classes (Ernaux, 1983) were included as well as works with a didactic perspective (Bruno, 1989). Feature films deemed to be particularly well suited to the study of cultural values and historical traumas (*Astérix*, *Le chat*, *Jeux interdits*, *Les dernières vacances*) were shown and discussed. In view of the teacher audience, a number of these sources were selected with regard to their relevance to childhood and adolescence: the works by Ernaux (1983) and Bruno (1989) as well as *Jeux interdits* and *Les dernières vacances* all have to do with the portrayal of children and adolescents, and *Astérix* is a cartoon primarily intended for young viewers.

It goes without saying, however, that in spite of their relevance, these sources were not meant to be used in the classroom. In fact, because of cultural incompatibilities, what is meant for children in one country is not necessarily usable in the U.S.: *Astérix* is a perfect example of material that would not be deemed acceptable in most American classrooms. The study of such sources, therefore, is meant to provide additional understanding of the dominant values and characteristics of the target culture but does not and cannot translate directly into classroom activities. These must be developed separately with the help of documents culturally suitable to American schools (hence the importance of the book of activities composed by the participants).

Project Setting

The twenty-eight teacher participants in this project all came from school districts in the Washington, D.C., metropolitan area. The districts represented were: Washington, D.C., a large urban district located in the nation's capital; Montgomery County Public Schools and Fairfax County Public Schools, both large county districts composed of urban, suburban, and rural settings.

Although the teachers represented four different program models for teaching foreign languages (total immersion, partial immersion FLES, and middle school), these differences were enriching. A healthy exchange of opinions and perspectives resulted in greater understanding among participants of the goals and objectives of each program model. Five participants taught in K–5 or K–6 French or Spanish total immersion programs. Four participants were K–5 Spanish partial immersion teachers. One teacher taught all K–5 students Spanish in a content-based FLES program. Fifteen participants taught students in grades 7 and 8 in either junior high or middle schools. The remaining three participants taught in unique settings. One participant taught French to all K–12 students who selected French language instruction in a private school. A Spanish-speaking teacher taught an English kindergarten with a high percentage of Spanish-speaking students. Her goal was to develop culture-rich lessons with some Spanish language to promote increased self esteem and pride among Spanish-speaking students and to introduce Spanish-language and cultural knowledge to English-speaking students in the class. One teacher of English worked with students enrolled in a Spanish immersion program. Although her primary responsibility was to teach English language arts, she worked closely with her grade 5 Spanish immersion team member during the seminar to develop culture lessons that were complementary to the grade 5 curriculum and culture lessons in Spanish developed by her

Spanish immersion counterpart.

Over a two-year period, approximately 2,484 students benefitted from the knowledge gained and the instructional materials developed during the three-year project. It is difficult to make general statements about students, parents, and the community in which project participants taught. Some schools were located in an urban setting; many were located in suburban locations and several were in rural settings. All districts represented in the project had student populations with diverse ethnic groups, and from different social and economic backgrounds. Results of a post-project survey indicate that students continue to benefit as teacher participants continue to use an integrated approach to teaching culture, supported by activities developed during the project.

Project Implementation

Development of a K–8 Culture Scope and Sequence

During the first year of the project, MCPS project staff developed curriculum guidelines for teaching culture in grade K–8 in consultation with national leaders in the field of presecondary foreign language instruction (see Appendix). Project staff reviewed: literature related to the teaching of culture; secondary guidelines for teaching culture; and K–8 curricular documents for reading and language arts, social studies, math, and science. During the three years of the project, these guidelines were reviewed and revised eight times with extensive input from the teacher participants and other foreign language practitioners with experience in K–8 classrooms. The revision process included project participants' use of the guidelines as they developed lessons to teach culture in K–8 classrooms.

In order to develop a user-friendly Culture Scope and Sequence, objectives were clustered in the following categories: Primary—Kindergarten, grades 1 and 2; upper elementary—grades 3,4, and 5; and middle school—grades 6, 7, and 8. This approach was used to accommodate the diversity of grade-level implementation points for K–8 foreign language programs across the U.S. For example, some FLES programs begin in kindergarten and continue to grade 5 with a smooth articulation to grades 6–8 at the middle school. Others begin at grade 3, while yet other districts do not begin study of a foreign language until the middle school years.

The clustering of objectives was intended to provide for some flexibility in use of the framework.

An additional differentiation in the Culture Scope and Sequence is represented by two categories of objectives. Because of differences between FLES and immersion programs, the objectives are divided into Core Objectives and Enrichment Objectives. Core Objectives are those that should be taught to all students in all programs. An example of a Kindergarten–Grades 1 and 2 Core Objective is that students will identify selected community helpers in U.S. and target cultures. Enrichment Objectives include objectives appropriate to but not limited to students in immersion programs. An example of a Kindergarten–Grades 1 and 2 Enrichment Objective is that students will name and describe selected community helpers in U.S. and target cultures. Related K–2 Enrichment Objectives that require a higher level of language proficiency than might be appropriate for students in FLES programs are: Students will name career options available to peers in U.S. and target cultures (e.g., When I grow up I want to be …); students compare and contrast work activities of people in selected occupations in U.S. with same or similar occupations in target cultures. Decisions as to which of these objectives to teach is best made by individual programs or teachers. While Enrichment Objectives were included primarily with immersion students in mind, teachers of FLES or middle-level programs may choose to include Enrichment Objectives in their instructional programs. As outlined in the introduction to the K–8 Scope and Sequence, selection of objectives should be guided by considerations such as the amount of time available for instruction, the availability of appropriate instructional materials, and/or teacher's knowledge.

Many of the objectives reflect the connections made with other disciplines. For example, a K–2 Core Objective states that students will identify and name clothing common in U.S. and target cultures. This objective connects with a social studies area of study for primary students (kindergarten through grade 2) about the need for clothing and how this need is met in different climates. A grade 3–5 Enrichment Objective states that students will read, demonstrate understanding of, and discuss fables from selected target cultures. This objective connects with an upper elementary (grades 3–5) reading and language arts objective requiring students to read and discuss fables from other countries. Finally, a grade 6–8 Core Objective states that students will draw a map to scale of a target culture country or city or region from that country. This objective connects with a math objective that requires students to plan and execute scale drawings.

Material Development Seminars

The materials development seminars were organized so that all participants met daily during total group sessions to discuss planning, instructional strategies, and teaching culture using an integrated approach. During the first week of the summer seminar, project personnel presented a template for lesson planning that was organized to include content objectives, language objectives, and culture objectives. The intent of this organization and its immediate introduction and discussion to seminar participants was to focus on a mind set that would always include these three instructional objectives as lessons were developed and planned.

Language-specific sessions were conducted separately and facilitated by university professors or other invited guest speakers who served as subject-matter experts. Discussions in each of the language groups during each summer session focused on the role of the linguistic and ethnic diversity in Francophone and Hispanic cultures. Specific topics included: the interplay of geography and history; family and social life; contemporary leisure activities; housing patterns; the diversity of contemporary culture reflected in food, clothing, housing, transportation, and attitudes and values represented in the most common practices of daily life; art, architecture, games, songs, and authentic children's literature. Reading selections in either French or Spanish were coordinated with seminar topics to enrich participants' background knowledge and provide them with reference materials to use to develop lessons.

Sessions were conducted in the target language to enrich participants' language proficiency. As part of the application process for the seminars, a language assessment (written and spoken) was used to ensure that participants would be comfortable in an all French or Spanish environment and be able to sustain small- or large-group discussions in the second language. One teacher who taught English to Spanish immersion students successfully demonstrated in a personal interview that her Spanish proficiency would allow her to participate actively in all aspects of the project. In addition to the unique perspective that she brought to project activities, she noted that her Spanish language skills had improved considerably at the end of seminar activities.

Participants used the academic content discussed in language groups to develop activities and materials for use with K–8 students. They worked collaboratively and individually to synthesize topics covered in the seminars with their pedagogical knowledge, to make the cultural content age-appropriate and interesting to young learners. A resource library of authentic materials in French and Spanish was available to develop lessons. During each of the summer materials development seminars, participants examined and evaluated resource materials for their usefulness and appropriateness to elementary and middle school instruction.

Two volumes of selected lessons, one each for French and Spanish, were published during the last year of the project. *Teaching Culture in Grades K–8: A Resource Manual for Teachers of French* and *Teaching Culture in Grades K–8: A Resource Manual for Teachers of Spanish* (Lorenz and Met, 1994) contain lessons organized by grade level and topic. An interesting outcome of the distribution of these resource manuals has been their appeal to teachers at the secondary level who have noted that they use many of the lessons in the manuals with few adaptations.

A brief summary of several lessons from the resource manual for teachers of French follows. (References in these examples are to page numbers in the manuals and the name of the teacher-author).

A Grade 5 lesson (p. 117, Gouin) developed for French immersion includes math objectives for multiplying and dividing factors of two and three place numbers by 10 and multiples of 10 and a culture objective to promote understanding of the importance of the rail system as a means of transportation in France. In this lesson, students discuss their personal experiences with various types of transportation for travel outside of their immediate city. They compare their experiences with the most commonly used types of transportation in France. The lesson provides background information about railways in France that students use to solve six word problems. As an extension and evaluation activity, students use the information about trains in France to develop original word problems to exchange with classmates. An example of a word problem from the lesson is:

> *Marie voudrait rendre visite à sa grand-mère qui habite à 273 km de chez elle. Elle voudrait voyager en 1ère classe. (a) Estimez le prix de son billet aller-retour. (b) Calculez le prix de son billet aller-retour.* Students solve this problem using the following information provided in the information section about trains: *Le 1er janvier 1991, les 100 km coûtaient 62 francs en 2ème classe et 92 francs en 1ère classe.*

In a Grade 7/8, Level-1 French lesson (p. 185, Ryland), students learn to name and describe articles of clothing. Working in pairs, they examine the contents of several imaginary students' closets and determine how many different outfits the students can wear, based on the combinations of clothing. Finally, students read a simple description of certain unwritten rules of dress in France and use this information to identify similarities and differences between U.S. and French unwritten practices regarding clothing.

A brief summary of several lessons from the resource manual for teachers of Spanish follows. A kindergarten lesson (p. 287, Russell) developed for Spanish partial immersion integrates use of a floor map representing the Panama Canal and different colored manipulatives to represent boats, to promote development of logical reasoning and problem solving in math. Although the physical aspects of the Panama Canal are introduced only briefly, the floor map is the setting in which students identify which boats (identified by color) and how many boats are located in a certain area of the map. A sample problem from the lesson is: *En total hay ocho barcos que esperan a cruzar el canal en el Océano Pacífico. (Place boats). Algunos barcos son rojos y otros negros. Si tres de los barcos son rojos ¿cuántos de los barcos son negros?* In a lesson for older students, a Grade 8, Level-1 Spanish, students review number names while they construct and learn to play the Aztec game of Patolli. The lesson presents a simple *Sí/No* questionnaire about Patolli to help students identify its characteristics; students use a Venn diagram classification activity to compare the two board games, Patolli and Parcheesi.

Field Testing Lessons to Teach Culture

During the academic year following each of the Materials Development Seminars, project staff and participants continued to work together. In addition to follow-up weekend seminars, the specialist conferenced with and visited each of the participant's classes during field testing of lessons. Participants welcomed opportunities to continue professional dialogue about teaching culture using an integrated approach. These discussions often led to lesson revisions.

Project Evaluation

Although the frame of the project remained essentially the same as that described in the original proposal, staff used three tools to gather feedback from participants. Participants and facilitators met informally each morning for coffee and frequently ate lunch together. These unplanned moments during the day provided a valuable forum during which discussions sometimes included reflections on the facilities, program, and need for specific materials. One such discussion led to an adjustment of the syllabus to better meet participants' needs and interests. In a more formal fashion, project staff used weekly surveys to gather feedback from participants. Finally, an external evaluator, a well-known expert in the field of early language learning, visited each seminar for two days. During her visit, she asked participants to respond to an extensive questionnaire about seminar activities and also met with small groups of participants to discuss the seminar. She met with core faculty members to gain their perspective on seminar activities. Information from her report about the first Materials Development Seminar was used to plan for the second seminar. In the final evaluation, participants identified the following outcomes of the seminar as significant to their professional growth and development: development of activities and instructional materials for teaching about culture; skill in developing interdisciplinary units; improvement of teaching; intellectual stimulation. One notable direct result of project activities was that many participants expressed a strong interest in visiting one of the countries studied during the seminar in order to enhance and expand further their new knowledge.

Reflections

Two areas were the most challenging during implementation of project activities. The first was the amount of time and energy needed to communicate the interests and needs of K–8 teachers to core faculty and consultants. The second was the stress and frustration expressed by many teacher participants during the process of developing instructional activities.

The first challenge centered around the need for communication. University members of the core staff and outside consultants were highly qualified experts in their fields who devoted much time and energy to ensuring the success of project activities. Only four consultants had ever received any formal training in working with students in the K–8 age group and therefore a great deal of time was required prior to and during the seminars for dialogue between presenters and participants. An important role for the project specialist was to emphasize and reiterate project goals that the academic focus of seminars be on content most useful to K–8 teachers of French and Spanish. Flexibility and openness to discussions during seminar sessions resulted in adjustments by core staff as well as teacher participants. Both groups recognized that a blending of perspectives was necessary to meet project goals, which encompassed a strong academic component leading to the development of usable classroom lessons with which to teach culture. As mentioned earlier, many materials (videos, film, autobiographical works, etc.) were selected with regard to their portrayal of children and adolescents in order to provide a relevant basis for crosscultural analysis.

Another case in point took place during the year 1 seminar. The French core faculty specialist explored the structure and geographic density of cities in France using a variety of texts (video, audio, and print). He began by looking at the French sense of privacy reflected in the personal interactions among the French and the use of barriers (fences and walls) to limit private space. Discussions focused on similarities and differences between U.S.–French use of space, openness in geographic organization, and interactions among people. The texts and discussions assisted participants in gaining a better understanding of how the French sense of privacy relates to the structure, organization, and geographic density of cities in France. As a result of this seminar topic, several teachers developed lessons about the organization of cities in France, highlighting similarities and differences with U.S. cities. These lessons did not include the same texts, level of detail, nor the adult-level sociological concepts and explanations that were a critical part of seminar discussions. Rather, teachers synthesized, selected, and adapted information that they included in developmentally appropriate activities, such as identifying, comparing, and contrasting important elements of cities in the U.S. and France. Teachers realized that a portion of texts and information discussed during the seminar was needed to promote and expand adult understanding but was not directly applicable to the K–8 classroom setting. They recognized that greater knowledge and a deeper understanding was needed to develop accurate lessons that presented complicated concepts at a developmentally appropriate, interesting level for students.

Another area of give-and-take was the willingness of some core faculty to try out new pedagogical approaches from the K–8 setting, such as the integration of cooperative learning techniques into their lecture/discussion format. Core faculty and guest presenters recognized that project participants represented a unique audience with focused interests and needs and therefore adjusted their university syllabus and approach to the audience.

The experiences of this project underscore the often discussed and obvious need for frequent contact and increased exchanges between classroom teachers and university faculty from language departments who are, or should be, involved in the professional preparation/continued professional development of K–8 second language teachers. What should this dialogue include? University faculty should be made aware of the rationale, content, and instructional strategies that are used in K–8 classrooms in order to participate effectively in the process of continuing professional development of teachers. If early-start/long-sequence foreign language programs are to be successful, then dialogue among all teachers in such a sequence (kindergarten–16) is needed to promote articulation and realistic expectations for students as they move through the education system. Increased communication will benefit programs, students, teachers and university personnel. Whose responsibility is it to make sure that such a dialogue happens? The range of possibilities is great—from school districts and universities, professional organizations, and conference organizers, to the individuals who make up the infrastructure of the foreign language profession.

The second challenge that surfaced was the stress experienced by participants during the development and writing of instructional materials and activities. While as a matter of course, most teachers write daily, weekly, and monthly lesson plans, few have been formally trained to develop activities and lessons for others. Additionally, new cultural knowledge and the relatively new, integrated (language, content, culture objectives) approach to the teaching of culture that were the core of project activities necessitated a change in mind set for core faculty and participants alike. The project specialist used whole group sessions and demonstration lessons to model an integrative approach. For example, one lesson was organized around graphing the modes of transportation routinely used by participants (first-hand experience/math). Using the whole-group graph as a point of departure, slides were used to discuss common forms of transportation in Mali (culture). Finally, participants constructed a Venn diagram comparing modes of transportation from their graph and those from Mali presented through the slides.

The project specialist conferred with participants during the seminars and the academic year as teachers field tested activities. Participants worked cooperatively, exchanging ideas to problem solve and identify interesting and developmentally appropriate topics and practices for classroom implementation. Peer review of draft lesson plans yielded insightful comments about ways that concepts might be presented and expressed differently.

It is interesting to note that during the second Materials Develop Seminar, most participants expressed less frustration and anxiety about the process of developing lessons than during the first seminar. Perhaps the experience of having successfully written, field tested, and revised a first set of lessons provided a sense of confidence and a framework that put participants at ease. Just as learning a second language takes time and practice, so, too, does the teaching of culture through an integrated approach and the development and writing of instructional materials for a particular age group. What can we learn from the frustrations encountered by participants during this project? Should teacher preparation coursework or continued professional development focus more on preparing teachers to undertake such endeavors? Curricular frameworks, cultural knowledge, and innovative instructional strategies are all tools available to K–8 foreign language teachers. Is preparing materials to share with others an area that needs further attention or is it an area of responsibility that belongs elsewhere in the profession?

A University Perspective

The lack of collaboration between school systems and universities is notorious. And yet, collaborative endeavors involving both parties can be immensely fruitful, as we learned from the project described in this article. It is a platitude to say that teaching is a reciprocal form of exchange, and that in many ways the teacher learns as much from the classroom experience as the students, but it was particularly true in this case. The audience was composed of very experienced, immensely dedicated, and highly specialized school teachers who did not merely "learn" about foreign cultures, even though they wished to acquire up-to-date accurate information. They were looking for solutions to difficult problems relating to the pedagogy of culture teaching. Learning from their needs was a very enriching experience, and it put the traditional teaching of culture at the college level in an entirely new perspective.

For one thing, even though the participants claimed that they needed a "refresher" culture course, it was more for their own pleasure, motivation, and satisfaction than for practical reasons. It was clear that their need for additional exposure to the French or Spanish cultures was more emotional than factual. Several objectives had to be achieved through the workshops, but conveying new information to the teachers was probably not a major one. The workshops were infinitely more useful to promote an atmosphere conducive to reflecting on pedagogical issues, and first and foremost—how to incorporate culture into the curriculum.

How to teach culture and what to teach are two prevalent concerns in school systems. Immersion teachers, in particular, are faced in their jobs with a serious difficulty: they have to teach all their subjects in another language while adhering to the cultural guidelines imposed by their U.S. school system. It is important, therefore to focus on their specific predicament.

The question for them is not simply how to teach culture, but how to convey the target culture within a pedagogical framework which is only designed to support American cultural values, and which does not allow for radical departures from those values. Within this framework, which is entirely monocultural and ethnocentric, issues are naturally addressed in a way which are not necessarily pertinent to the societies of the target cultures. The problem of immersion teaching, therefore, is not unlike a cultural dilemma. For example, French immersion programs, from that point of view, have little to do with French Government programs in this country, which essentially reproduce a French environment abroad. A "lycée" in the U.S. is not essentially different from its counterparts in France. The only minor difference is that lip service is paid to the teaching of American Studies, in compliance with federal laws. By and large, this added "subject," perceived as culturally foreign within the French schools, is not taken very seriously. Thus, while French immersion programs attempt to teach the target culture from within the context of the national one (hence the conflict), dealing by definition with the difficulty of biculturalism, French schools in this country mostly ignore the host culture, and therefore simply do not address the concept of biculturalism.

In French immersion programs, the numerous translation difficulties commonly encountered reveal this cultural quandary (teachers will ask how to say "Social Studies," for example, or "the four food groups", etc.) It is often impossible to find an adequate translation for a term, simply because the pedagogical approach, which reflects cultural priorities and a national ideology, is different in France and Francophone countries where issues are not dealt with in the same manner as in this society.

Furthermore, when foreign language teachers use culturally authentic materials, they know that these materials must be selected so as not to threaten the cultural integrity of the U.S. system. Many documents which would be quite acceptable in schools of other nations simply cannot be used in the United States. In particular, textbooks from other cultures have to be avoided because they cannot be integrated into the American curriculum, although one would imagine that using them would be the easiest way of teaching the target cultures. And there are countless instances of cultural incompatibilities. An example is the much greater tolerance for nudity in France, and even though paintings by French artists can certainly be used as "authentic" documents, their selection (with particular attention to the deletion of nudity) is hardly authentic. Another example: French comic books like *Astérix* and *Lucky Luke* are commonly used in French schools to teach reading. The language used in those stories is in no way offensive, and in view of their well-known appeal among children, they are well suited to the task. However, politically correct concerns in this country preclude their use in U.S. schools (they may portray smoking and the drinking of alcoholic beverages, for example, which does not offend anyone in Europe but which is often regarded as unacceptable here, and the graphic representation of minorities may be offensive). The choice of "authentic" documents, in other words, reflects the dominant American cultural ideology and becomes far less authentic than one may imagine.

From this perspective, the foreign language classroom environment in general, and the immersion classroom environment in particular, is artificial, since it portrays the target culture through American eyes. But this artificial dimension is probably less problematic than one might think, essentially because it forces teachers to deal in an imaginative manner with the clash of the two cultures. One of the goals of the workshops was thus to address this apparent artificiality and the benefits that can be derived from it.

Another focus of the workshops was the current perception of the target language in this country. For example, identifying and discussing the nature of the prevalent images associated with the foreign language and the cultures it conveys, and even stereotypes—whether positive or negative—are essential within this "artificial" system, whose aim is to promote biculturalism or even multiculturalism. Negative stereotypes, for example, should hardly be counterbalanced by an inordinate use of positive ones, although it is clear that students should have a positive image of the foreign culture as well as the American one. Ideally, both cultures should be on a par. This may be more difficult to attain than it appears, but it is obvious that the teacher who has a clear understanding of the use of target-culture stereotypes in this country should be better equipped to deal with the teaching of the cultures.

Finally, in order to generate intellectual stimulation, the workshops also addressed less practical issues, although this was not its main focus. It was not inappropriate, for example, to discuss the validity of opposing "c" to "C" cultures, to wonder why the term "culture" is by and large preferred to that of "civilization", etc. These issues are relevant to the more practical matters already alluded to, since addressing them helps assess the ideological status of the target culture and perhaps ways to change it, if necessary. At the university level, for example, the current trend to rename departments is well known. The move has been from "literature" to "studies," a broader and more encompassing term. Besides reflecting a more global perspective, what this trend indicates is that not only the traditional supremacy of "literature"" (clearly associated with "C" Culture) is more and more challenged (at least at the undergraduate level), but also that the line between literature and culture has become more and more blurry. Needless to say, not everyone agrees with this present tendency (see, for example, Petry, 1995). As one would imagine, this change of self-image has already had a significant impact on the curriculum (away from "traditional" literature survey courses) and, consequently, on the education of future language and culture teachers.

Personal Voice of the Teacher

A pre-project questionnaire about the teaching of culture, distributed during the first year of the project (May, 1992) to K–8 foreign language teachers in the greater Washington, DC, metropolitan area yielded 28 responses. Teachers ranged in experience from 1 year to 18 to 20 years in the profession. FLES, immersion, and middle school programs were represented by the respondents. The primary intent of the questionnaire was to gather teacher input about what should be included in the K–8 Culture Scope and Sequence.

Additional information gathered from this questionnaire offers a glimpse of these classroom teachers' perspectives on the teaching of culture. Seventeen teachers expressed three major concerns about teaching cultures: (1) insufficient and/or up-to-date background knowledge about cultures; (2) lack of appropriate materials with which to teach cultures; and (3) inadequate time in a normal school year to teach cultures. Discussions with foreign language colleagues reinforced the need for a framework to address the teaching of culture because although some K–8 foreign language programs have generally stated goals for teaching cultures, few have articulated guidelines, activities, and materials to support and ensure implementation of the goals. When asked if they taught culture, all teachers replied affirmatively. However, when asked if they had a year-long plan or an articulated program plan for teaching culture in a K–8 sequence, most did not. While the incidental teaching of cultures may be better than none, when this approach it used, it is conceivable that students enrolled in a K–8 foreign language sequence exit grade 8 with an unbalanced or even inaccurate view of the target culture.

The results of a post-project questionnaire compiled in April 1996, three years after the formal end date of this project, indicate that 16 K–8 FLES, immersion, and middle school teachers (28 questionnaires sent) continue to use and apply the knowledge gained from their seminar experiences. All 16 respondents stated that they currently use activities that they developed during the seminar in an integrated way in their classes. One teacher uses lessons to differentiate instruction for students who are at varying levels of academic and cognitive development. Another teacher stated that she has used only a small part of what she could potentially use because of time constraints. Asked if they make connections in their classroom between second language, culture, and content objectives, all teachers responded affirmatively. Some comments were general in nature, such as, "The students can understand better that everything is related." Others were more specific, referring to areas of the curriculum where connections are most easily made, such as social studies. Less encouraging were responses to a question about the continued use of the K–8 Culture Scope and Sequence. Eight replied that they had used it to identify topics to teach culture and 8 replied that they had not. All but one respondent felt that participation in the culture seminars had changed how they teach culture in their class. Generally comments underlined that culture is not being taught in isolation or during "cultural moments," but integrated with the teaching of other topics. One respondent commented that participation in the seminar had increased her self confidence and that she has gone on to conduct more research on her own.

Because the university professors played such an integral role in seminar activities as core faculty, the questionnaire included a question about their contributions to participants' learning experiences. Respondents described university professors' participation as a major contribution to the seminar and felt that they brought a different perspective to the experience. One participant described seminar discussions and intellectual arguments of some sessions as "mind stretching." Others described their contributions as: Expertise; Created an atmosphere of questions and answers that was nonthreatening; Enthusiasm was infectious. In summary, all respondents expressed positive comments about the core faculty.

Nine of the sixteen respondents have participated in other professional development activities on the teaching of culture since the seminar. Activities cited included: award of a National Endowment for the Humanities summer independent study grant; French government summer seminar on Francophone cultures in Dakar, Senegal; participation in a seminar on culture organized by the National Foreign Language Center in Washington, D.C.; and several presentations at national conferences.

Results of the Project

Dissemination

As a final summary of project activities, two volumes of selected activities to teach the cultures of French- and Spanish-speaking countries were published by Montgomery County Public Schools. Each volume begins with the K–8 Culture Scope and Sequence, which is then followed by lessons that detail procedures, instructional strategies, instructional materials, and in some cases illustrations that support the lesson. Because the spirit and intent of the project was to promote the teaching of culture, all materials included in these two volumes may be copied for classroom use. In addition to field testing lessons, project participants, core faculty, and project staff were involved in the lengthy process of reviewing and revising these materials prior to their publication. As was the case throughout the Materials Development Seminar, communication was a key factor in making sure that the materials included were accurate and could be realistically used in the K–8 foreign language classroom.

Continued Collaboration and Connections

The Standards for Foreign Language Learning (1996) were being drafted as this project began. Early drafts had already included Culture Goals in strong terms; the interdisciplinary, or Connections Goal, followed quickly. In many ways, this collaborative project illustrates how the standards' goal areas link with one another, as shown in the icon of interlocking circles used with National Standards Project work. Readers of this chapter will certainly find resources for the teaching of culture, but one of the powerful messages this project sends lies in the crosscultural approach embraced and the strong ties to the K–8 social studies, math, or science curricula.

The initial collaboration between Montgomery County Public Schools (MCPS) and university staff from the University of Maryland, College Park (and other universities) that began with a project proposal has led to other joint endeavors. In June, 1996, a national seminar for French and Spanish immersion teachers organized by MCPS was held on the College Park campus of the University of Maryland. A number of facilitators at this seminar were University of Maryland faculty. In July, 1996, a ten-day institute on the teaching of culture and authentic children's literature for teachers of French and Spanish was sponsored by the National K–12 Foreign Language Resource Center at Iowa State University, Ames, Iowa. This seminar was planned and implemented with two university staff that participated in the original project described in this paper. As with most collaborative endeavors that involve an exchange of ideas and approaches, this institute included some of the components of the project *Teaching Culture in Foreign Language Programs in Grades K–8*, while at the same time, new and revised approaches have evolved.

One of the promising areas of cooperation is probably that of foreign languages for specific purposes (business, engineering, the legal profession, etc.), although one should be careful not to exaggerate its likely impact on the teaching of foreign languages in general. Teaching language for a specific purpose will not revolutionize the field but may add a new dimension to it. At the University of Maryland, International Business and Foreign Languages (IBFL), a program created in 1990 for students majoring both in a language and business has been quite successful. It requires some additional training on the part of the language instructor, mainly in terminology and business culture. This training could be offered to interested high school teachers through specially designed workshops, for example, although it should first be determined how this business language component could be best incorporated in the curriculum at the secondary level. It may also be useful to look into the specific language needs of high school students who wish to embark on technical studies at the college level. In the fall of 1996, for example, prospective engineering students were invited to the University of Maryland. Half of them had some training in Spanish and the other half in French. They all wished, if possible, to further their study of these two languages. Clearly, a specific program adapted to the needs of these students should be contemplated at the university level, but it might be important to start a more tailored form of language preparation at the high school level. The main objective is to make sure that the transition from high school to college is done smoothly and that students who have the desire to continue learning a language beyond the secondary level be given the opportunity to do so, however demanding the course of study they select outside of the humanities may be.

Summary

Teaching Culture in Foreign Language Programs in Grades K–8 was a three-year project that made connections within and beyond the K 8 setting. Development of a framework for teaching culture, teacher seminars that focused on a collaborative atmosphere led to the development of student-centered learning activities in which connections were made among three important learning areas in the foreign language classroom: language, content from other disciplines, and culture. Because project activities were developed collaboratively by project staff from the public school setting and university professors from a near-by state institution, rich resources and varied perspectives were also connected. Drawing on their experience as K–6 total and partial immersion teachers, some participants came to project activities with a rich understanding of the math, science, social studies, and reading/language arts objectives that can be taught in a foreign language and the ways to teach them. However, the additional goal of bringing culture connections to the planning table was both challenging and enriching. At the end of the project, connections between the foreign language objectives (language and culture) and those of other disciplines resulted in the development of successful activities for use at the K–8 level. Moreover the project experience led to connections and continued collaboration among project staff, K–8 teachers, and university professors in an on-going dialogue that continues to impact teaching and learning.

References

Bredenkam, S., (Ed.) (1987). *Developmentally appropriate practice in early childhood programs serving children from birth through age 8.* Expanded Ed. Washington, D.C.: NAEYC.

Bruno, G. (Madame A. Fouillée). (1989). *Le tour de la France par deux enfants.* Paris: Librairie Classique Eugène Belin.

Byram, M. (1989). *Cultural studies in foreign language education.* Clevedon, England: Multilingual Matters.

Campbell, S. F. (1976). *Piaget sampler.* New York: John Wiley & Sons, Inc.

Carroll, R. (1987). *Evidences invisibles.* Paris: Seuil.

Curtain, H., & Pesola, C. A. (1994). *Languages and children.* White Plains, NY: Longman.

Ernaux, Annie. (1983). *La place.* Paris: Gallimard.

Galloway, V. (1985). A design for the improvement of the teaching of culture in foreign language classrooms. ACTFL project proposal.

Indiana Department of Education, Division of Curriculum. (1986). (Center For School Improvement and Performance). *A guide to proficiency-based instruction in modern foreign languages for Indiana schools.* Indianapolis, IN: Author.

Indiana Department of Education, Division of Curriculum. (1987). *A Guide to proficiency-based instruction in French for Indiana schools.* Indianapolis, IN: Author.

Indiana Department of Education, Division of Curriculum. (1987). *A Guide to proficiency-based instruction in Spanish for Indiana schools.* Indianapolis, IN: Author.

Kimmel, A. (1992). *Vous avez-dit France? Eléments pour comprendre la société française actuelle.* Paris: Hachette/CIEP.

Lorenz, E., & Met, M. (Ed.) (1994). *Teaching culture in grades K–8: A resource manual for teachers of Spanish.* Rockville, MD: Montgomery County Public Schools.

Lorenz, E., & Met, M. (Ed.) (1994). *Teaching culture in grades K–8: A resource manual for teachers of French.* Rockville, MD: Montgomery County Public Schools.

Lafayette, R. C. (1988). Integrating the teaching of culture into the foreign language classroom. In A. J. Singerman (Ed.), *Toward a new integration of language and culture* (pp. 47–62). Middlebury, VT: Northeast Conference.

Mermet, G. (published yearly). *Francoscopie.* Paris: Larousse.

Michaud, G., & Kimmel, A. (1990). *Le nouveau guide France.* Paris: Hachette.

National Standards in Foreign Language Education Project. (1996). *Standards for foreign language learning: Preparing for the 21st century.* Yonkers, NY: Author.

North Carolina Department of Public Instruction, Division of Communication Skills, Instructional Services. (1985). *North Carolina Competency-Based Curriculum. Teacher Handbook Second Language Studies K–12.* Raleigh, NC: Author.

Omaggio Hadley, A. C. (1993). *Teaching language in context.* Boston, MA: Heinle & Heinle.

Pesola, C. A. (1991). Culture in the elementary school foreign language classroom. *Foreign Language Annals, 24,* 331–346.

Petry, S. (1995). French studies/cultural studies: Reciprocal invigoration or mutual destruction? *French Review, 68,* 381–392.

Rhodes, N., & Oxford R. (1988). A National profile of foreign language instruction at the elementary and secondary school levels. Los Angeles: UCLA.

Seeyle, H. N. (1993). *Teaching culture: Strategies for intercultural communication.* Lincolnwood, IL: National Textbook.

Wylie, L. (1981). *Village in the Vaucluse.* (3rd Ed.). Cambridge, MA: Harvard University Press.

Wylie, L., & Brière, J.-F. (1995). *Les Français* (Second Ed.). Englewood Cliffs, NJ: Prentice Hall.

Films and Documents on Video

Astérix le Gaulois. (1976). Goscinny, R. , Uderzo, A., and Dargaud, G. Dargaud Films Production.
Le chat. Granier-Deferre, P. (Director). (1971). Joseph Green Pictures.
De Gaulle: Une certaine ideé de la France. (1990). (Distributed by FACSEA).
Les dernières vacances. Leenhardt, R. (Director). (1948). Films Constellation.
L'histoire immédiate. (1988). (Distributed by PICS/The University of Iowa).
Jeux interdits. Clément, R. (Director). (1952). (Distributed by FACSEA).
La mort monumentale. Descamps, O. (Director). (1984). Secrétariat d'Etat auprès du Ministre de la Défense chargé des Anciens Combattants and Modom Productions.
Laurence Wylie in Peyrane. (1983). Petit, B. (Producer)

Appendix. Excerpts from Kindergarten through Grade 8 Scope and Sequence Objectives for Teaching Culture

The Arts

Kindergarten – Grades 1 and 2
Core Objectives

Students will:

- recite and use gestures to demonstrate understanding of traditional rhymes from target cultures used by caregivers with preschool and young children
- use illustrations in target culture children's literature as context to demonstrate understanding of the story line of simplified short narratives and folktales
- listen to and demonstrate understanding of simplified short narratives and/or folk tales from target cultures
- identify illustrations in target cultures children's literature as a reflection of the culture
- dramatize simplified, authentic folktales from target cultures
- sing songs from target cultures used by caregivers with young children
- use authentic instruments and/or replicas of authentic instruments from target cultures to explore music and rhythm from target cultures
- make simple replicas of authentic instruments from target cultures
- perform simple modern and/or folk dances from target cultures
- identify selected popular and/or classical music originating from target cultures
- identify colors using artifacts, works of art and illustrations in children's literature drawn from selected target cultures

- identify artifacts and works of art as creations from the target cultures and use them to discuss topics that are a familiar part of the daily world of kindergarten, grade 1 and 2 students, e.g., family, pets, holidays.
- create own artwork related to target cultures
- identify artifacts or works of art from selected target cultures as examples of artistic creations
- identify geometric shapes in works of art from target cultures

Enrichment Objectives: Immersion

- read and demonstrate understanding of simplified short narratives and/or folktales from target cultures
- read and demonstrate understanding of simple proverbs from target cultures
- name colors using artifacts, works of art, and illustrations in children's literature drawn from selected target cultures
- name and/or describe artifacts and/or works of art as examples of artistic creations from selected target cultures
- name and describe geometric shapes in works of art from target cultures
- identify and describe how families, in the past and currently, meet their needs for food, clothing, and shelter using works of art from selected target cultures

History and Geography

Grades 3, 4, 5
Core Objectives

Students will:
- identify and name at least two monuments and/or symbols that represent important values of target cultures
- locate main geographical regions of selected target culture countries on maps
- identify a region in a target culture country that is similar to the state in which students live
- identify selected characteristics of the environment, ecology and conservation attitudes in target culture countries
- identify and name flora and fauna indigenous to selected target culture countries
- use a line graph to compare and contrast temperatures in regions (north, south, east, west, central) of U.S. and those in regions of selected target culture countries
- name and describe attitudes toward the environment, ecology, and conservation in selected target culture countries
- identify and locate capitals and major cities in selected target culture countries
- name target culture countries that are characterized by racial and ethnic diversity

- demonstrate understanding of the role of religious values in target cultures
- identify sources of mutual influences between U.S. and the target cultures e.g., entertainment, literature, architecture
- identify examples of culture-specific practices that are contemporary and/or traditional
- identify customs from target cultures that have been assimilated into daily life in the U.S
- identify customs from U.S. that have been assimilated into daily life in target cultures

Enrichment Objectives: Immersion

- describe the importance of monuments that represent historic events or values for target cultures
- locate important natural resources of selected target culture countries on a map
- name and describe geographic regional features, such as mountain ranges, that could foster ethnic separation in selected target culture countries
- use a line graph to report research on average temperatures in various regions of selected target culture countries during the four seasons of the year
- explain prevalent attitudes towards the environment, ecology, and conservation in selected target culture countries (include economic, religious, and cultural factors)
- name and describe ethnic groups that currently live in selected target culture countries
- explain how the natural environment has influenced the way people of selected target culture countries meet their needs (vegetation, animal life, water sources, soil)
- explain the role of religion in historical events that may have contributed to the exploration and settlement by people from target culture countries of the state in which students live (as appropriate to the state)

Daily Life Patterns

Grades 6, 7, 8 Middle Level
Core Objectives

Students will:
- read and complete standard forms from target culture countries, e.g., application forms, etc.
- research and report on the significance of one major holiday from a target culture country
- name major religions in target culture countries
- name and describe important religious practices in target cultures
- understand and explain how religion influences customs in daily life of target cultures
- identify folk beliefs held by some people in U.S. and target culture countries
- understand and use appropriate language and behavior necessary for interacting with strangers in target cultures in a variety of situations, e.g., small shops, public transportation, restaurants, and places of entertainment
- demonstrate understanding of attitudes and values of target cultures as reflected in daily

practices in public life and private life (e.g., pasta shops open on Sunday morning in Buenos Aires; French practice of closing doors in all rooms in the home)
* describe parent-child or adult-child relationships in target cultures
* identify and explain generally accepted target culture guidelines for making decisions about teenage activities
* describe or demonstrate (as appropriate) display of affection among family members and friends in target cultures
* name other languages spoken by large portions of the population in target cultures
* identify the status of various occupations in selected target cultures
* understand and describe the attitudes of the general population toward police, fire, and other public service institutions which provide safety and security in target culture countries

Enrichment Objectives: Immersion

* explain folk beliefs held by some people in U.S. and target cultures
* adjust register to reflect the level of formality required, depending on a given situation and the individuals present in a variety of situations from target cultures
* explain attitudes and values of target cultures as reflected in daily practices in public life and private life (e.g., pasta shops open on Sunday morning in Buenos Aires, Argentina; and French practice of closing doors in all rooms in the home)
* identify differences between written and spoken language in target cultures (e.g., identify forms of language that may be spoken, but not usually written—ça/cela; chévere [réquete] + adjective/excelente)
* compare and contrast modes of transportation in U.S. and target cultures, from early settlement to modern times

Linguistic and Cultural Comparisons: Middle School African American Students Learning Arabic

Zena Moore

Mark Anthony English

University of Texas at Austin

I had a wonderful day. I'm starting to know Arabic. I can barley speak Arabic but that's better than nothing. I can help my brother Aziz when he need help. I like helping my brother cuz he don't under stand Arabic like I do. I'm starting to want to take Arabic home and studie.
[from student journal]

Comparisons Goal

The Comparisons Goal of the new National Standards for Foreign Language Learning (1996) reflects the widely held belief that students who learn a second language and the cultures in which that language is used benefit cognitively and affectively beyond the immediate curriculum. By going beyond the parameters of their native language and culture, they acquire insights into the very nature of language and cultural systems. As students learn a new language, it is thought that they discover different patterns among language systems and become more aware of how languages operate. Learners soon recognize similarities between their first and second languages, as well as categories and structures in the second language that do not exist, or that differ significantly, in their own. Students also discover that acceptable behaviors or practices in their culture may not be acceptable or may carry different meanings in other cultures. Indeed, one value of language study, particularly if it is over an extended period of time, may be the realization that cultures see the world from quite different perspectives.

The Comparisons Goal includes two standards.

Standard 4.1
Students demonstrate understanding of the nature of language through comparisons of the language studied and their own.

This standard focuses on the effect of learning the new language system on students' ability to develop hypotheses about how language works. It may enable them to go beneath the surface structures of their own language to understand more fully how forms carry meaning.

Standard 4.2
Students recognize that cultures use different patterns of interaction and can apply this knowledge to their own.

Throughout language learning, students continue to learn about the similarities and differences with respect to the perspectives, practices, and products of the native and second cultures. An awareness of how two cultures have developed patterns in different ways may lead students to suspend judgments of cultural perspectives as simply right or wrong, strange or familiar.

Exploring the Goal in the Context of Teaching All Students

The National Standards through the Comparisons Goal would have students focus on drawing comparisons between L1 and C1 with L2 and C2. The standards imply that teachers should create opportunities and learning experiences that allow students to make these comparisons throughout their language study. While insights occur over time, teachers can direct students' attention to linguistic elements and cultural factors from the very first lessons. This issue of linguistic and cultural comparisons as a by-product of L2 study is particularly interesting as we face today's challenge of teaching foreign languages to *all* students, not just to those who do well in language arts. Exploration of this goal area may help to reach more effectively students who have experienced a lack of interest or failure in learning a foreign language or students who have not been offered the opportunity to study one. Helping students see connections between their own language and culture and the second language and cultures may enable them to be more successful in language study. With this goal as the focus, this project was designed to explore linguistic and cultural comparisons within the context of teaching Arabic to African American students in an inner-city middle school.

Why a Case Study of African American Students?

Too often in our country, students in inner city schools who were not considered to be "college bound" or in the "academic track" were not included in foreign language courses. Given that African American students make up a large percentage of inner-city school populations in many areas of the country, they often became marginalized from foreign language programs. Additionally, research findings, such as that of Ganshow, Sparks and colleagues (1991, 1992, 1994) that looked at the relationship between L1 and L2 with high school and college students led them to propose a Linguistic Coding Deficit Hypothesis (LCDH) that speculated that foreign language learning problems are linked to native language learning difficulties in mastering the phonological, syntactic, and/or semantic "codes" of language. The population for these studies, it must be noted, was not an African American one.

Some researchers (Bereiter and Engelmann, 1966) have posited that African Americans, principally those from "culturally disadvantaged" environments, are linguistically deficient. According to the deficit theory (Dummett, 1984), the language spoken by African American students is undeveloped and unstructured. The theory further posits that because of their language deficiency, speakers of AAE suffer a cognitive deficiency that renders them unable to excel in the study of Standard English and other academic subjects (Orr, 1987). In fact, at one time, there were proposals in this country to teach Standard English as a foreign language to speakers of African American English as a means of eradicating the "culturally deprived" stigma associated with the African American student (Bereiter and Engelmann, 1966).

During the past twenty years, however, the field of sociolinguistics has made great strides in combating the deficit theory. Research on the phonology and syntax of African American English has convincingly concluded that it is a well structured and systematic language (Dillard, 1972). Moreover, the use of AAE does not interfere with a person's ability to excel in any academic endeavor if the proper instruction and learning environment are provided. Sociolinguists and language educators (DeStefano, 1971; Dummett, 1984; Miller, 1953) argued that the attitudes of teachers toward AAE contributed significantly to the academic failure of many African American students who had to deal with instructional materials in Standard English. Miller (1953), for example, in a study on the teaching and learning of foreign languages in historically Black colleges and universities, concluded that many foreign language teachers felt their students suffered from certain communication handicaps that interfered with their ability to learn a foreign language.

The AAE issues being discussed today derive from studies and ideas originating in the 1960s and 1970s which have carried over to the 1980s and 1990s. But there is a new phenomenon of language vernacular being used by the African American youth who were born in the 1980s which is quite distinct from the traditional perceptions of typical AAE usage among older generations. These differences are not the normal ones associated with teenagers in their use of street slang in order to speak differently from the older generation. This behavior is universal among all teenagers. The irony, of course, is that the very groups of adolescents who have been described as linguistically disadvantaged, are creating a new non-standard form of African American street speech which was itself derived from the previous non-standard dialect that thrives within the black street culture. Baugh (1983) describes this so-called non-standard dialect as constantly fluctuating and adjusting to the new terminology flowing in and out of colloquial vogue. So, as teachers we can be sure that there will be manifestations of this variety of English in the classroom.[1]

One goal of the present study was to examine the connections between the variety of English students speak, in this case AAE, and foreign language learning. A second goal was to help this particular group of inner-city middle-school students, considered at-risk by their school, to achieve success in foreign language study.

The Project: Background

Case Study Approach

The project was designed as a case study. The case-study approach has had a long history in educational research and has also been used extensively in other areas of research such as clinical psychology and the study of individual differences. In its simplest form, the case study involves an investigator who makes a detailed examination of a single subject or group or phenomenon. Until recently, this approach was rejected by many educational researchers as unscientific, mainly because of its lack of research controls. However, the increased acceptance of qualitative research methods such as educational ethnography and the use of participant observers has revived the case-study approach. Case studies often incorporate a variety of data-collection methods. Such information sources may include public archival records, private archival records, and direct response data. This study utilizes all of these sources in order to obtain specific information, perceptions, and opinions that are relevant to the study.

The present investigation is particularly suited for what may be viewed as an *observational case study.* As Yin (1984) posits, one of the purposes of a case study is "to arrive at a comprehensive understanding of the groups under study" (p.11). The focus of this study, together with the setting and subjects involved, naturally lends itself for such a comprehensive investigation and follows what Yin (1984) suggests as four essential characteristics of a substantive case study. First, this study is *particularistic* in the sense that it will concentrate attention on the way a particular group of people confront a specific problem, taking a holistic view of the situation. Secondly, this study is inherently *descriptive.* Compilation of data from the diaries, questionnaires, observations, and interviews will make the end product a rich, "thick" description of the phenomenon under study. Third, this study will be *heuristic,* meaning that previously unknown relationships and variables can be expected to emerge which may lead to a rethinking of this particular phenomenon involving African American students and foreign language study. Finally, this study is *inductive* in the sense that generalizations, concepts, or hypotheses will emerge from an examination of data which is grounded in the context itself.

Inherent in the qualitative assessment will be an attempt to arrive at a comprehensive understanding of this particular language learning group under study and to develop general theoretical statements about regularities in the students' social structure and process. Because this is primarily a qualitative study, statements of statistical significance will not be given. The data will be presented and analyzed inductively and will be analogous to constructing a picture that takes shape as the parts are collected and examined.

University and Middle School: Professional Development Site

The project was designed to allow the researchers, a university professor and a doctoral student, to take a closer look at African American students in a foreign language classroom. Relatively few studies have focused on the factors affecting the performance and attitudes of African American students in foreign language programs. Over forty years ago, Miller (1953) pointed out that during a period of thirty-five years prior to his study, there had been only four scholarly studies on the topic and only two of those dealt with student performance and evaluation. From 1940 to 1991, a few studies (Nyabongo, 1946; Miller, 1953; Clark and Harty, 1983; Davis and Markham, 1991) focused on African American students' perceived needs, performance, and attitudes toward foreign language study. The current study attempts to build on the previous research and to offer another dimension of critical inquiry relevant to this important yet often neglected topic.

The college of education, in which the foreign language education program is housed, is actively involved in a Professional Development Site with an inner-city middle school in the area. Professional Development Sites (PDS) have been advocated by the Holmes Group as a way of encouraging university professors, preservice, and inservice teachers to work together for the improvement of teaching and learning. (The Holmes Group is a national organization made up of university professors, college students, and classroom teachers who dedicate time and effort to developing working partnerships with schools in their area.)

University Professor and Graduate Student

The university professor comes from a multiethnic, multilingual, and multicultural society. She became interested in discovering reasons and explanations for the low enrollments of minorities, in general, and African Americans in particular, in foreign language education programs. She was specifically puzzled by the virtual absence in enrollment figures of African American student teachers, when national figures suggest ever increasing numbers of minority students in public schools. The student/researcher/teacher in this study is an African American male. He is the sole African American graduate student in the foreign language education program in a large state university. The FL/ESL/EFL program boasts of being one of the strongest in the nation enjoying an average number of 120 applicants from countries all over the world. The startling reality of his single presence in the program engendered interest in the topic of research.

Language of Instruction

Three main reasons guided the selection of Arabic as the L2. In an earlier study conducted in the same city among African American college students (Moore, 1995), the authors found that several students expressed a preference for studying a language that was "easier to identify with," a language that was spoken by "black people." The students in the case study were aware that there are many Africans who spoke Arabic, such as those in Egypt, Sudan, Chad. One student said that he wanted to learn Arabic so he could talk "to those Arab dudes" in the school. The opinions of students appeared to support the cultural distance theory that learners may be more motivated to learn a foreign language that is linguistically and culturally closer to their own. The second reason for selecting Arabic was that there was a real-life reason for doing so. There is a locally based active community of Black Muslims who are allied to the National Black Muslim League. Some students wanted to learn to read Arabic in order to read the Koran and find out about the teachings of Islam so they might possibly become a member of the Black Muslim religious organization. The third reason was more practical. The teacher who taught the students is fluent in Arabic. He is also African American.

The primary instructional material used for this study was an exploratory language unit created by the Middle East Area Studies Center at the University of Texas in consultation with the Texas Education Agency and with assistance from the U.S. Department of Education. Targeted toward adolescents, the Arabic teaching material was a unique and challenging course of study meant to build self-esteem, confidence, and motivation for future learning. The specific Arabic unit offered students an introduction to the language through the study of Middle East culture, history, and geography. A major goal of the funded project was to design materials for instruction at an early level, with the hope that it would provide a foundation for continued study. The material is clearly designed to develop all four skills as well as to provide cultural information. For example, the lesson on Greetings and Introductions is presented in the form of cartoons. It features an African young man greeting a friend on the road.

One lesson, focusing on reading road signs, is set in a market in Damascus; another uses authentic material from a restaurant menu (see Appendix).

Exploratory language units at the middle school level vary widely in the amount of time allotted to a particular language program. A successful exploratory language course anticipates this and allows for flexibility of use. Thus, although the materials are sequentially organized in terms of vocabulary and writing system acquisition, they contain a substantial non-sequential set of activities centered around cultural and regional information as well as language learning techniques. Much of the instruction was augmented by incorporating some of the experiences of the teacher who has taught Arabic at the undergraduate level and who has traveled extensively throughout the Middle East.

Students as Collaborators

Based on the standards, we thought that the students had to be collaborators in this study as well. To obtain glimpses of their feelings, opinions, and experiences, they received instructions to keep a diary. Defining what is meant by a diary study in second language research is probably best described by Bailey (1991):

> A diary study in second language learning, acquisition, or teaching is an account of a second language experience as recorded in a first-person journal. The diarist may be a language teacher or a language learner—but the central characteristic of the diary studies is that they are introspective: The diarist studies his own teaching or learning. Thus he can report on affective factors, language learning strategies, and his own perceptions—facets of the language learning experience which are normally hidden or largely inaccessible to an external observer. (p.189).

Diary instructions to the students of Arabic were as follows:

> This journal has two purposes. The first is to help you with your language learning. As you write about how you think and feel as a language learner, you will understand yourself and your experience better. The second purpose is to increase the overall knowledge about language learning so that learning can be increased. You will be asked to leave your language learning journal at the end of the semester. However, your journal will be read by myself and researchers interested in language learning. Your identity and the identity of others you may write about will be unknown to anyone except the researchers. You will be given 15 minutes at the end of every class period to write. Please write as if this were your personal journal about your language learning experience.

The teacher also developed guidelines for himself:

Self Instructions: Develop a habit of writing down observations immediately after the end of class. Try to be as specific as possible. Be sure to cover perceptions, strategies, styles, feelings, etc with the intention of formulating a list of factors which learners consider important in their language learning process.

School Setting

Demographics, Teachers, and Students

Sanchez Middle School (a psuedonym) is a sixth-through-eighth-grade school and is considered an "inner-city school" by its Independent School District. It is located in modest surroundings primarily consisting of minority and low-income families. The teacher population at Sanchez during the time of this study was 51.6% white, 29% Hispanic, and 19.4% African American. The student population was 61.3% Hispanic, 24% African American, 13.4% white, 1.0% Asian/Pacific Islander, and 0.3% Native American.

Many inner-city schools suffer from a lack of infrastructure and resources in terms of adequate classrooms, facilities, equipment, etc., when compared to schools in primarily high income neighborhoods. However, Sanchez Middle School does not appear to be lacking in any of those categories. It is a well maintained school with computer and science laboratories, modern industrial technology equipment, bright and lively classrooms, and a variety of extra curricular activities for the students.

The initial subjects for this study were 10 African American students ranging in age from 13 to 15 and in either the 7th or 8th grade. Two of the subjects were subsequently removed from the school for disciplinary reasons. All the students were from low-income families. School records indicated that there were no adult male members in their respective households. There appeared to be a range of cognitive abilities and approaches to learning with some students demonstrating appropriate use of their assumed L1—Mainstream American English (MAE)—in the skills of reading, writing, and speaking ability for their grade level while others demonstrated lesser abilities. The verbal behavior among all of the subjects was a mixture of MAE and some of the pronunciation characteristics of African American English (AAE). This was their first exposure to foreign language instruction. They were randomly selected from a pool of initial volunteers of African American students who expressed an interest in learning a foreign language. School records also indicated that most of the subjects appeared to have developed a resistance to educational achievement as evidenced by heavy absenteeism, sporadic suspensions from school, and generally marginal performance in other classes.

Their cultural values and norms have been oppositional to school norms which may have led to a conscious avoidance of intellectual engagement, in part because any intellectual activity and achievement is presumably viewed as the domain of whites. As Fordham and Ogbu (1986) posit, these subjects may have internalized facets of the dominant group mythology, notably that African Americans are intellectually less competent than whites, and thus, to achieve academically among students is an instance of "acting white." There was no evidence that this group of students shared that view. Selections from their journal entries certainly support awareness and pride in achieving. Students' entries are reprinted *exactly as the students wrote them* to capture accurately the students' reflections on their L2 learning.

It should be mentioned that this was the first time the students were ever given the task of journal writing or composing of any sort in their L1. Their entries demonstrated their emotions and thoughts about their learning experiences. They were open and insightful in expressing their emotions and they were hopeful and positive about their abilities. In Figure 1, a student expressed the belief that he would move on to study another language now that he recognizes that "he has become very good in learning things."

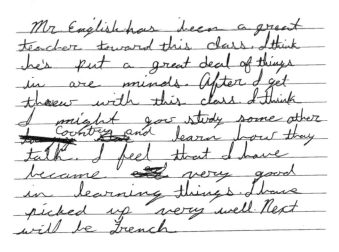

Figure 1. Journal Excerpt

Foreign Language Curriculum

There were two foreign language teachers in the school—one for Spanish and the other for ESL and French. Conversations with these two teachers revealed that their respective classes were well structured and involved the use of a variety of language instructional material that included film, video, newspapers, magazines, music, and other realia. Testing of student knowledge consisted of vocabulary and grammar exercises, content questions, and multiple choice questions. Although the two teaching styles were relatively different, their commonality of style reflected active and direct involvement in the classroom similar to a director of a stage play with students as actors. They also saw themselves as providing a safe environment in which students could learn and grow. The counselling/parenting analogy was evident. Both teachers considered appropriate student behavior as: willingness to try a new language, positive and cheerful attitude, attentiveness, and willingness to participate. Their views of inappropriate behavior consisted of talking, being out of seat, being disrespectful toward teachers/others, being unwilling to try a new language, and being off-task.

These teachers did not feel that there was a cultural gap between themselves and the minority students in their class. They handled difficult students (in terms of performance and behavior) by insisting that the students follow classroom procedures, scheduling extra time for remedial work, and adjusting their teaching style to learning and behavioral differences.

This project introduced for the first time to Sanchez Middle School one of the less commonly taught languages. Although the students were not utilizing a specific text book for this project, they received a number of worksheets and general handouts which covered all the areas in a foreign language curriculum of instruction. Though purposefully generic in nature, pictures and other drawings from the exploratory teaching materials still reflected a bias against minorities in general and African Americans in particular. The way in which African Americans have been portrayed in textbooks and other illustrative material has been an issue for many years. Even with this exploratory language unit, that bias still persisted. While students were doing a dialogue exercise, one of them remarked, "How come there are no black people in these pictures?" (There were no real pictures, just illustrative drawings of adolescents talking). Many studies have cited the fact that illustrations of any form can have a lasting impact on an individual. This is particularly true when these visual images carry non-verbal messages about race, even if such messages were not intended by the author (Boben, 1985; IABC, 1982; TEA, 1979). Since the nature of illustrations and pictures can be instrumental in transmitting ideas and cultural values, this is still a crucial issue in the education of children, regardless of ethnic background. This issue needs to be explored further.

Parents and Community

There is little to no involvement in the life of the school community by the parents of the students in this project. This may largely be a function of the students in this study coming from low income single parent households. The teacher/researcher had an opportunity to talk to some of the parents of the students. They were all working mothers who expressed a sincere interest in their child's education and progress but who rarely interacted with teachers or school administrators.

Implementation of Project and Results

The university professor held preliminary discussions with the principal of the school about the possibility of conducting the study. The graduate student and the professor then had a second meeting with the principal to discuss in greater detail what the study entailed. The principal is an alumna and part-time faculty of the university and is very interested in the success of the Holmes Professional Site. She offered full cooperation and showed genuine pleasure at the possibility of augmenting the foreign language curriculum and increasing the number of electives offered to students.

Project Phases and Time Frames

The project was planned to last two semesters (a six-month period), sufficient time to allow for the students to learn some basic language skills and to be evaluated. Since Sanchez Middle School is an all-year school, its academic calendar facilitated structuring the two semesters to run without interruption of a long vacation period.

Using the exploratory language unit described earlier combined with other language material, the teacher taught Arabic to the subjects for one semester in a schedule where class met three times per week: one day for a 45-minute period, and the other two days for two hours each. The 45-minute-period class was used primarily for review and more casual classroom interaction. The other two periods focused on specific language learning skills.

Language learning material integrated the oral, aural, and visual skills into productive output. Some of the more specific language skills being introduced were the following:

- discriminating and articulating Arabic sounds in isolated words
- discriminating and articulating sounds in connected speech (e.g., assimilation)
- recognizing and manipulating Arabic script
- recognizing the stem and root of an unfamiliar lexical item
- understanding and producing information orally and in writing at the sentence level
- understanding and expressing implicit meaning based on context
- understanding and expressing conceptual meanings such as relational concepts, time, quantity, frequency, etc.

Mastery of the skills required a great deal more than just functional memorization. It required a shift to a higher level of comprehension and manipulation of basic language skills. Pushing toward skills at the intermediate level proved to be quite a leap in cognitive ability for most, if not all, of the students. Given the time available for learning, targeting proficiency at the Novice level (ACTFL Proficiency Guidelines, 1989), in Arabic is a substantial challenge.

Student and Teacher Comments and Reactions

The students maintained a diary and wrote down their thoughts, ideas, and impressions as they went through the language learning process. In addition, two videotaped sessions, one taken at the early stages of the project and the other at the final stages, provided much information about the students' classroom behavior, their learning styles, their language, and their opinions. Clips from the videotapes along with excerpts from their journals provide much of the students' comments which we report here.

On Learning Arabic

An initial question and answer period about the learning of foreign languages in general and about learning Arabic in particular, revealed that most students had a negative attitude toward Arabs as a group. Most seemed uninterested in learning a new language, especially Arabic. One student asked, "Do they speak Arabic in Africa?" while another student commented, "I don't want to learn that Arabic stuff. Why should I since I can't use it anywhere?" The teacher explained to them the possible advantages of learning a foreign language and Arabic in particular for future schooling and professions, but most seemed unimpressed with those explanations. However, most of the students did express interest in knowing more about the cultural aspects. The interest and enthusiasm generated from the cultural sessions were captured on videotape. In one lesson, each student dressed in a different Arabic outfit and had to make an oral presentation on Arabic ways of dressing. The videotapes revealed that the students had acquired a lot of information. For example, one student demonstrated how the *Kaffiah* is worn and the different styles used with it. He knew why it is worn, (to protect the wearer from the sand), the material of which it is made (tightly woven cotton cloth), and the name of the black cord (*aggaal*) that holds it in place. Similar scenarios that made the cultural practices come alive seemed to motivate and fascinate the students and led to discussions of various countries, dress, costumes, food, geography, etc. of the Arab world. During his presentation, one student said (phonetically transcribed):

> Now I understand why dey wear all dese clothes and why dey different from American clothes. Before I t'ought that dey were just weird!

Comments like these showed a gradual awareness of cultural differences and the reasons for the differences.

During the introduction of the Arabic alphabet, phonology, and writing and recognition of letters, most students were eager to learn how to write and went ahead of the instruction when completing the writing worksheet tasks. Some were hesitant to get up in front of the class and recite the phonetic sounds of the alphabet, but they all pronounced most of the new letters with minor mistakes. One student said that "this stuff was too easy…" and he was bored and restless. He could not stay seated for more than a few minutes at a time. The teacher told him it would become more challenging as the lessons progressed. Again, the videotaped interviews gave them the opportunity to talk about their Arabic skills. All the students said that they liked writing in Arabic, and they liked speaking the language. They all said that learning to write Arabic helped them become more aware of writing in their own language. One student wrote:

> In Arabic, you have to take your time and pay attention to all the lil tings.
> I like dat, becuz I feel good when I get it right.

After several weeks, most of the students had changed their minds about learning a foreign language. They said that they liked the class because it was fun, and they had tangible proof that they were learning. By this time, too, the students had become used to their Arabic names, which they seemed to like, since the names carried their own meaning. They seemed flattered by names like Assad, which means "the lion," and Mubarak, which means "the generous one." The following two comments reveal the importance of having an appreciative, warm teacher, and Figure 2 captures the importance of personalizing instruction.

> The class was a little hard because of the lettering and the writing. The lesson was a fun and interesting but I am going to need practice. I am glad am taking this class it lets you express your feeling. The class is one of my best classes. The letters are a little bit hard but I can manage it.

I like class today. It was fun I was not at all scared, the class is well behaved.

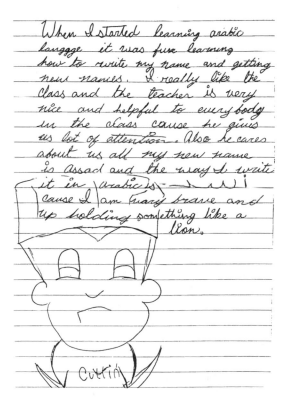

Figure 2. Journal Excerpt

Learning Styles

Most students appeared to be visual learners with a strong desire to touch, feel, act out, or improvise on new material. Some students were more verbal than others, but most showed an interest in verbalizing variations of new words and sounds to see how they fit into their very stylized African American English vernacular with its unique rhythm and harmony. Some students were trying to use their initial knowledge of Arabic sounds to compose "rap" songs in order to aid in memorizing the sounds.

After the fifth session, (approximately two weeks), most of the students had marginally mastered the sounds of the Arabic alphabet. A couple of them still had difficulty with memorization and concentration and needed some assistance when reciting the alphabet, but they all learned to write their assigned Arabic name and to formulate some simple sentences in Arabic.

All students appeared to be at ease in the class and learning now took place within the framework of a highly affective domain. The students were very people oriented and sensitive to the nuances of body language, facial expressions, and the use of nonverbal cues. Raising my voice to emphasize a point in class was only temporarily effective, but when they worked together to solve a problem or I looked at them in a certain way (sternly to get them to behave in class or more congenially when they performed a certain task correctly), that appeared to have a more lasting effect. I began to see a connection or bonding between the students and myself. They began joking around me and with each other in friendly fashion. A feeling of social solidarity in the classroom was growing.

Although I was still an authority figure, my teaching style began to reflect a non-authoritative attitude. For example, I started to allow the students to design their own learning material. During a role play scenario, the students came up with their own settings for meeting someone and introducing themselves and a friend. With a mixture of African American street slang and basic Arabic greetings, the students enjoyed the exercise and hopefully retained some of the vocabulary from that experience. One student captured this feeling of accomplishment in the first excerpt shown in Figure 3. Notice that, although the student's L1 writing in this excerpt contained spelling mistakes which may have been due to carelessness, he was scoring excellent grades in Arabic. The same student's entry is in the next excerpt about *hatha*. These entries indicate L1 writing skill at the novice level. It is an example of a Grade 2 or 3 writing sample. However, his ability to write in Arabic and to score 100% in every

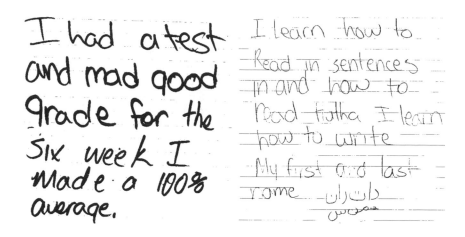

Figure 3. Two Journal Excerpts

test were evidence of his academic ability and seemed to suggest that with more effective teaching in the L1 this student could perform better.

Classroom Setting

After the first month of instruction, the social dimension of the classroom appeared to take a new turn (see Figures 4, 5). The students felt more comfortable around me and I too began to feel the same around them. The result was an environment in which I came to appreciate certain modal cognitive styles and behavioral characteristics. For example, all of the students had short attention spans and were unable to persist toward the completion of a task without a great deal of assistance. There was a great need for physical contact among themselves, and they thrived on competition. In short, the setting evolved to a physical and visual style of learning. The classroom was rarely quiet, a fact that was very discommoding, since classrooms are expected to be like quiet cemeteries. Even when asked to perform individual focused tasks, there was constant bantering and joking and drawing while they were attempting to accomplish the task. Most of the students were very bright and liked the challenge of learning a new and difficult language but they were easily bored with the drills, which the material designers believed to be important for language foundation building.

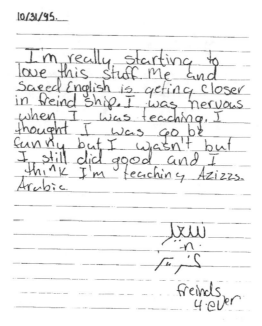

Figure 4. Journal Excerpt

L1 and L2 Transfer

Although some of the students demonstrated weaknesses in their L1 reading (specifically, pronunciation), and writing skills (spelling and cursive writing), those problems were not transferred to the L2 when more vocabulary and other grammar functions were introduced. In fact, the opposite was true. It seemed that the more the students became familiar with the cursive writing style in Arabic script, the better they became at it. This was particularly revealing for one of the students who could not write cursive in his L1 yet became quite proficient in writing in Arabic script as the semester progressed. Further, there were no noticeable reading errors in the L2 in terms of the pronunciation of recognizable letter combinations. Mastering these skills was quite a remarkable achievement given the difficulty most Westerners have in learning to read and write from right to left.

In order to make the introduction of new vocabulary words more relevant, I asked the students to tell me some of the favorite "slang" words that African American adolescents use these days and what their translation was for those not socialized in that vernacular. For example, "kitch" meant a girl, "loc" (pronounced "loke") meant a friend (when greeting), e.g., "What's up loc?" and "sax" meant someone's personal business. One student wrote in his journal:

> So far we have taught Mr. M. 5 slang words. These are Kitch,Cuz,Loc,Saks and tight. Also we learned how to say the same words in Arabic.

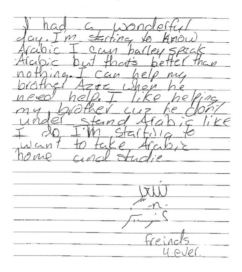

Figure 5. Journal Excerpt.

These and other slang words were put on the chalk board. I first constructed a transliteration of the English words using Arabic letters and then I translated the words into Arabic. After the new Arabic words were introduced to them, I asked them to use the Arabic instead of their usual slang equivalent from now on inside the classroom and outside if possible. The students enjoyed this new way of communicating by using their L1 words of slang in combination with new "cool foreign sounding" words. They liked to impress their other friends and teachers by initiating conversations among themselves that no one else could understand. This ability to combine L1 and L2 expressions in real world settings was instrumental in giving the students more confidence in their ability to learn a different language. I hoped this would be one way of aiding the memory of some basic vocabulary words or expressions in Arabic that they used on a daily basis among themselves.

One lesson called for the introduction of vocabulary used when ordering food and going to a restaurant. I told them that if they could verbalize in Arabic what they wanted from Mc Donald's and also write it down correctly, then if I could comprehend what they had said and what they had written down, I would go to Mc Donald's and buy what they had ordered. To assist them, I had a placemat from a Mc Donald's in the Middle East which had all of the items written in Arabic along with colorful pictures. Surprisingly, they wrote down their respective orders better than they could articulate what they wanted. This was understandable because they had not been introduced to some of the oral constructions to ask for something. However, I wanted them to interpolate and be creative with their vocabulary. I wrote down their respective orders while at the same time attempting to teach them some new expressions and vocabulary. Needless to say, they had a great time with this little exercise. The next class meeting I showed up with their orders and we had a "Mc Donald's" afternoon of eating and learning while we ate.

This exercise was revealing in terms of how the students reflected on their L1 (AAE) phonological cues. For example in order to help them better comprehend the sounds of Arabic letters, they were told to write the English words in Arabic script. Thus, instead of trying to memorize for example, the Arabic word for milk *(haleeb)* and its corresponding Arabic script, they were practicing Arabic script on known L1 vocabulary. Later when sounds of Arabic words were introduced, the students had a better comprehension of the L2 phonological cues because of earlier practice on L1 phonological cues.

Students as Teachers

In one class period, I asked Assad and Saeed to teach certain portions of the class. They both seemed willing and eager to do so. Assad was a talented artist, and the class was challenging for him. He introduced the class to new vocabulary items. I did not tell him how to approach his teaching of the class, but I wanted him to ensure that he was satisfied that everyone could understand the definitions and that everyone could pronounce the words correctly. I was totally impressed with the way he conducted the class. He wrote down each new word in its morphological components and explained how each word should be pronounced; he then called on individual students to pronounce and define what the new word meant. The change in the students' attitudes, as witnessed in the videotaping of this lesson, was remarkable. Throughout the approximately thirty minutes of instruction, all the students were very quiet and attentive, al-

though there was the usual casual bantering. They were respectful of Assad and gave him no problems. The incident gave cause for reflection on
the part of the university professor and on my part. It showed that the
students knew how to comport themselves in the classroom. Why, then,
did they give other teachers problems? There was no doubt that what
teachers considered "discipline problems" may be more accurately interpreted as acts of defiance and resistance.

I later asked Saeed to introduce some new expressions that involved the
use of the interrogative and of verbal expressions using the newly introduced
verb "to like." Saeed took his new responsibility seriously and was more
strict with the students than Assad in terms of attention to detail of pronunciation. This caused some turmoil in the class, primarily because some of the
students did not think that Saeed knew the material better than they did and
were therefore peeved that he should extract such exactitude from them.
Overall, however, the students probably had more fun and presumably
learned more from their peers than from me, which raises the broader issue
of how interactive pedagogy and student-centered classrooms can possibly
bring about effective language learning at the middle school level.

Application of Learned Material
(or, Can They Use the Language in Real Situations?)

For one lesson, I took the students on a field trip to an Arabic restaurant. The purpose was to introduce them to Arabic food and to augment
previous instruction on the eating habits of people from the Middle East.
I ordered a sampler of appetizers to go along with their selected entrée.
They had a brief introduction to the different types of Arabic food and
how the dishes are prepared. My professor and one of the assistant principals also joined us. Discussion at the table was lively with a variety of
questions about how certain foods tasted, etc. Students were all curious
and respectfully ate some of the more exotic appetizers. For the most part,
they ordered the kabobs, which were essentially grilled chicken or beef
with a plate of saffron rice. The waitress was thoroughly impressed when
they all introduced themselves in Arabic! In fact, I was pleasantly surprised (and so was the vice-principal who knew these students only in the
roles of underachievers and troublemakers), at the ease and fluency with
which they spoke. I was even more impressed when they tried to elevate
the conversation by asking the waitress what her name was in Arabic. Not
one mistake or hesitancy by anyone during this brief exchange! I now had

tangible evidence that not only were they definitely learning something from the instruction, but that they were willing and able to demonstrate their new knowledge outside classroom settings and in conjunction with casual L1 usage.

Findings: Reflection on Comparisons Goal

To say that the project was a tremendous success is an understatement. It may be more productive and helpful, especially to foreign language teachers of African American students who may be interested in similar projects, to present a summary of what worked.

An Ethnographic Case Study

An ethnographic approach, as used in the study, provided us with much data. We were able to get an in-depth look at learning styles and teaching strategies. We followed the growth and progress of the students simply by being there week after week. We were able to modify what did not work and improve or repeat what did work. Most of all, we had evidence that the group of students, badly labeled as they were, were capable of learning and functioning in Arabic. We witnessed their performance in and out of the classroom.

Student and Teacher as Collaborators

We included the students as collaborative partners in the teaching and learning process. They were data providers and data collectors. Their voices were part of the database. Only from them could we get accurate pictures of their world. The use of the journals provided the researcher with an outlet for capturing his own learning experiences as well as documenting the class events and feelings of the students. It was also a means of accessing the student insights targeted in the Comparisons Goal of the National Standards.

The Videotaped Recordings

Especially useful was the use of the video recorder. An hour long videotaping of the students captured personal interviews in which they expressed their feelings and experiences as students in that particular school setting. Through the recordings we saw the actual class activities, the visuals in the classroom, and the students' behavior. The videotaped sessions of the two students teaching the class allowed us glimpses of a type of peer interaction behavior that we had not seen in any other setting.

L1–L2 Comparisons: Facilitating FL Learning

While the relatively short duration of this project limited the insights of a comparative nature envisioned in the Standards, it was evident that interactions between L2/L1, and C2/C1, were occurring. One of the more revealing findings from this project was how certain grammatical constructions of the students L1 (AAE) actually helped to facilitate the understanding of new constructions while the students were learning Arabic (L2). Therefore, we suggest that discussions on Arabic, African American English, and Standard English phonology and syntax can provide the type of analysis which may help foreign language teachers to better understand the important linkages that exist for comparing and contrasting L1 and L2 constructions. This understanding should facilitate instructional approaches.

One of the major teaching points in learning grammatical structures in Arabic is that forms of the verb "to be" do not exist. Although generally a difficult concept to grasp for students who have been socialized into structures of Standard English, the students in this project who exhibited some features of AAE vernacular, readily understood this concept. This may be explained by the fact that one of the major syntactic features in AAE is the existence of the zero copula: "I think they in the kitchen," "the principal in his office now," "they walking to school," etc. These sentence structures are patterned similarly in Arabic except that the verb comes before the subject. When this concept was introduced, the students may have readily grasped the L2 constructions after consciously or unconsciously recalling their use of some L1 (AAE) syntactic features.

This finding challenges commonly held beliefs that AAE may be an inhibitive factor in learning a foreign language. This study challenges the work done by Bereiter and Engelmann (1966) for its genuine lack of appreciation for the intricate structural components of nonstandard vernaculars such as AAE, which, according to evidence from this study, have features that can readily facilitate and even enhance the language learning experience of speakers of those vernaculars.

A Comparison with the ACTFL Proficiency Guidelines

Mid-way through the course (approximately three months) the teacher estimated that the students were demonstrating selective performance at the Novice-High level in the primary skills of speaking, reading, writing, and listening. According to the ACTFL Arabic Proficiency Guidelines (1989), this equates to the following:

Speaking: Able to satisfy partially the requirements of very basic communicative exchanges. Partial ability to make short statements using simple formulaic phrases and ask a few simple questions. Vocabulary focuses on basic objects and activities. Pronunciation will often be faulty, and delivery will still be strongly influenced by first language.

Listening: Comprehends a number of memorized utterances in areas of immediate need, involving situations where context is an aid to understanding. May require repetition, rephrasing and /or a slowed rate of speech for comprehension.

Reading: Can identify a number of set expressions and memorized material in areas of immediate need. Can recognize all Arabic letters as they occur in any position in a word, including *hamza* and *alif maqsuura*. Where vocabulary has been mastered, can read for instructional and directional purposes, standardized messages, phrases or expressions, such as some items on menus.

Writing: Can reproduce all the symbols of the alphabet in a form recognizable to a native-speaker and write frequently used memorized material such as their own name. Can write some memorized short sentences. Ability to write rudimentary personal communication is partial. Sound to symbol correspondence is developing, but reproduction in written form is still erratic.

The availability of the ACTFL Arabic Proficiency Guidelines provided us with an objective national measure to judge the students' performance across skills.

Addressing the Comparisons Goal

In an explanation of how he teaches African American students to appreciate languages and their own language and culture, James J. Davis, an African American professor at Howard University, states simply that "we tend to look at culture in the foreign language context in terms of the big icons of civilization such as the Eiffel tower—culture with a big 'C.' But what we foreign language teachers need to do is teach culture with little 'c' by taking students inside the map to the people who inhabit other places, to learn what makes them tick, how they behave" (1992). Indeed, the Cultures Goal in the National Standards takes this to a new but extended paradigm. By encouraging students to delve into practices and products of cultures as a means of understanding the perspectives of peoples, the standards also compel students to look likewise at their own culture prior to making comparisons. This takes on special dimensions as African American students compare their language and culture with second ones.

Whether it is used in the classroom or not, the study of the use of AAE as a student's L1 when compared to other languages can be an instrument for students to understand how certain languages and vernaculars have shaped both low and high cultures of the African diaspora, as in the creole dialects of the Caribbean and Louisiana. For example, in dealing with African American students, it can be posited that any cultural matrix of the African diaspora is not uniquely "black" or African but an amalgamation of diverse cultural and linguistic influences. Exposing African American students to this type of analysis supports the contention that through language and literature, links can be formed with other people that transcend national definitions. Language crosses political, cultural, intellectual, and ideological boundaries and can introduce all students to new ways of looking at the world by connecting people of all colors across the globe. Interest in foreign languages by African American students can be enhanced when classes show the inter-connectedness of one's own language and culture and that these students belong to a world that reaches beyond the borders of the United States.

Personal Voice of the Teacher

What Did I Learn about Myself as a Teacher/Researcher?

One aspect of this experience in which I was particularly pleased as a teacher/researcher was the demonstrated ability of these students to ignore what other teachers have said about what they could not do in terms of learning and achievement. Instead, these students focused on what they could do. In order to contribute to this atmosphere of positive development, I wanted to create an environment in which the students could, in a very real sense, *construct* knowledge— in contrast to a situation in which the learner would be given that knowledge by someone else (parents or teachers for example). Bruner (1990) calls this teaching approach *Discovery Learning* where learning takes place when students are not presented with subject matter in its final form but rather are required to organize it themselves. This approach requires learners to discover for themselves relationships that exist among items of information. The most important and most obvious characteristic of a discovery approach to teaching is that it requires far less teacher involvement and direction than most other methods. However, this method does not imply that the teacher ceases to give any guidance once the initial problem has been presented. In fact, this approach takes far more preparation of teachers (both professional preparation and individual preparation for each lesson) than "regular" pedagogies. The advantages of a discovery approach are that such learning facilitates transfer and retention, increases problem solving ability, and increases motivation.

For example, when I introduced English words of Arabic origin, it was necessary for the students to understand the concept of the definite article *al* [the] in many Arabic words and that this definite article was still present in many English words. When I introduced words such as *algebra* (*al-jabr* [the reduction]) and *almanac* (*al-manakh* [the climate]), it was much easier for students to arrive at a concept that related certain vocabulary words once it had been discovered that they were all derived from words with the *al* as the definite article. They learned that alphabet, and alfalfa, alcohol, alkali are words derived from Arabic. This knowledge, in turn, permitted the students to make inferences (as the Comparison Goal advocates) about other specific words which allowed them to go beyond the information given. The capabilities of these students, exemplified through discovery learning and through other demonstrated abilities, suggest that they were not only willing to learn but also capable of mastering intellectual challenges beyond what may have been expected of them.

There have been few programs designed specifically for African American students enrolled in foreign language study that relate their unique cultural experiences to the study of foreign languages. In the past, African American student experiences in the classroom have often been viewed negatively by some educators. Deviations from the norm were seen as a problem where students had to be "corrected." This examination may help to reveal, in part, that the problem may not be with students but instead may be with the attitudes and perceptions of teachers. Through this experience, I have learned to be more receptive to new ideas in pedagogy which may be viewed as radical or outside the status quo. I also hope that I may have contributed in some measure to questioning notions of what constitutes academic success. This may be the first step in recognizing that learning a foreign language, like any other academic endeavor, is well within the intellectual capabilities of many African American students.

What Did I Learn about Myself as an Innovator?

In order to accommodate the synergistic learning styles of these students, my teaching reflected a combination of several influences which I adapted to my particular situation. Most notably were the Natural Approach (Krashen and Terrell, 1983) and what some literature suggests as Discovery Learning or the Constructivist Approach to teaching based on a theory of cognitive learning (Bruner, Goodnow, and Austin, 1956; Bruner, 1990). Over the years, language teachers have intuitively recognized the value of associating language with physical activity and that there was a need to create an environment that was a stress-free as possible, where learners would not feel overly self-conscious and defensive. I tried to incorporate this knowledge into the way I presented material and the way I interacted with the students.

I structured the classroom as a free-flowing environment where students did not have assigned seats and where they could sit with whom and where they wanted. Material was presented in a cooperative fashion in terms of what particular subjects the students felt were relevant to them. Instead of the use of textbooks, handouts, and lectures, teaching was more interpersonally oriented with frequent interruptions for anecdotes from both student and teacher. The students preferred, and seemed to benefit from, peer-oriented seating, review sessions, study questions, and student presentations. Because these students were very physically oriented and extroverted they related physically to their cognitive work through role plays, jokes, and games. They appeared to learn or absorb the material better when they related physically to their peers in the classroom. The difference in orientation might create problems for the teacher used to traditional methods of instruction but not unsolvable ones if teachers are willing to make adjustments.

In a sense I allowed the classroom to become a stage where interaction with others was important. From the perspective of teaching a foreign language, this proved to be quite effective in introducing certain phrases and grammatical structures in real situations where the students could physically act out or relate to the meaning. Similar settings, or simulated settings like hanging out in a mall or on the basketball court or at the movies can provide settings that may make learning more successful and purposeful. Such real or simulated settings provide synergists, who often come from limited experiential backgrounds, a means of expanding their perception of the world and of acquiring information.

I emphasized cooperative learning. Slavin (1983) and Johnson and Johnson (1985) demonstrated rather clearly that the use of cooperative learning can result in improved achievement. This also ties in with the fact that the social structure of a classroom sets the stage for a learner's self-concept. Quiz results showed that the more the students interacted with each other, the more easily they retained information and the more productive they became. Some of the students appeared to be challenged by those who were doing better and tried to emulate them. The smarter ones in turn were always trying to help the others with their in-class work. The key here is that the students were never alone during the learning process and there was a constant sharing of information and explanation.

I find that the use of a multisensory approach to teaching new material facilitates the learning process. Instead of the traditional approach to teaching, I chose to show the relationship between concepts, to use active/interactive discussion, and to bring in concrete objects that demonstrated the relationship of the concepts to the world and environment through the use of art forms, pictures, and drama. For example, in teaching new vocabulary items, I took the class on a field trip to real world places such as a restaurant and other places in the community so they could actually see certain objects that they could not otherwise visualize or touch or feel. This change of environment coupled with real-world objects greatly enhanced the ability to associate an object with a word and its corresponding pronunciation and spelling. This was particularly acute because of the different alphabet, sounds, and formation of the different letters. Unfortunately, many teachers equate the need for concrete, factual, motor manipulatives with low intelligence rather than as a perceptual preference.

I tried to tailor my presentation of new material with structures that complemented the cognitive learning style of the students. Often, the students preferred to be told how to do a problem rather than discern the way of approaching the solution. Unfortunately, this often led me to focus purely on the knowledge level rather than moving the student through the application, synthesis, and evaluation stages. This was obviously a limitation in the classroom and I tried to rectify it by trying to have a blend of both the analytic as well as the synergetic approach to learning. As mentioned earlier, my style was more a hybrid of both the Natural Approach and the Discovery Learning Approach. Insights and intuitions from these approaches to teaching not only accommodated the learning styles of these students, but they may also have been instrumental in analyzing the effect of the language learning experience on the students' use of Standard English or perhaps more importantly, the effect on the use of their L1—African American English.

What Changes Will I Make in My Own
Practice as a Result of this Project?

I will try to incorporate a more cooperative, interpersonally-oriented type of instruction that involves student presentations and more interactive discussions and multisensory presentations. For example, incorporating blocks of instruction that include a hands-on demonstration of the use and function of cultural artifacts. For this project, the students had the opportunity to dress up like an Arab person and became familiar with the various types of clothing worn. They also had the opportunity to burn some frankincense in the classroom to gain an appreciation for what Arabs value as pleasant smelling. They were also introduced to *Misbaha* ["worry beads"] and their function in Islam. These vignettes illustrated that the students were interested in and seemed to enjoy the look and feel of real objects from the Arab world. I must continue to incorporate more manipulatives in the classroom to augment instruction.

There are other practical steps that I can take as a teacher to help students bridge the comparisons of other languages and cultures with the students' own language and culture. One of these steps would be to create a culturally compatible classroom which addresses the perceptual, motivation, and behavioral styles of students from different backgrounds. Through various techniques such as developing activities and a classroom environment that is moderately structured, praising frequently acts of learning rather than negatively commenting on behavior, and using small groups and cooperative learning, I can be sensitive to the social and emotional factors in the classroom and use them as positive influences on learning. Teaching *all* students is not an impossibility when one adjusts approaches in the belief that all can learn.

Dissemination of Project Results

All foreign language educators should be gathering information from studies such as this one. As the challenge to teach all students a language other than English is taken up, teachers must learn the ingredients of success. Specifically, those educators in middle schools and in inner-city schools where ethnic diversity is great must create programs that include all young people in learning other languages and cultures as a means of learning more about their own language and culture. It is clear from this study that the group of young African American students can be motivated to learn and can accomplish a lot. Teachers should be trained in diverse methods of being effective teachers with these young people. The classroom setting and classroom interaction that played an important part of putting the students at ease are generally at variance with the average classroom setting. The study indicated that the students must be given opportunities to develop friendship and support for each other.

Foreign language teachers and educators must become familiar with cultural differences in learning. The study showed how exposure to the cultural instruction about attire, food, names, and religious behavior made language learning more meaningful to the students. Students in the study took pride in teaching their classmates. The interactive teaching/learning approaches used with the students were effective. Foreign language teachers need to build more interactive activities into language learning for all students.

Foreign language researchers interested in investigating African American presence in foreign language instruction can gain from this study. We need to develop more studies that are guided by the naturalistic inquiry mode. Long periods of time spent with students as they perform in the classroom can reap tremendous insights into their learning styles and abilities. The students in this study did not demonstrate hostility and resistance to learning, as is so often cited in the literature. Rather they showed eagerness and pleasure in learning although they admitted that it was not easy.

The myriad social, political, and economic issues which surround the unique niche that many African American students occupy in our schools is beyond the scope of this study. However, findings from this examination may contribute to the further study of the salient issues related to the education of these students within a specific context of learning. In the past, African American student experiences in the classroom have often been viewed as a "problem" with fervent discussions about what this problem entailed and what to do with it. This study contends that the problem may not be with the student but instead may be with teacher attitudes and perceptions. We must relinquish notions of what constitutes academic success and recognize that learning a foreign language, like any other academic endeavor is well within the intellectual capabilities of many African American students.

In recent years, researchers have posited several factors as major contributors to successful L2 learning: intelligence, language-learning aptitude, teaching methodologies that utilized age, motivation, and psychological and social distance factors which may be related to both the target language speaking community and the actual learning environment. The influence of these factors on successful language learning is universal for all students and does not necessarily affect African American students any differently. Consideration of these factors suggests that communicative competence, where language is used in pragmatically appropriate ways to fulfill social functions, implies the need for language learners to perceive and understand more than the structural factors or linguistic components of a language.

Teaching All Students

This study was fundamentally an endeavor to determine the effect of culturally relevant teaching and other social and cultural factors which can have a positive influence on foreign language learning among African American adolescents as a step toward more-inclusive language classrooms. A secondary objective was to focus on the Comparisons Standards in this short-term course. Some of the factors identified included those which the literature has discussed as important to language learning and those derived from actual classroom observations. The degree to which these factors compare with Schumann's (1975) taxonomy of social, affective, personality, and cognitive factors may contribute to a better understanding of the effect of foreign language learning situations on African American students. Additionally, sociolinguistic factors such as the influence of cultural values and norms on classroom learning may also be viewed as valid predictors of how certain students may approach language learning situations. Results from this study may have substantive pedagogical implications on the learning of a second language—not only for African Americans but also for other minority students. Among the recommendations are:

1. Foreign language coordinators must be encouraged to design special workshops for teachers of minority students. Workshops of this nature have traditionally catered to language arts teachers at the K–5 levels, and foreign language teachers have not profited from such professional development.
2. As part of a movement toward teaching all students, foreign language teachers must expand their training to include linguistic and sociolinguistic courses that deal with ethnic groups in the USA.
3. Foreign language teachers in inner-city schools must receive special training in teaching non-mainstream English speakers
4. The foreign language teaching profession should focus more attention on issues of instruction for all middle-school students.
5. The foreign language teaching profession must begin looking at preparing its teachers to teach in truly diverse school settings.
6. There is need to undertake more research on L1 and L2 and C1 and C2 interactions.
7. The Northeast Conference may consider having its next conference on topics dealing with teaching and learning foreign languages in diverse classrooms.

Note

[1]A thorough evaluation of phonological structures in African American English according to current linguistic theory is beyond the scope of this study. Such an undertaking can occur only after more basic syntactic and morphological problems have been solved. Instead, it may be more relevant to present several phonological features demonstrated by the subjects which are also often noted among African American non-standard speaking populations and to contrast those features with a brief analysis of Arabic and Standard English phonology. It goes without saying that these students clearly are not representative of the non-standard speaking populations and that there is a great deal of phonological variation within those populations. Further, these generalizations are perhaps not exclusively valid for any one speaker. Eight features and their relevance to students in this study include:
(i) Vowels in General

The low front vowel /a/ (as in *father* in most American white dialects) is present in most versions of African American English. It also occurs in Southern white dialects, and may have spread to them from earlier forms of African American English. This vowel is between the /a/ of *hot* and the /ae/ of *cat*; even when lengthened, it sounds like the vowel of *cat* or *cap* to many speakers of Standard English. A common expression that the students used in class was "Yo, what's up dawg?" It is this *dawg* expression that most closely resembles this vowel in their vernacular. In the early 1970s it was not uncommon to hear of unexpected discoveries of "new homophone pairs" such as *island* and *Allen* in the so called Negro Non-Standard. Dillard (1972) asserts that although the homophone set of African American English is different from that of Standard English, these two would not be examples; /a l n/ contrasts with /ael n/, but some speakers of Standard English can't hear the difference. The lengthened /a / of *island* in African American English is, of course, /ay/ ("long *i*") in Standard English.

This "replacement" by African American English is shared with many Southern white dialects and in fact was used by some of the white native Texans teachers at the middle school where the study was conducted Any theory of the direction of influence would require long and careful consideration. In some places where there is a large African American middle class such as Washington, D.C., there may be less tendency to this phonological development before voiceless consonants /bdg/; that is, the /a / sound will occur in *ride* but the /ay/ sound will occur in *write*. The more extreme forms of African American English have the "substitution" everywhere. African American English vowels, like Southern white dialects, have a marked tendency to lengthen: /pI g/ for /pIg/ *pig*. Instances of students using this vowel lengthening is quite common and is evidenced by such phrases as *"I'm tired a dis..."*

(ii) The initial "th"

The initial "th" of *the, then, that, those, though, there, this, these* is pronounced as /d/. The students in this study frequently used the pronunciation in such expressions as "gimmee dat pencil" or "dis ain't right.".

(iii) The Final "th"

The final "-th" of *with, both, birth, mouth, truth,* etc., is sometimes pronounced as /f/. One of the 7th graders in the study who was most likely functioning at the 4th grade in his L1, was more noticeable with this particular pronunciation feature although it was used by the others sporadically. We see an example of the transference of /th/ to /f/ in the name of the national basketball player Anfernee (Anthony) Hardaway.

(iv) The medial "th"

The medial "th" of mother, other, brother (always voiced / / in Standard English, not voiceless / /, is pronounced as /v/. Although a characteristic of African American English pronunciation, it was not noticeable in any of the speech patterns of the students.

(v) The final /r/

The final "r" is "dropped," as in many other dialects of English; but in African American communities, this persists in geographic areas which do not have the feature otherwise. In the South, it is more widespread among African Americans than in the white community. As Labov (1972) points out, the "r-dropping" is also common in certain Northeastern United States dialects—which, however, often have a difference in the existence of "intrusive" /r/ *(idear of it)*. In at least some versions of African American English, intervocalic /r/ is "dropped," so that mad=/maed/; mired=/mad/and married=/maeid/ are almost identical sounds and differ only in the vowel nuclei which are so much alike, from the viewpoint of Standard English, that distinctions are not easily made. In almost all instances where the /r/ should be used in Standard English speech forms, most of the students habitually dropped it.

(vi) The range of vocal pitch

The range of vocal pitch is probably greater. There is not much in the phonological literature of African American English that addresses this subject. However, there is habitual use of beginning impressionistic statements with such words as "Niggah!" or "Cuz" or "Dawg", "My maan" These are all used very casually as terms of address as opposed to pejoratives.

(vii) Lexical items

Several features often referred to pronunciation are really matters of lexicon rather than of phonology. That is why some base forms of African American English are: des = desk; was = wasp; aks = ask (Dillard, 1972).

(viii) The use of profanity.

The aforementioned seven lexical differences were most obvious in the speech patterns in the classroom. If any correction is required, it should be on reducing the extensive use of profanity so prevalent today. This appeared to be a common and largely accepted (by fellow adolescents) feature of the speech patterns that the teacher observed, not only in the classroom but throughout the school in general. Although the researcher/teacher was initially surprised at the frequency of use, he gradually realized that it was not intended as a slight against anyone nor was it intended to have any pejorative or negative connotation. Most of the profanity was uttered in the context of casual conversation among the students themselves. It appeared to be such a normal part of discourse that the teacher often had to reprimand them for the use. The reaction was usually one of surprise, accompanied by phrases such as "Man, you have no ide' what's goin' on," or "what chu' talkin' bout? I ain't sed nuttin wron'." Although there were clearly language use implications arising from this persistent use of profanity, this issue is probably better addressed in a social-psychological context.

References

Apple, M. & Christain-Smith, L. (Eds.) (1991). *The politics of the textbook: Politics, policy and pedagogy*. New York: Routledge.

American Council on the Teaching of Foreign Languages. (1989). ACTFL Arabic Proficiency Guidelines. *Foreign Language Annals, 22*, 373–392.

Bailey, K. M. (1991). Diary studies of classroom language learning: The doubting game and the believing game. In E. Sadtono (Ed.), *Language acquisition and the second/foreign language classroom* (pp. 60–102). Singapore: SEAMEO Regional Language Centre.

Baugh, J. (1983). *Black street speech: Its history, structure, and survival*. Austin, TX: University of Texas Press.

Baugh, J. (1995). The law, linguistics, and education: Educational reform for African American language minority students. *Linguistics and Education, 7*, 87–105.

Bereiter, C., & Engelmann, S. (1966). *Teaching disadvantaged children in the preschool*. Englewood Cliffs, NJ: Prentice Hall.

Boben, D. (1985). *Guidelines for equity issues in technology education*. Reston: International Technology Education Association.

Bruner, J. S. (1990). *Acts of meaning*. Cambridge: Harvard University Press.

Bruner, J. S., Goodnow, J. J., & Austin, G. A. (1956). *A study of thinking*. New York: Wiley.

Carroll, J. (1962). The prediction of success in intensive foreign language training. In R. Glaser (Ed.), *Training and research in education* (pp. 87–136). Pittsburgh: University of Pittsburgh Press.

Clark, B., & Harty, H. (1983). *African cultural elements in language learning*. Washington, DC: National Endowment for the Humanities.

Comer, J. P. (1990). Building quality relationships. In J. G. Bain & J. L. Herman (Eds.), *Making schools work for underachieving minority students* (pp. 13–24). New York: Greenwood.

Davis, J. J. (1992). African American students and foreign language learning. [ERIC ED 345 583].

Davis, J. J., & Markham, P. (1991). Student attitudes toward foreign language study at predominately black institutions. *Foreign Language Annals, 24,* 227–237.

Defense Language Institute Foreign Language Center. (1986). *A contrastive study of English and Arabic.* Presidio of Monterey, CA: Author.

DeStephano, J. S. (1971). Black attitudes toward Black English: A pilot study. *Florida Foreign Language Reporter, 9,* 23–27.

Dillard, J. (1972). *Black English.* New York: Random House.

Dummett, L. S. (1984). The enigma—The persistent failure of Black children in learning to read. *Reading World, 24,* 31–37.

Fordham, S. (1996). *Blacked out: Dilemmas of race, identity, and success at Capital High.* Chicago: University of Chicago Press.

Fordham, S., & Ogbu, J. (1986). Black students' school success: Coping with the "burden of 'acting white.'" *Urban Review, 18* (3), 176–206.

Foster, M. (1995). Talking that talk: The language of control, curriculum, and critique. *Linguistics And Education, 7,* 129–150.

Ganschow, L., & Sparks, R. (1991a). A screening instrument for the identification of foreign language learning problems. *Foreign Language Annals, 24,* 383–398.

Ganschow, L., & Sparks, R. (1991b). Foreign language learning difficulties: Affective or native language aptitude differences? *Modern Language Journal, 75,* 3–16.

Ganschow, L., Sparks, R., Javorsky, J., Pohlman, J., & Bishop-Marbury, A. (1994). Identifying native language difficulties among foreign language learners in college: A "foreign" language learning disability? *Journal of Learning Disabilities, 24,* 530–541.

Ganschow, L., Sparks, R., Javorsky, J., Pohlman, J., & Patton, J. (1992). Identifying native language deficits in high and low risk foreign language learners in high school. *Foreign Language Annals, 25,* 403–418.

Hancock, C. R. (1994). Cultural roots and academic achievement: Is there a problem in foreign language study? In G. K. Grouse (Ed.), *Meeting new challenges in the foreign language classroom* (pp. 9–19). Lincolnwood, Il.: National Textbook.

Johnson, R., & Johnson, D. (1985). Student-student interaction: Ignored but powerful. *Journal of Teacher Education, 36,* 22–26.

Johnson, S. O., & Johnson, V. J. (1988). *Motivating minority students: Strategies that work.* Springfield, IL: Charles Thomas.

Krashen, S. D., & Terrell, T. D. (1983). *The natural approach: Language acquisition in the classroom.* Englewood Cliffs, NJ: Prentice Hall.

Labov, W. (1972). *Language in the inner city: Studies in the Black English vernacular.* Philadelphia: University of Pennsylvania Press.

Miller, K. C. (1953). The teaching and learning of modern foreign languages in colleges for negroes. Unpublished doctoral dissertation, Ohio State University, Columbus.

Moore, Z. (1995, November). *African American college students and foreign language instruction.* Paper presented at the ACTFL Annual Meeting, Anaheim, CA.

Nerenz, A. G. (1990). The exploratory years: Foreign languages in the middle-level curriculum. In S. Magnan, (Ed.), *Shifting the instructional focus to the learner* (pp. 93–126). Middlebury, VT: Northeast Conference on the Teaching of Foreign Languages.

Nyabongo, V. S. (1946). Modern foreign language study in negro colleges. *French Review, 20,* 153–158.

Orr, E. W. (1987, November 1). Does Black English hinder learning mathematics? *The Washington Post.*

Pimsleur, P. (1963). Predicting success in high school foreign language courses. *Educational and Psychological Measurement*, *2*, 349–357.

Schuhmann, A. M. (1990). Improving the quality of teachers for minority students. In J. G. Bain & J. L. Herman (Eds.), *Making schools work for underachieving minority students* (pp. 147–154). New York: Greenwood.

Schumann, J. H. (1975). Affective factors and the problem of age in second language acquisition. *Language Learning*, *25*, 209–235.

Schumann, F. E. (1978). Diary of a language learner: A further analysis. In S. D. Krashen, & R. C. Scarcella (Eds.), *Issues in second language research* (pp. 118–131). Rowley, MA: Newbury House.

Slavin, R. (1983) *Cooperative Learning*. New York: Longman Press

Seliger, H. (1983). Learner interaction in the classroom and its effects on language acquisition. In H. W. Seliger & M. H. Long (Eds.), *Classroom oriented research in second language acquisition* (pp. 17–40). Rowley, MA: Newbury House.

Sparks, R., & Ganschow, L. (1993). Searching for the cognitive locus of foreign language learning difficulties: Linking first and second language learning. *Modern Language Journal*, *77*, 289–301.

Texas Education Agency. (1979). *Guidelines for establishing equity in languages and illustrations*. Austin: Author.

Yin, R. K. (1984). *Case study research: Design and methods*. Newbury Park, CA: Sage.

Appendix

Examples of Classroom Language Learning Material

Pleasantries: Arabic Cartoon

LOST IN THE MARKET

Zein is from Cairo, Egypt and is visiting his cousins in Damascus, Syria. His cousins were taking him on a tour of their city when Zein became separated from them and lost in the market area. Can you help him find his way home? He can only pass through streets

whose total is five. Remember to read mathmatical problems from right to left. حظاً سعيداً   Good Luck!

/sa-?ii-dan   ha ð-ᵹan/

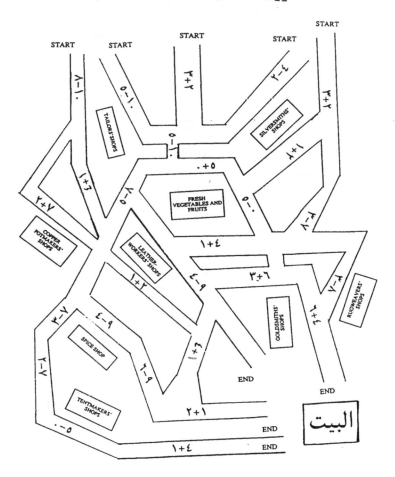

صحتين !

SAH-TEYN !!

PICTURE IT......

    You have just arrived in Cairo and are eating at The Arabic Restaurant, a well known eating spot by the Pyramids. Your good friend Leila was supposed to meet you there, but she got stuck in traffic and will be 2 hours late! GACK!!! You're starving!!

    The good news is that The Arabic Restaurant takes American money which is all you have since you just arrived in the city a few hours earlier. The bad news is that your Arabic is a little rusty and you only have $10.00. You'll have to do the best you can at deciphering the menu without going over your budget. Here are some helpful tips:

1. Read through the entire menu as best you can. Some words you will know and some will be completely new. Not to worry! You know better than to get frustrated. Focus on the words you DO know.

2. Use the information you can gather from the menu to answer the questions below:

    [A] The name of the restaurant is written in Arabic on the menu. Find it and copy it here.

_____

    [B] The following list of words are new to you. Guess their meaning based on the context in which they appear on the menu:

الخضروات   المقبلات   ساندويش

الفاكهة   سلطة   المشروبات

3. Now go back to the menu and make your choices. You must spend between 8 and 10 dollars and your meal must include one meat dish, one vegetable dish, and a drink. In the spaces below at left write your food choices in Arabic, on the right record the cost for that item. When you are finished choosing, add up your bill.

صحتين !

(صحتين   _sah-_teyn!   "to your health!"   Said before eating.)

FOOD ITEM   COST

_____

_____

_____

_____

Communities of Learners: From New York to Chile

Mari Haas

Teachers College, Columbia University

Margaret Reardon

*Pocantico Hills Central School,
Sleepy Hollow, New York*

Me alegré mucho cuando recibí tu mensaje, oye amiga o amigo

Eiden Saez, Padre las Casas, Chile

The first letters arrived via the Internet from Chile! The students in Peggy Reardon's Spanish class, at Pocantico Hills Central School in Sleepy Hollow, NY, were excited. Antonio received his letter, and as he walked back to his desk he began to read the greeting aloud to himself. His face lit-up as he read, *Hola Antonio*. He returned to his desk and, like the other students, tried to understand his letter. The first line was hard. What did the word *sorteo* [lottery] mean? He needed help from the dictionary or the teacher to find out. Many of the other letters also included the word *sorteo* because the Chilean teacher had put the names of the students from New York in a hat for each Chilean student to choose. Was *Karis* a boy or a girl? Her full name, *Karis Andrea Mellado Fabres* gave Antonio a clue. And her description, *soy delgada, de ojos café oscuro* [*I am thin, with dark brown eyes*] helped confirm that Karis was a girl's name. She told him her parents' names, Hugo Mellado Otarola and Sonia Fabres Jimenes, and that she liked to listen to music and to dance.

Connecting Communities via E-Mail

This e-mail letter exchange is part of a unit on Chile designed by Peggy Reardon, in collaboration with Mari Haas, a teacher-educator from Teachers College, Columbia University, for Peggy's 7th grade Spanish class. The students have been studying Spanish for three years, since 5th grade. Peggy chose this particular class to work with because they are an active group and do not often get the opportunity to participate in special projects or to go on fieldtrips. She felt that this unit on Chile would be engaging for them and could channel their energy into an exciting learning experience. The students live north of New York City where children from several small towns all attend a pre-K-to-grade-8 public school. The students come from a variety of backgrounds. Most are from middle-class families and about 27% are African American, Latino, or Asian. There are 19 students in the Spanish class. They study Spanish five days a week for 44 minutes each day. The language curriculum follows the text, *Viva el español* (Belisle-Chatterjee et al., 1990) from 5th to 8th grade, but Peggy often plans special thematic units. Her emphasis on teaching language thematically comes from her participation in the National Endowment for the Humanities/Teachers College, Columbia University grant-funded project called Project Pluma.

Project Pluma gave Peggy the opportunity to study the history and culture of Mexico and creative writing at Teachers College in New York City and in Mexico. After teaching her Pluma curriculum project, a unit on Diego Rivera, to an eighth-grade class, she was interested in creating other thematic units that integrate language, content, and culture. Mari, a K–8 methods instructor at Teachers College and the Director of Project Pluma, has worked with Peggy for the last several years on teaching strategies for thematic, content-centered lessons. The Chile unit combines activities designed by Peggy and Mari as well as activities from a thematic text, *The Language of Folk Art* (Haas, 1996). The teaching strategies and student activities were written to let the students learn about Chile in the classroom as well as through interaction with Chilean people. The emphasis in this project on using language as a tool to communicate with native speakers of Spanish exemplifies the fifth goal of the National Foreign Language Standards, *Communities* (National Standards, 1996).

The Communities Goal

This goal takes the perspective that in our global society today, with an economy that is more and more based on information, technology, and service, students who study languages other than English will be better able to participate in the multilingual communities within their own neighborhoods and states as well as around the world. It is a goal that is facilitated when students complete long sequences of language study that provide them with many opportunities to use the language. The Connections Goal is made up of two standards: the first asks students to apply what they have learned by using the target language in the classroom as well as beyond the school setting; the second standard reinforces the notion that because knowing other languages gives students access to information and people from the target culture they are able to participate in many rich and enjoyable opportunities that contribute to their becoming lifelong learners. Projects that stress the application of certain language skills give students meaningful experiences with the language and culture. These include: communicating with people who speak the target language through e-mail, telephone, or letters; interacting with peers around a language or cultural topic; planning a trip (real or imaginary) to a target country; playing games, and listening to music or viewing art work from the target culture. These activities will help them understand the interdependence of people throughout the world as well as expand the avenues of information open to them. Although the goal of *Communities* incorporates the other standards, especially those of *Communication* and *Cultures*, it is an extremely important comprehensive goal because it allows students to put their language learning into action and to experience "the power of language" (National Standards, 1996) first hand.

When Peggy and Mari were planning the unit, the Internet connection to Chile was the obvious activity that would let the students "leave" the classroom and connect with students in Chile. As the planning progressed they discovered additional resources in the school, the community, and nearby that could also enrich the project. Therefore, the National Foreign Language Standards goal of *Communities* was emphasized throughout this project in a variety of ways. Progress toward the goal was manifest when the Pocantico students exchanged e-mail letters with Chilean students, interviewed a first-grade teacher in their own school who is originally from Chile and the author of a reading passage about Chile, and visited a Chilean bakery in the village nearby. They also sang a song from

Chile, learned about *arpilleras* (see Figure 5) and made their own *arpillera*-inspired collages.

Planning the Project

Together, Peggy and Mari outlined the project, incorporating activities from the *Language of Folk Art*, creating additional activities, and shaping the unit to the needs of this class. Peggy was concerned that the students continue to learn the vocabulary and structures they would be responsible for on the exam at the end of the school year. She wanted to see how a thematic unit could reinforce the school language curriculum and how new ways of using language (the e-mail letters and communication with unfamiliar native speakers) would enhance the students' learning. The connection between Chilean students and Pocantico students was particularly exciting for Peggy. Both Mari and Peggy were curious about what the students would learn about their own culture and the culture of the Chilean people through their participation in this unit (a focus of the Comparisons Goal). Mari was glad to have the opportunity to watch an excellent teacher in action, to observe the teaching strategies she used and the ways in which she facilitated students' language use inside and outside the classroom. Since teaching a thematic unit was still new for Peggy, Mari's presence in the classroom several times each week gave them both the time to reflect on the methodology and to learn from each other.

The project was a true collaboration in several ways as diverse communities of educators worked together. The first collaboration involved Peggy and Mari, a classroom teacher and a university-based educator. Through this collaboration, Peggy and Mari strengthened their sense of community that had begun during Project Pluma. Even though they had had many positive experiences together in the past, during the Chile unit Mari was a more frequent observer and an occasional teacher in Peggy's classroom. It took a lot of trust on Peggy's part to open her classroom to this scrutiny and to allow the teaching to unfold as she tried new techniques and incorporated successful, tried and true activities.

While teaching the unit, Peggy also worked with other teachers at her school. The computer teacher assisted with the logistics of sending and receiving e-mail messages, and the art teacher explored, with the students, ways to think about designing the culminating folk-art project. When Peggy realized that the first-grade teacher was originally from Chile, she invited her to visit the class. Arranging for the interview required Peggy and the first-grade teacher to switch classes. This sense of community spirit at Pocantico Hills School was evident throughout the Chile project. The other teachers were interested in the project and excited to facilitate and contribute to it in any way possible. It allowed all the teachers involved to step out of their traditional roles and teach from a new perspective. They each learned something new about their colleague's teaching field, thus strengthening the Pocantico Hills School community.

Folk Art

Unidad 6 in The *Language of Folk Art* focuses on Chile and uses an *arpillera* (an appliqué picture made with scraps of colored material sewed on a burlap background) of a small town to teach about this South American country. Coincidentally, this chapter added yet another layer to the focus on the Standards goal of *Communities*. The context of the chapter is created by the *arpillera* and the language lessons expand on the elements that make up a community in a small South American town. The reading passage about Melipilla, a small Chilean town, gives the students a sense of what growing up in a small town was like and allows them to compare and contrast Melipilla with their own town. The students learn Spanish as they are studying the geography of Chile; they learn what towns and cities are like (the stores, services, and places of interest), and how *arpilleras* are made. As she prepared to teach the unit, Peggy first worked on familiarizing herself with the activities in this chapter. Then she started to explore the Internet to find a connection with a school in Chile. Previously, she had researched Argentina, Peru, and Colombia and worked with an 8th-grade class on a keypal project (Reardon, 1995). She used her experience from that project to begin her exploration of a link with Chile and eventually made contact with Elena Herrera, a teacher at the Dario Salas School in Padre Las Casas, a small town near Temuco, Chile.[1] Elena and Peggy began corresponding through e-mail (see Figure 1). They decided to have three student letter exchanges. The first message would discuss the students' appearance, their family, and their likes and dislikes. The second would describe their schools, school subjects (Peggy's students were interested to know if the Chilean students studied English or other foreign languages), and their interests (sports and music). They planned to include a description of their towns in the third exchange.

Date: Wed, 27 Mar/Thurs. 28 Mar. 96 10:56:29
From: Elena Herrera A. <Coordinador@dsalas.plasca.plaza.cl>
To: Peggy Reardon <poco@transit.nyser.net>
Subject: =?iso-8859-1?Q?Comunicaci=F3n?=

Hola Peggy
Te saluda Elena,Coordinadora de la Red en la Escuela Darmo Salas. Soy
profesora de Educación General Básica, coordinadora de la sala de computación
en el proyecto Enlaces.

Nuestra escuela está ubicada en la comuna de Padre las Casas en la novena región.
Tenemos lugares de verano preciosos, como el balneario de Licanray, Villarrica,
Pucón, Cerro Qielol etc.

Tú me dices y comenzaremos a intercambiar información. Deseo tener comunicación con ustedes para hablar de los temas que planteastes, trabajaría con
alumnos de 7 año.

Saludos desde Chile
Espero me contestes pronto. Me despido deseándote un gran éxito en este año.

Elena Herrera Alveal

Figure 1. A combination of two letters from the computer teacher in Chile.

Beginnings

And so the unit began. On the first day Peggy asked the students to
list, in English, any facts they knew about Chile. She wanted to gauge
their background knowledge about the country. As it turned out, their
knowledge was limited to facts about the geography. They said that Chile
was a long, skinny, Spanish-speaking country on the Pacific coast of South
America, with the Andes Mountains running through it. Peggy then
changed the sign hanging in the front of the classroom from the "English"
side to the "Español" side (Curtain and Pesola, 1994, p. 300). Using a
large map of South America, Peggy and her puppet friends presented a
dialogue about Chile. One puppet was in a hurry to leave for a trip to Chile.
The other puppet began asking questions about the country:

1. Hola Miguelito, ¿qué pasa?	Hi, Mikey, What's happening?
2. Pues, tengo prisa.	Well, I'm in a hurry. Leave me
¡Déjame en paz!	alone!
1. ¿Adónde vas?	Where are you going?
2. Voy a Chile en una hora.	I'm going to Chile in an hour.
1. ¿Dónde está Chile, en los	Where is Chile, in the US?
Estados Unidos?	
2. Me vuelves loco. Está en Sud-	You drive me crazy! It's in
américa.	South America.
1. ¿Está cerca de un océano?	Is it near an ocean?
2. Por supuesto, el Océano	Of course, the Pacific Ocean.
Pacífico.	
1. ¿Cómo es Chile?	What's Chile like?
2. Es largo y estrecho.	It's long and narrow.
1. ¿Cuál es la capital?	What is the capital?
2. Es Santiago.	It's Santiago.

From the dialogue, Peggy created a Total Physical Response (TPR) sequence using the map and giving commands to the students such as:

Toca Chile.	Touch Chile.
Enséñame el país al norte de	Show me the country to the
Chile.	north of Chile.
Toca el país al este de Chile.	Touch the country to the east of
	Chile.

During the first class Peggy also showed slides she had taken on a trip to Chile many years before. This activity added to the background knowledge the students were collecting on Chile. Afterwards, she asked them a series of questions about the country, and they were able to reply with more in-depth information. Mari suggested Peggy write a *language-experience story* with the students on chart paper to help synthesize the information they were discussing in Spanish. A language-experience story is a description, usually written on large pieces of chart paper, of a shared experience students have had or know about. The teacher begins the "story" and asks questions or pauses frequently so that the students can add information or sentences about the experience. The teacher reads the sentences as they are finished, always starting from the beginning so that the students have many chances to listen to the story as well as read the words on the chart paper. The next class session, Peggy began the story. She started writing about Chile, eliciting much of the information from the students. The students were engaged in the activity and eager to participate.

Chile

> Chile está en la América del Sur o Sudamérica.
> Es estrecho y largo.
> Los países al norte se llaman el Perú y Bolivia.
> La Argentina está al este de Chile.
> El Océano Pacífico está al oeste.
> Las montañas son muy altas y se llaman los Andes.

Language Experience Story

Peggy reflected in her journal:

Mari suggested that I do a 'language learning experience' and I liked that idea. ...I knew it was a technique that would help me consolidate what the students were learning...I like keeping the chart paper because it gives my slower students a reference....I can pull these charts out again.

The First Letter Exchange

Soon, the first letters arrived from Chile on the Internet. When they were printed, Peggy and Mari began to read them and realized there was a minor glitch in the transcription. Many of the Chilean students had included accent marks, tildes (ñ), and upside-down question marks in their writing, but the program on the library computer at Pocantico Hills School was not set up to take them. So, when the computer read an accented letter, it changed it to a completely different letter. For example, the letter "ú" was changed to "z" so the word *música*, which appeared in many letters, was *mzsica*. The word *años* (years), was *agos*. This last example was easy for the students to figure out since it was used in the context of how old the students were, so the "g" must really be an "ñ." At least the mysterious letters were consistent and together the class was able to decipher the messages. The computer teacher collaborated with Peggy to resolve the problem of the incompatible character set on the computers.[2]

The letters from the Chilean students contained a wealth of Spanish language and interesting insights into the culture of students from Chile (see Figure 2). Mari was fascinated with the content, which contained

Date: Tue, 16 Apr 96 16:08:46
From: Eider =?iso-8859-1?Q?S=Elez? <Alumno7@dsalas.plasca.plaza.cl>
To: Chema <poco@transit.nyser.net>

Hola Chema.
Mi nombre es Eider Alvaro Saez Paredes, nací en Temuco, el dia 21 de Febrero de 1984, soy bajo, de pelo castaño, de ojos verdes. Mi padre se llama Fidel Humberto Saez Gallardo, trabaja en una contructora, de chofer, es alto, moreno, su pelo es negro. Mi madre se llama Eliana Paredes Sanchez, es ama de casa, pelo negro y mide 1.58, tiene los ojos café claro, es morena, mi hermano se llama David Heliacer Saez Paredes, nacio el 28 de Diciembre de 1974, es alto. Lo que mas me gusta hacer es jugar al futbol, también escuchar música de la radio. La televisión me aburre.

Bueno amiga me despido deseando que lo pases bien.
Escribe pronto.
Tu amigo
Eider
Padre Las Casas, 09-04-96

Date: Tue, 16 Apr 96 16:08:46
From: Cesar Moncada =?iso-8859-1?Q?S=Elez? <Alumno7@dsalas.plasca.plaza.cl>
To: Cristina <poco@transit.nyser.net>
Padre Las Casas, 16 de Abril
Hola Cristina
Mi nombre es Cesar Moncada y estudio en la escuela Darmo Salas, de Padre Las Casas. Estoy en 7:año basico, tengo 14 años. Soy un chico responsable en mis deberes cuando tengo que hacer algo en clase. A mi me gusta tocar la flauta dulce. Vivo en Galicia 2, tengo que viajar todos los dias para asistir a clascs, demoro casi una hora en llegar a la escuela. Tengo dos hermanas, soy el mayor, practico un deporte que te contaría mas adelante cuando tu me escribas. Mi padre se llama Miguel Moncada, es militar y mi madre se llama Rosa, es dueña de casa.
Por ahora me despido esperando tu pronta respuesta.

Tu amigo
Cesar

Figure 2. First Letters from Chile (some punctuation added).

Date: Tue, 16 Apr 96 16:08:46
From: Juan Pablo Gutierrez =?iso-8859-1?Q?S=Elez? lumno7@dsalas.plasca.
plaza.cl
To: Catalina <poco@transit.nyser.net>

Hola Catalina
Es un placer escribirte estas letras.
Soy Juan Pablo Gutierrez Gutierrez. Mis Padres son Cecilia Veneranda Gutierrez
y Juan Carlos Gutierrez, por considencia mi madre es Gutierrez y mi padre
también. Me gustaría conocerte, yo tengo 12 años, me gusta el fútbol, no juego
por ningún equipo. Me gustan todas las verduras menos el morrón. Me gustaría
que me respondieras esta carta para saber de tu país, ¿cómo es todo lo que hay
aca? Bueno amiga por el momento te dejo, cuando me contestes conversamos
otro poco.

Se despide tu amigo
Juan Pablo. Chaooooooooooooo

Figure 2 (cont'd.).

material for many Spanish lessons. When the first set of letters arrived,
she examined them with the class. Using overhead transparencies of the
actual letters, the students figured out the code for the punctuation. Then
they focused on the messages, listing the many greetings and farewells
used in the letters (*Hola, Buenos días, Buenas tardes* and *Adiós, Hasta
luego, Chao, Chaooo, Tu amigo/a*). Often, sentences included interesting
words such as *callejero* [a boy who likes to "hang out" in the street] and
useful phrases the Chilean students used in their letters that could be repeated in the replies from the Pocantico students. Some of Peggy's students talked about their *aspecto físico* [appearance], one replied using the
verb *cumplir* [to turn a certain age] to say when he would be 13 years old,
and another borrowed the phrase, *Estoy muy alegre de escribirte* [I am
very happy to write to you]. The Pocantico students also saw examples
of concepts they already knew about from their Spanish lessons. They
discovered that the Chileans *do* often use their mother's and their father's
names, that numbers *do* go after street names, and that the day goes before
the month. They explored the metric system as they calculated how tall a
Chilean correspondent was. They learned new descriptive adjectives such
as *risueña* [smiley] and *cachetona* [a person with chubby cheeks]. They
were very interested in the fact that the Chilean students started school at
8:00 and finished at 1:00 or 1:30 (they also used the 24-hour clock) and

that they wore uniforms. And they saw evidence that the Chilean students were like themselves in many ways. They liked sports and music (*el Meneito, Macarena*), they studied similar subjects (English begins in 5th grade and French in 7th) and the students live in many types of families.

For the next activity, Peggy asked her students to brainstorm information they could use in their replies to the students in Chile. They picked a topic such as school and listed all the relevant vocabulary (*dos pisos* [two floors], *un gimnasio* [a gymnasium], *una biblioteca* [a library], etc.) Later, as they wrote their letters, the students expanded this information into sentences. They were also encouraged to think of questions they wanted answered by their keypals such as, *¿Juegas deportes en la escuela?* [Do you play sports in school?], *¿Te gusta leer?* [Do you like to read?] *¿Cuál es tu música favorita?* [What is you favorite music?] *¿Es tu escuela pública?* [Is your school public?]. It was amazing to see the amount of Spanish they reviewed in an interesting context during this process, language that would help them complete a real task. The first responses (Figure 3) were e-mailed off to Chile, and the students anxiously awaited the replies.

¡Hola Alex!
Hola me llamo Rena. Yo vivo en Elmsford, NY. Mi familia es buena y ¿tu familia? Tengo un hermano Max 2 y una hermana Dana 8. Tengo trece años y vivo en un apartamento. Me gustan los deportes y mi deporte favorito es basquetbol. Me encanta español e inglés. No tengo un novio todavía. Tengo muchos amigos y amigas. Tengo ojos azules y pelo pardo. Soy delgada. ¿Cuánto tiempo andas con Luz? Envia me una foto a mi escuela de Luz y ti.

Adios Alex. Espero conocerte bien.

Quierido Karis,
Hola! Me llamo Antonio. Cumplo trece años en junio el veinte y ocho. Tengo un papá Felipe, una mamá Maria, un hermano Felipe, y un hermana Christina.

Me encanta jugar los deportes. Mis deportes favoritos son fútbol y beisbol. Yo juego los deportes todo el tiempo. Vivo en una casa mediana en Briarcliff Manor, NY. Yo tengo el pelo rojo, y los ojos pardos. Yo soy alto. Mis pies son 29 cm.

Hasta Luego

Antonio

Figure 3. Samples of the first replies written by the Pocantico students.

Culture Research: Products and Perspectives

When Peggy's students were not working on their letters she was continuing with the unit on Chile. After teaching a bit of the geography of Chile, Peggy divided the students into groups of four or five students. Each group was assigned a specific aspect of Chile to research and report back on to the whole class. The topics were: a detailed map of Chile; the Chilean flag and the meaning of its colors; a topographical map that highlighted the rivers, lakes, and mountains; and one that showed the major cities and depicted where Temuco (the largest city near where the Chilean students live) was located. Each group created a visual for their report and wrote a description on a large piece of chart paper (Figure 4) and then presented them to the class.

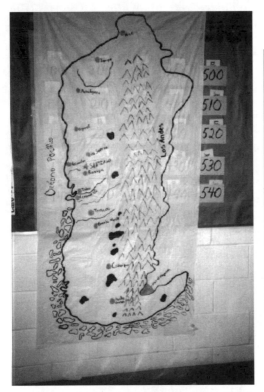

Las montañas en Chile se llaman los Andes.

Los ríos importantes son:
  el Maule
  el Maipo
  el Itata
  el Bío Bío

Los ríos van de las montañas al océano Pacífico.

En el sur hay muchos lagos.

Figure 4. Floorcloth map of Chile and written description.

Later, the students used the floorcloth map (a shower curtain liner with a map of Chile drawn on it with permanent markers), created by one group, to give each other commands such as *Camina a Concepción* [walk to Concepción], *Nada en el río Itata* [swim in the Itata River], *Sube las montañas* [climb the mountains]. Peggy placed signs around the room with the names of the other countries in South America written on them. She asked the students to go to the country by role playing different means of transportation including *maneja* [drive], *monta a caballo* [ride a horse], and *vuela* [fly].

Using the poster of the Chilean arpillera from *The Language of Folk Art* (Figure 5), the students discussed what they saw. They talked about the houses, the mountains, the trees, the people. They knew the word *pan* [bread] and Peggy pointed out that the *panadería* [bread shop] was where *pan* was sold. Later, the class discussed (in English) the two types of *arpilleras*, the original ones from the '70s with a political message and the more contemporary ones that depict daily life. For many women, making arpilleras has become their livelihood. Students also watched the movie *Missing* that illustrates life in Chile during the late '70s.

Figure 5. A Chilean Arpillera.

Integrating Language and Culture

Next the students learned the names of other stores in a town and the products they sold. To practice the new vocabulary they did a pair activity in which they asked each other what was sold in a certain store. Partner A asked, *¿Qué venden en la heladería?* [What do they sell in the ice cream store?] and Partner B answered, *(En la heladería venden) helado* [In the ice cream store they sell ice cream]. The following day the students played a progressive reading game. Each student had a card with a product from a store written on the top and a question written on the bottom (see Figure 6). They had to listen until they heard their product mentioned, answer the question, and then ask the new question printed on the bottom of the card. Peggy found that the students were attentive and interested in both activities and wanted to play the reading game again and again after switching cards.

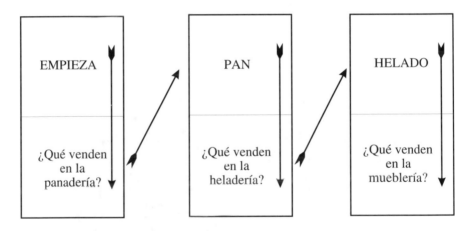

Figure 6. Example of progressive reading game cards (Haas, 1996, p. 211).

Once the students knew the relevant vocabulary, Peggy used masking tape to create a large town on the floor of the classroom (Curtain and Pesola, 1994, p. 350). She made a grid of the streets and the plazas and placed pictures of stores throughout the town map grid. Using TPR she introduced the vocabulary for getting around town and had the students stand up, turn to the right, turn to the left, go straight ahead, stop on the corner, cross the street, etc. Then she gave individual students a series of commands to carry out on the map. When they arrived at the appropriate store, they identified where they were and what they were going to buy. The students continued by instructing their peers how to get to a certain store. Peggy's journal entry reflects how this activity gave the students an experience that allowed them to understand the directions right and left and what a plaza really was. She said,

> I have found that this activity is great for the kinesthetic learners. They volunteer and want to participate...[During] this activity the others watch and comment if they [their peers] make a wrong turn. For whatever reason, [the Spanish words for] right and left are very hard to assimilate into their vocabulary.

Later the students wrote a series of commands on index cards for another student to choose and role-play on the town map. Peggy wrote similar cards and, as an evaluation, asked each student to select a card, read the commands, and carry them out. During the next activity the students wrote concrete poems about a store. They read a poem (see Figure 7) about *una zapatería* [a shoe store]. Several students then recited and role-played the poem.

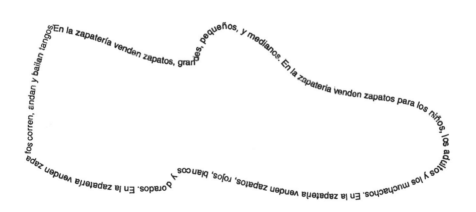

Figure 7. En la zapatería venden zapatos (Haas, 1996 p. 154).

Next, in preparation for writing a class poem, they created a web (Figure 8) about a *librería* on the board. Since many of the words were cognates they quickly assimilated the new vocabulary. Finally, they chose a store and wrote their own poems, first in pairs and then individually (see Figure 9).

Figure 8. Web of words for a poem about a bookstore.

Figure 9. Example of a concrete poem by Catalina Zegarelli.

Literature to Learn about Communities

During the next activity the students read a short passage about a small Chilean town called Melipilla. The passage was written by Angela Roa, a Spanish teacher at Bank Street School for Children in Manhattan. Through the eyes of a young girl named Rosita, Angela wrote about her experiences growing up in Melipilla. The students were already familiar with much of the vocabulary in the first paragraph that described the location of Melipilla. Peggy retold the beginning of the story several times to the students substituting vocabulary and verbs the students already knew. She also illustrated the story with magnetic board pictures of a river, mountains, a house, and people swimming in the river and used the chalkboard to illustrate words like *rodeado* [surrounded]. By the third recitation she used the exact words from the text and asked the students questions about the story.

After hearing it so many times, several students were already able to narrate the story in their own words, illustrating with the magnetic board pictures. Then, they read the first paragraph in *The Language of Folk Art Activity Book* and confirmed that Melipilla was 60 kilometers from Santiago toward the coast, surrounded by foothills, and near the Maípo River. Peggy repeated a similar sequence with each of the four paragraphs. In the second paragraph Angela wrote about Rosita's small house near *una panadería, una carnicería* and *una farmacia* [a bakery, a butcher shop, a pharmacy]. Next the readers learned what her family did on Sundays: going to church in the plaza, meeting friends and buying *maní* [peanuts] from the *manicero* or *barquillos* [wafer tubes with a cream filling], listening to the band, or browsing at the craft fair on the edge of the plaza. On Sundays, Rosita's parents bought delicious things to eat like *empanadas* [meat-filled turnovers] and her mother made *pastel de choclo* [corn pie]. In September there were rodeos on the farms around Melipilla where the *huasos* [cowboys] roped cows and in the afternoon the people danced the *cueca*. The passage ends with a description of what Rosita did on rainy days. The students enjoyed reading the story and retelling it in their own words, often embellishing the story with details about the weather or a description of Rosita.

Interviewing a Guest from Chile

Mari invited Angela to visit Peggy's Spanish class. The students prepared interview questions to ask the author. For the first question, Diego asked *¿Cómo se llama usted?* An interesting discussion ensued when Angela explained why her name was Angela Roa Pérez de Arce. The students knew that Pérez de Arce was her mother's name, but Angela explained that because *Pérez* was such a common last name the *de Arce* was added long ago to distinguish her family. The students found out the details of Angela's life including where she lives, what her apartment is like, how many brothers and sisters she has, and what her favorite color is. They also learned that her parents still live in Melipilla, eight kilometers from the town. When asked, *¿Cómo es Santiago?* she described Santiago for them as a large, sprawling city with lots of space and gardens. She added that it is five times as big as the city of Rome with four million people and now has lots of traffic. She said that it is special because it is surrounded by the Andes Mountains. When Cristina asked *¿Cómo es la ropa de Chile?*, Angela described the traditional clothing of *el huaso* [the cowboy], a small poncho, black pants, black boots, and spurs.

All the activities in the unit worked together to support each other. The students were able to build on their knowledge about Chile through the interview with Angela which also served to enrich their knowledge about communities in Chile and expand on the reading passage. The language-content-culture activities gave the students more of a context in which to place the additional knowledge they were learning about their keypals through the e-mail exchanges. A community of learners in Chile and New York was forming as the unit progressed. Although many students asked their interview questions with soft voices, they continued to raise their hands to ask yet another question. Some of the questions merited longer answers than others, but each student felt a sense of satisfaction when they asked a question of the classroom visitor and, in turn, received a response. The information they had been learning about Chile came to life for the students.

The Second Letters

When the second letters arrived (Figure 10), it seemed that the students had begun to form relationships. Questions were being answered, and more were posed. They shared information that was interesting to them and were excited to receive their letters. Some even consulted with Peggy during lunch or recess about their responses.

Date: Thu, 23 May 96 13:55:32
From: Alex Urrea <Coordinador@dsalas.plasca.plaza.cl>
To: Rena <poco@transit.nyser.net>
Subject: Respondiendo a Rena
Hola Rena resibi tu carta, veo que no sabes muy bien el idioma del castellano.
Me gusto mucho que escribieras, porque asi puedo conocerte un poco. Me pides
una foto de Luz, no la puedo mandar poque no tengo ninguna y tambien termine
con ella hace una semana porque ella se cambio de casa y no puedo comunicarme
con ella escepto llamarla por telefono. Lo siento mucho pero no podre mandartela
a lo mejor la mia. Me gustaria que me mandaras una foto tuya. Amiga cuentame
algo de tu vida en el colegio .
Se despide de ti y deseando que te vaya bien en todo lo que realices. Y que pronto
me escribas nuevamente.

Tu amigo Alex.

Date: Wed, 22 May 96 15:06:45
From: Eider Saez
To: Chema <poco@transit.nyser.net>
Subject: Respondiendo a Chema
Hola Amiga CHema Couniotes
Me alegre mucho cuando recibi tu mensaje, oye amiga o amigo aclárame cual es
tu sexo, Ahora te cuento de mi escuela:
Mi escuela es muy bonita. mi deporte favorito es futbol en octavo y sepimo
año tambien se aprende.frances e Ingles. mi materia favorita es matematica, la
musica favorita es treno choni. la hora que entramos a clases es 8.15 y salimos
a las 13.00 hrs, a veces salimos a la 1.30. Mi fruta favorita es la manzana y el
platano. Me despido deseando estes bien, en compania de los tuyos.
Tu amigo Eider.
Responde prontoooooooo

Figure 10. Samples of the second letters.

¡Hola Alex!

Recibí tu carta. Lo siento sobre Luz. En mi escuela entramos a las ocho y es grande. Hay muchas clases y materias son matematicas, estudias sociales, inglés, ciencias de la vida, banda, educación física, y español. Mi escuela es pública y ¿tu escuela? Mi escuela es de prekinder hasta el octavo. La escuela tiene cuatro deportes, volibol, fútbol, basquetbol con chicos y chicas y beisbol. Mi clase favorita es inglés porque es fácil y cómica y español es difícil y interesante. ¿Cual es su clase favorita? ¿Cambias los salones de clases? ¿Tiene la misma profesor para todas sus clases? Toco la flauta en la banda y en educacion física juego al beisbol. No me gusta matemáticas porque es aburrido. Hay noventa estudiantes en la escuela middle. Mi casa es mediana y tengo un patio mediano. Hay un parque cerca de la piscina. ¿Cual es su cuarto favorito en su casa?

Adios amigo, Rena

el 30 de mayo

Querido Karis,

Hola! ¿Cómo estás? Yo estoy así así. Gracias por tu carta. Es muy interesante. Te contaré sobre mi escuela.

Mi escuela se llama Pocantico Hills Central School. Es muy pequeña. Tiene un gimnasio grande, seiz canchas de tenis, dos piscinas, el campo de fútbol y beisbol. La cafetería de mi escuela tiene la comida terrible. Tiene cuatro pisos. Tiene muchos carteles y retratos en las paredes de la clase de arte.

Yo tomo siete clases. Estudios Sociales, Inglés, Español, Música, Ciencia, Matemáticas, y la clase de educación física. La clase de educación física es muy divertida. Juegan todos los deportes. Mi profesor de la clase de educación física es chevere. El es muy atlético.
Yo juego al beisbol ahora para mi escuela. Mi equipo es terrible.
Estamos 1-8.

Mis notas son buenas. Recibo muchos 90s. Yo estoy en la sociedad nacional de honor.

Escribe me por favor. Adios.

Figure 10 (cont'd.).

A Fieldtrip in the Community

The day to visit the Chilean bakery finally arrived. The students boarded the minibus for the short trip to town. Although Pocantico has a small percentage of Latino students, the majority of the students in Peggy's class did not know about the wonderful Chilean bakery located a mere five minutes from school. And, when Mari went to buy film at the store across the street, she found that the *bodega* was run by a family from the Dominican Republic. Besides being a valuable language learning and cultural experience as well as a culinary pleasure, the fieldtrip allowed the students and the teachers to learn more about their own multilingual community.

The students were greeted at the door of Los Andes Bakery by Fran cisco Mejías, who, with his wife Jessica, owns the store. Once everyone was inside, he pointed to his native city, Viña del Mar, on the map. The students understood him as he talked about the map and explained that Viña was located *cerca de Santiago* [near Santiago]. Then Francisco walked behind the glass case filled with goodies. He pointed to each pastry and told the students what they were called in Spanish: *merengues, pan de huevo* [egg bread rolls], *queque de frutas* [fruit cake], *pan dulce* [sweet rolls], *pastel* [cake], *empanadas de queso* [cheese turnovers], and *mantecados* [butter cookies sprinkled with powdered sugar]. He described the different breads displayed in baskets on the side of the case. Ready for the students to taste was a tray filled with warm *empanadas de queso.* Everyone was impressed by Francisco's warm welcome and generosity as he encouraged them to try an empanada saying, *sírvase.* Later, he took the group to the back of the bakery. He introduced them to the *panadero* [baker] and the *pastelero* [pastry chef] and pointed out the machines brought from Chile that are used to make the bread. The *pastelero* had trays of *repollos* [small round eclairs] for the students to dip into chocolate or brush with pineapple glaze. He explained and demonstrated the process. Then he asked for volunteers to whip the filling, *crema chantilly.* Diego wanted to try immediately. The filling was spooned into a pastry bag and several students helped fill the centers with cream. Of course, the best part was eating the delicious *repollos.*

As the visit came to an end, the students were able to buy pastries or bread to take home. They asked, *¿Cuánto vale?* [How much does it cost?], pointing to items in the case. Diego, who wanted to buy a baguette, said, *Quiero este pan largo* [I want this long bread]. Students left the store saying *gracias* to Francisco. The experience was rich and exciting in many ways. The students listened to native speakers from Chile as they explained familiar concepts on the map and unfamiliar concepts about baking. Everything, though, was in the context of a here-and-now situation, and thus they had little trouble understanding the language. They enjoyed the experience of tasting the foods of Chile, the *empanadas de queso* and the *repollos*. The expressions, *¡Es delicioso!* and *¡Qué rico!* now have real meaning for the students. Several have even returned with a parent to purchase items at the bakery.

Endings: Culminating Activity

The third letters arrived from Chile just as the school year was coming to a close (Figure 11). The letters described points of interest around their town and region. But before the Pocantico students could write their replies describing their towns, Elena sent a message requesting that they write the third letter in English. The Chilean students wanted to know about points of interest in the United States including the Statue of Liberty, Disneyworld, and the White House. The Pocantico students were more than happy to comply with their request. Additionally, Peggy sent off a package to Chile (to reciprocate for a similar package received from Elena) that included pictures of the students and the school, information about New York State, and realia from Pocantico Hills School. Now each group had a visual idea of who their keypals were and where they lived.

Date: Wed, 11 Jun 1996 18:55:16-0400 (EDT)
From: Karia Mellado <Coordinador@dsalas.plasca.plaza.cl>
To: Antonio <poco@transit.nyser.net>
Subject: Tercer Mensaje

Tercera carta 11-06-96

Hola Antonio
¿Cómo estas? recibi tu carta estaba muy linda.
Ahora te contare sobre mi pueblo. Mi pueblo mi ciudad es linda tiene bellas playas
y campos aqui en Temuco hay muchos lugares lindos donde yo vivo hay muy
linda vista hay unos estanques de agua y vivo en el cerro Conunhueno es super
lindo.
Quicro que me mandes una carta y me cuentes sobre disneyworld.

Se despide de ti
tu amiga Karis
        chaoo Antonio

Date: Wed, 11 Jun 1996 15:39:58
From: Eva Arias <Coordinador@dsalas.plasca.plaza.cl>
To: Marcos <poco@transit.nyser.net>

Tercer mensaje.
Temuco 11-06-96
Hola Marcos Scott
Espero que estes bien;
Bueno recibi tu carta y la encontre super buena aunque venían algunas palabras
que no las entendi para nada, pero se que pronto mejoraras tu Castellano;
Me han contado que el idioma castellano es el más dificíl ¿que puedes desir en
cuanto a esto? porque yo lo encuentro super fácil.
Tambien quiero contarte sobre mi país CHILE: es largo y angosto tiene mucha
flora y fauna pero a la vez tiene mucha contaminación. Bueno eso es todo por
hoy Chaooooooooooo...
tu amiga
Eva Arias de Chile

From: Pamela Salamanca <Coordinador@dsalas.plasca.plaza.cl>
To: Josue <poco@transit.nyser.net>
Subject: Tercer Mensaje

Figure 11. Samples of the third letters.

Tercera carta 4/06/96
Hola
Amigo Josúe
¿Cómo estás? espero que bien.
Ahora te contaré que las comidas Típicas son las siguientes: Las empanadas, lacazuela y el peure.
El presidente de la república de Chile se llama: Eduardo Frei. La flor nacional es el Copihue, la capital de Chile es Santiago. Sabes que el arbol tipíco de la novena región es la Araucaría. Da un fruto llamado Piñon.
Chile tiene aproximadamente 13.000 mil habitantes. Temuco es muy bonito y desde que llegue aquí a crecido bastante. Padre las Casas es una comuna y hay muchos proyectos. Nuestra fiesta nacional son los días 17, 18, 19 de Septiembre, hay mucyhas actividades un desfile, y se hacen ramadas donde sirven la comida tipíca y la chicha de manzana que es muy rica cuando esta recíen hecha.
Cuentame algunas cosas de acá como por ejemplp: que ubicacion tiene tu casa, que distancia hay de tu ciudad a la capital y porque E.E.U.U. esta dividido en Estados, cuentame si has ido a Disney Work conoces la Estatua de la Libertad.
Escribe pronto.
     Tu Amiga Pamela

Figure 11 (cont'd.). Samples of the third letters.

The culminating activity for the Chile unit was to create paper collage *arpilleras* about the students' own towns. In order to prepare the students for making the collages, Peggy explained the history of *arpilleras*. The Pocantico students thought about what scenes would show the Chilean students something about their lives in New York. They chose to illustrate their houses and favorite pastimes as well as the village streets. Each student decided on a theme and they began cutting shapes out of the multicolored papers from old wallpaper books. Ruth Weyland, the art teacher, came to the classroom and discussed making collages with the students. They explored the shapes, colors, and textures they had cut from the wallpaper. They considered the space in the picture and how to decide where to place the pieces. The students began experimenting with moving the shapes around the background. They used different-sized shapes to build a picture of a house or a tree or another image in their *arpillera*. They then glued the larger shapes to the background and later added the smaller details such as the stitches around the border (Figure 12). They depicted their lives with vibrant colors and pleasing shapes.

Figure 12. Example of student *arpillera.*

Although Peggy had assessed the students' progress throughout the unit, she and Mari wanted to find out the depth of their cultural knowledge at the end of the unit. They designed a series of questions in English for the students and also asked them to write a paragraph about Chile in Spanish. The questions and examples of student responses follow:

1. What are two interesting things you have learned from your keypal?
   They don't move from class to class, the teachers do.
   They wear uniforms to a public school.
   They have the same classes as we do.
   Chile has regions not states.
   They are very close to their family.

2a. What did you like best about the trip to the bakery?
   I learned that Chile has very good food.
   Eating the food.
   The food was good, and we talked in Spanish to them.
   Learning how people really do talk from Chile—fast.
   They showed us how to bake the stuff and they gave us samples.

b. How were you able to understand what Francisco and the pastry chef were telling you in Spanish?
   Because I learned a lot of Spanish in Spanish class and they pointed

to what they said.

By his hand movements and what he was holding.

It was easy to understand, but he needed to slow down.

When I recognized words he said I just put as many as I could together and tried to figure it out.

c. How is the bakery Los Andes similar or different from the bakery you usually go to?

There were no donuts and different cookies.

They both have cookies and breads.

They sell Spanish food.

They talk Spanish and they have Chilian pastries.

It is similar because they use cookies and chocolate.

3. How is Rosita's town of Melipilla similar or different from your town?

It is much smaller.

It is different because they have a small, small house and a river.

It is small just like my town.

They're not as wealthy.

It doesn't have many stores.

4. Describe how you decided what to show in your arpillera.

Out of my imagination.

My house and what I like to do.

The places I visit a lot.

I decided to show Main Street because it has a lot of historic stores.

I just put together a typical town.

5. Write a paragraph in Spanish about Chile. Include any information you learned about the geography, the flag, what small towns are like, information about your keypal, etc. Just try to get your message across in Spanish and don't worry too much about making perfect sentences.

A compilation of the students' responses

Chile está en la América del Sur o Sud América. Chile es largo y estrecho. Santiago es la capital. En Chile es muy differente de los Estados Unidos. Chile tiene muchos lagos en el sur. Chile tiene muchos rios como Itata, Bío Bío, y Maipo. Los montañas en Chile es grande y se llaman Los Andes. Los colores de la bandera son rojo, azul, y blanco. La estrella representa el honor y progreso en la nacion. Al oeste de Chile es el oceano Pacífico, al este es Argentina.

Mi keypal es Veronica.

The responses show that the students, indeed, did gain insights into the cultures of Chilean people. They learned about the country, the food, what schools and families are like, that many things are similar in their lives and other things are different. Some also reflected on their own culture as they decided what to depict in their *arpillera*. The paragraphs in Spanish were interesting because the students almost exclusively wrote about the geography of Chile or the flag. Maybe this is because these are the only topics (excluding the letters and poems) they actually wrote about during the unit. Or maybe they understood much of what their keypals wrote or what the Chileans they encountered said but need a more structured activity in order to write about those topics.

Peggy found that the unit reviewed some of the information in the regular textbook, expanded other information, and added a tremendous amount of new language. Students who were not as successful learning topics from the textbook chapters seemed to do better during this unit. Peggy also found that this way of teaching, where students interacted more with each other and she wasn't always the "sage on the stage," strengthened her bond with the students. She also seemed to be sharing more ideas with the other teachers. The time spent preparing the students with the language they might need to complete a task was worth the effort. Activities such as reviewing the language contained in the letters and listing common expressions, brainstorming and listing questions for letters and interviews, and webbing concepts all helped to make the resulting student work better.

The Chile unit proved to be exciting. The students were active participants in a variety of activities that integrated language content and culture. They learned many things about their own community and another community in Chile including the geography, history, what towns are like, the names of stores and what they sell, typical foods, and a traditional folk art. They used their language to respond to commands, write letters to Chilean students, talk to peers, write poems, listen to native speakers living in their own community, buy pastries, interview Chilean people, and describe their own towns. The students were engaged in reading and writing the letters. They were interested in perfecting their Spanish and acquired useful language in the process of reading their letters and writing responses. They loved the trip to the bakery and making the *arpilleras*. The value of including the community as an integral part of the language learning experience was very evident to Peggy during the fieldtrip. She realized how important it is for students to interact with native speakers. She noticed that the meaning of common phrases, that usually don't appear in textbooks, are understood in context, such as when Francisco continuously repeated *sírvase* to each student gesturing toward the tray of *empanadas*. It was exciting to hear students use their language to buy pastries and find out information.

For Peggy and Mari the collaboration was a learning and growing experience. Their reflection on the teaching process added depth to Peggy's teaching and allowed Mari to experience the reality of classrooms for several months since she has not been teaching young students for several years. It also gave Mari a chance to see theory in practice. Every activity during the unit seemed to take longer than planned. It was evident to Peggy and Mari how long it takes to really teach a unit in depth. Although there were many other activities planned for which there was no time, the unit was a rich and meaningful learning experience for the students. Peggy was thinking ahead to how she would change and expand the unit during the next school year. In fact, the first question that the students asked when they entered the Spanish classroom as new 8th graders this fall was, "Can we continue writing to our keypals in Chile?"

Many goals were realized during this project. The students learned about Chile through classroom activities that integrated language, content, and culture. They used their developing language skills as a tool to communicate with Chileans from their own community and those who live in Chile. Experiences in and out of the Spanish classroom allowed the students to work together in groups collecting and sharing information about Chile with their classmates, interview native speakers from Chile, savor the taste of a freshly baked *repollo* dipped in chocolate, learn facts and information about Chile in general and about a small town called Melipilla, and tell their peers in Chile about themselves as well as ask questions to find out all about them. Many communities were formed and others were fortified, communities of educators, communities of students, communities within local communities, communities in cyberspace. Because of the e-mail exchanges, the interviews, and interesting activities in the classroom, students were empowered to use their language for real purposes and the Standards goal number five, *Communities*, became an exciting reality for them.

Notes

[1]Peggy began by e-mailing Inés Alvarez (malvarez@taurus.apple.com), a Latin American contact she had made during her previous project. She explained the Chile unit to Inés and her desire to have students exchange information about themselves, their school and town, and their daily lives. Inés sent Peggy's name to Monica Campos (mcampos@enlaces.ufro.cl) who coordinates Chilean projects on the Internet. Monica asked Peggy questions concerning the ages of her students and their interests and put her in contact with Elena Herrera.

[2]The character-set problem resolved itself when Peggy forwarded the letters from the library computer (which was the e-mail address the students in Chile were using) to one in the computer lab, which has a distinct e-mail address, but an updated program that read all of the punctuation. In addition, during each class period, Peggy could only send two pairs of students to use the one computer in the library hooked-up to the Internet, and therefore it was taking a very long time to send the letters. Peggy was frustrated and concerned with the loss of class time. Terry worked out the problem by allowing the class to use the computer lab to input their letters, saving them to the student's directory on the school computer network, and sending the letters all at once to Chile.

[3]Los Andes Bakery, 180 Valley Street, Sleepy Hollow, NY 10591.

References

Belisle-Chatterjee, A., Fernándex, M., Martinex-Cruz, A., & Tibensky, L.A. (1990) *Viva el español*. Lincolnwood, IL: National Textbook Company.

Curtain, H., & Pesola, C. A. (1994). *Languages and children: Making the match* (2nd ed). NY: Longman.

Haas, M. (1996). *The Language of folk art: An Introductory Spanish course* NY:Addison-Wesley-Longman.

National Standards for Foreign Language Education Project. (1996). *Standards for foreign language learning: Preparing for the 21st century*. Yonkers, NY: Author.

Reardon, M. (1995). Traveling on the internet to South America. *Learning Languages 1* (1), 13–17.

Reflections on the Collaborative Projects: Two Perspectives, Two Professionals

Dale L. Lange

University of Minnesota

Joseph A. Wieczorek

Howard County Public Schools, Maryland

The culminating chapter of the 1997 *Reports* is a transcript of a videotaped discussion held between Dale L. Lange, University of Minnesota, and Joseph Wieczorek, Howard County Public Schools, Maryland. After having read drafts of Chapters 1–7 of this volume, Dr. Lange and Dr. Wieczorek met to explore together key themes and professional issues that emerged from the project descriptions presented in the chapters. Their discussion took place at Rosary College, Oak Park, Illinois,[1] and was moderated by Eileen W. Glisan, 1997 Northeast Conference Chair, and videotaped by June K. Phillips, 1997 *Reports* Editor.

Through the dialogue format of this final chapter, we engage a university professor and a high school language teacher in collaboration to discuss the nature of these projects in terms of the realities of the classroom and future directions of our profession. Specifically, their dialogue addresses the following questions:

- How do the projects relate to our national goal areas and standards?
- What is the role of culture and communication across the projects?
- How do the projects use interdisciplinary connections and the community to extend language use beyond the classroom?
- What is the role of collaboration and action research in the projects?
- What can we learn from the voices of students and teachers who participated in these projects?
- What are the implications of these projects for teacher preparation and ongoing professional development?
- What issues and questions arise from the projects and remain to be explored?
- What next steps does the profession need to take in order to address the standards?

The information and ideas presented in the dialogue between Drs. Lange and Wieczorek provide an excellent overview of the projects. While the two conversants often express similar opinions about some aspects of the projects, they also articulate different viewpoints based on their experiences in secondary vs. postsecondary settings. Their individual points of view clarify and raise critical issues that face the profession as we attempt to help learners progress toward the new standards. This interesting and informative conversation is sure to serve as an impetus to continue the dialogue about goals and standards with our colleagues, our professional community, and the public.

How Do These Projects Relate to Standards and Goals?

Joe: In one sense, I think that the Standards effort has brought out the complexity of professional development issues for teachers; but, it also argues for the need for collaboration among high schools, K–12, and postsecondary education. The Standards also indicate that we need to develop materials to make these Standards realizable, so that student learning can reflect the standards. The issues are how can we use the standards, and, how do we take them from theory to practice?

Dale: In addition to the need for collaboration, I think I see three other things in these projects: (1) the learning of culture; culture permeates every one of the projects; (2) the focus of the projects is on the learner; each of the projects seems to not focus on teaching so much as what the learners are doing as they and the teachers work together; (3) communication. It is the learning of language to communicate a message, to both receive as well as to tell. One of the interesting aspects of these projects for communication is that the story is so important; it's the telling of what the learner has to say in all these instances. So to summarize, in addition to collaboration, we have culture, focus on the learner, and communication that come through for me very clearly.

Joe: I think it's really clear that teachers have seen the Standards as something that they can use in the classroom; I believe they have been very positively received. Implications from the Standards are far reaching and they raise the question, What's a teacher going to do now?

Culture as an Issue

Eileen: You mentioned that culture is a recurring theme throughout the projects. Do you think culture is defined any differently in these projects than we have previously defined?

Dale: Well, I guess I'd say that the focus of the projects is always on the interaction of the learner with some aspect of culture. I would say that the projects stay away from the dichotomy of large "C" and small "c" culture. I think that is a plus because it's really culture that is important and the broad array of elements which it includes. So what I see students working with here are elements of culture that relate to everyday life more than anything else. Take the PACE Project for example (Adair-Hauck and Cumo-Johannsen); it is an approach to culture which includes literature, and yet I would argue that the PACE project and the strategies used can open the door to any aspect of culture, even though this project deals basically with oral and written text. It feels to me as though all the projects are working toward the same basic goal, which is culture undivided into traditional categories of large and small.

Joe: We have to be careful at the K–12 level about the kinds of culture we are actually going to represent. It seems that our constraints are from on high: from administrators and boards of education. They dictate the kinds of materials that are appropriate for the classroom. If we take a look at the Video Culture Project (Schwartz and Kavanaugh), the selection of that would be a no-no.

Eileen: Why would that be a no-no in your district?

Joe: My district takes a dim view of commercial films that are not rated for U.S. audiences. For example, in the middle section of *El Norte* there is some swearing on the bus going to Mexico. Administrators and parents see such activity as something that we are teaching the students. The video didn't look at any stereotypes or anything about peoples' lives, yet the kids were clearly affected by that video and by the kinds of things they saw in Central America. In defense of my school system, we also have to look at maturational constraints for grades K, 1, and 2. The culture we represent is significantly different from what is real so sometimes we are reduced to doing the trivial kinds of culture, the four Fs: festivals, folk tales, food, and fun. We have to carefully watch what we do. We know that we should be reflecting the target culture, but we don't; we often reflect American culture, whatever is in at the moment, whatever is politically acceptable at the moment.

Eileen: Well, certainly we have seen throughout the chapters that the K–12 researchers have said time and time again that they feel at a disadvantage because they have no culture curriculum per se. The result is that they tend not to know what to do with culture. And, of course, they have mentioned the difficulty of being able to use the texts and kinds of cultural materials they think most appropriate.

Joe: Yes. And whose culture is it anyway? The burning question for us at K–12 is where do we find, where do we get, and how do we use cultural material in the classroom? I think the Materials Development Project (Lorenz and Verdaguer) clearly brought that out that we have to spend time in dialog with teachers indicating that certain materials, those that I have for example, could be used by others as well.

Dale: Well, I think you're right, Joe, the materials project with its scope and sequences is at least a place to start. For example, I would take the theme, "family," to determine how, through revisiting the theme from time to time in the curriculum, the learners' concept of the extended family in Hispanic culture could be spiraled, how it is different from that of Anglo culture. I think that we need to prepare people—administrators, language teachers, others teachers, and parents—to understand that in language programs we are going to approach culture from a different perspective and that it's OK for students to understand different perspectives. We are not asking learners to accept or adopt another culture; we are only asking for understanding. This idea is one of the important contributions of the Standards, not only in terms of the comparison of cultures, but in the comparison of languages as well.

Joe: The Standards are visionary, I agree, but the fact that I feel we must reflect only American culture is something that I cannot change. Family is a typical unit in a K–12 sequence where we cannot ask questions about the kids' families ... that's not something we can do, although we know that non-typical family units exist, but we could say in the Hispanic culture, this is a typical x or y or z, and these rules are changing. We have to be very careful ... there is no academic freedom with us [in public schools], we cannot say I want to teach about this or that ...

Eileen: Well, as Dale has suggested, can parents be convinced, can school boards be convinced?

Joe: If the parents are convinced, the school boards will be convinced. I think it has to begin with that order. Yet, I think that community sensitivities may not allow us to work with the culture standards. If the community is viewed positively, then we start with the parents saying that the classroom is a community of learners, and that the Standards provide us with direction for what is to be accomplished with culture in the classroom. That is our vision. But again, it's not solely ours to say from the classroom; the four walls are a little constraining in that way.

Dale: Well, I think that the people in postsecondary education need to understand what you are saying. We have a tendency to say, because we have all kinds of academic freedom, "just go ahead and teach what you want to teach."

Collaboration as a Key: Issues and Problems

Eileen: Can collaboration play a role in solving this problem?

Joe: Absolutely. I think the Video Culture Project clearly demonstrated that, as a result of the postsecondary teacher coming into the school classroom and observing, bonding took place between the postsecondary teacher and the students. This teacher understood the constraints at the pre-university level. The project is a success because of collaboration; we probably need to do more of that; but once it is done, the question is, "now what?" We need to research the collaboration. From my perspective at the high school, we look at research as something done by the "other." It is not something that we do, that we have control over, or that we have interest in.

Dale: I think it is important for postsecondary and K–12 teachers and researchers to work together. In these projects, collaboration has demonstrated that the two levels can work together for success. On the other hand, I think it's also necessary to recognize limits for the postsecondary level as well. The close collaboration of these projects is something that cannot continue indefinitely. That is not to say that collaboration cannot continue at all, but it does suggest that collaboration has to take a different form. For example, with these projects, because an interest level has been built up, an informal, continuing mentorship is one way that collaboration could continue. Yet collaboration is necessary to grapple with larger issues such as articulation between K–12 and postsecondary where we can work both formally and informally together. One of the major issues in these projects is that of articulation or a practical understanding of the curriculum, instruction, and assessment of learners so that they can pass smoothly from one educational level to another. How do we talk to each other about such issues? What are the ways that collaboration on important matters such as articulation can be ongoing?

Joe: And the seeds were planted here! It's clear from these projects that the seeds were already planted ...

Dale: Yes, exactly.

Eileen: But isn't it challenging for a K–12 teacher to engage in collaboration, given the demands put upon them during the day?

Joe: Absolutely. One of the levels of hierarchy that we have to go through is getting permission from our immediate supervisor, the building supervisor, somebody in the central office. That's just to plant the idea of somebody's coming in! If a researcher is going to work with students in my district, we have to go through another level; we have to have a plan written out and have it approved. There is a question of energy and time here. Many of the projects brought out the fact that research takes time and energy; probably for us, the biggest issue is budget. Is there a budget for buying materials? Is there time for creating materials? Typically in a day, we have five or six classes, 130 students per day, and all other assigned duties: bathroom, lunch, and cafeteria duty. Those are constraints that take our energy away from the classroom.

Dale: And those are important constraints. I think that postsecondary faculty do not understand those constraints. But, there are constraints on our side as well if we are going to do research in schools: permissions of all kinds (human subjects committees, our own departments as to how the project fits our loads, as well as permissions from schools). Yet, these projects show that the importance of collaboration between these educational levels is just terribly important in creating an atmosphere in which the standards can work. This collaboration leads to the issue of articulation between K–12 and postsecondary levels. How do we bridge the expectations of both levels? How do we make expectations seamless between levels so that students are benefited in the process?

Joe: There is another point as well. It is clear in these case studies that teachers were re-energized. It happened in every single instance. I want to be involved and re-energized because a happy teacher makes a happy learner, and a happy learner means more enrollments. We want kids to go on; we want them to learn and love language, to be involved in the global community. So if we are re-energized by these collaborations, then they are successful; these case studies were clearly successful.

Eileen: Now we could see that it wasn't always easy for the K–12 teacher to accept a postsecondary person in the classroom, that there were lots of concerns, and it wasn't always easy for the postsecondary researcher to go in and deal with the demands of today's students so …

Dale: Yes, throughout these projects, negotiation and understanding took place about each other's assumptions. That is a key to further collaboration and future work on the standards. It sets the scene for the work that is yet to come, and we have a lot of work to do.

Eileen: We certainly do.

Joe: And look at how the students reacted; they were so positive; they could have written the standards themselves. They intuited the standards as they reflected back: this is what we are doing; this is why we are doing it. They prove that these standards are workable in the classroom. And, the standards are very usable, very user friendly.

Communication: Another Goal Area

Eileen: Let's come back to another goal area. Talk about how communication is manifested in each of the projects. As people look at the standards, particularly, the goal area of communication, we are hearing the comment, "Yes, I already do that in my classes." My question to you is: "Was there anything novel about the way in which communication came through in the projects that would perhaps give us a different view of communication as it's addressed in the standards framework?"

Joe: Certainly, the example of whole language. The whole language example (Adair-Hauck and Cumo-Johannsen) demonstrated that it isn't that "grammar is the be all and end all," as well as the opposite "they'll intuit it someday"; it provided a guided approach, gave language learning another view, which can inspire both teacher and learner.

Dale: I guess I would come at your question with a slightly different perspective. In these projects, it appeared that learners were given the freedom, opportunity, and the expectation that they were going to communicate. Consequently, in the whole language project, learners are able to retell stories after working though them. In the Austin, Texas, project (Moore and English), learners see that they can not only use the language, but after having been given some models, they can adapt and use the language for their own purposes. Through E-mail in the communities project (Haas and Reardon), learners were receiving language which wasn't much different from that which they were creating. So, in these projects, we are seeing a focus and an expectation that communication can really take place. In these projects, we can see that communication is important to students at a relatively low level of proficiency. The next question is: how do we continue developing communication into more advanced language competency and broaden it? Our curricula in foreign languages have a tendency to be convergent rather than divergent. We need to continue to develop this competency to communicate so that learners can take the initial experience and run with it, so they can communicate their stories to others.

Joe: We rarely think of lower-level language as extended and authentic discourse. We don't even use those terms. We tend to think of the notion of language for communication as an upper-level concern; something that learners get later on. That is certainly true with the non-traditional learners; they communicated and they liked language.

Communities

Eileen: We've certainly seen communication as a means to open students' minds to learning about another culture and connecting with the community, which brings us to the question of communities. This is another goal area that we have seen included across the chapters. Can you talk about some ways in which the community goal was addressed in these projects, despite the fact that students were not in the target language culture per se?

Joe: When I first read the community standard, I thought, "I don't live in East LA; I don't have that global community I can bring my kids to and say, 'All right, speak.'" I don't have a bakery, for example. The E-mail project (Haas and Reardon) brought the real world to the classroom. And, it certainly brought the students to see their peers in another country; they were communicating; it was for personal enjoyment. This project did bring that global community home to them. The whole situation was instantaneous; there were immediate responses, and bonding took place. One of the major things we need to do in the classroom is give students enough language to go out there and use it with another group of people, native speakers, I mean. The students saw their peers responding in Spanish with extended discourse. We think of activities, and that's it ... sort of discrete-point examples, discrete-point activities, or exercises. This project was a nice way of showing that this community comes out of the very place where I live.

Dale: Joe, I like what you said and I think you've hit on two of the three communities that are demonstrated in that particular project: the Internet community with Chile and the classroom students, and the local community as well. There is a third community, namely the classroom. It is a community that is also important to consider and develop. Communication can take place right within the classroom because it can be considered a culture and a community of its own.

Joe: Yes, we teach language; we don't teach about language. As from the cultures video project, one of the students said, "culture is life." And so is language by the way. And so is literature, all the things that the PACE project is … language is what we do.

Connections

Eileen: If we think about culture and connecting with other disciplines, we've also seen a lot of connections made from one chapter to the next. One of the ideas that has grown out of these projects is that we don't necessarily have to connect with a music teacher to have connections to other disciplines. Can you comment on that idea of making connections with other disciplines?

Joe: When I hear "interdisciplinary" approach, I think I have to do it all … clearly I don't. I need to find people and resources, but I don't need to be an expert in every area. I mean, do I need to be a singer to teach music? No! But other subject areas work on different issues; they work on multiple intelligences (Gardner, 1983; Gardner, 1993); they stimulate the right brain. They have a very positive effect on the classroom.

Dale: I would say that an overlooked connection in terms of interdisciplinarity is the student. The interests that student have can serve as a means of bringing other disciplines into the classroom. Thus, we don't have to go to the music teacher and say, "Have you got time for us to sit down and talk about bringing music into the foreign language classroom?" It is the interest of students we can draw on to help us create the interdisciplinary classroom that we otherwise do not have time to formulate.

Joe: Absolutely. I think the main point here is that we do not have the time, energy, or materials for interdisciplinary programs. In interdisciplinary programs, science and math go together, and English and social studies or history go together; we in foreign language are the fluff. Foreign language is often left out of any of those groups. Yet, the materials project

(Lorenz and Verdaguer), in a collaborative fashion showed that we can build an interdisciplinary approach with knowledgeable people and with community resources. We can look at foreign languages as part of the whole, and the whole would be greater than the parts themselves.

Dale: And, again I would say the student as a source of interdisciplinarity is a theme that emerges from these chapters as well. It is in the co-construction of language that students and teachers find the resources. Student interest becomes a source of materials to which the teacher adds knowledge of language, text, and other information that helps prepare the student for what s/he wants to do with these resources. I am simply saying here that the student is an overlooked resource in creating materials and connections to other disciplines.

Joe: I think this very point was brought out in the project with minority students. With their interests, they became the teacher-learner. For example, I know the kids like basketball, and I know some people who play basketball. If I bring this knowledge into the classroom, it will bring the students back saying, "OK, this is my little community, this is how French or Spanish or whatever language is going to relate to my life."

Eileen: So you're saying that there are connections that perhaps we don't bother with that are right here in our classrooms!

Joe: Yes, but for whatever reason, we ignore them. We just don't know who the students are. But the language is for them and they're our greatest resource. It sound a little hackneyed, but they're our future; they're the ones that are going to be speaking the language; they're the reason we do what we do.

Student Voices

Eileen: Well, you've both brought up the importance of the student, attention to the student. What did we learn through the voices we heard in each chapter? What did we learn from the students? What were some interesting ideas that you thought came forward?

Joe: Once again, in the cultures video project (Schwartz and Kavanaugh) a student pronounced that "culture is life." I found that astounding. I thought that this student is going to be a researcher in the future. Further, they felt the impact of the standards. The case studies positively influenced them. What I am assuming or hoping will happen is that these kids are going to use their language in meaningful contexts and will continue their study, not only in the K–12 sequence, but again in postsecondary education.

Dale: I think that the honesty of the voices is really refreshing. I think that anybody reading these chapters will have to reflect on their practice and how to include students. Students really want to take the lead in their own learning. So honesty about materials, activities are something that I heard specifically. In one of the projects, I remember students came away very clearly stating that worksheets were boring and something that they did not want to do. However, the activities where they had the opportunity to use language were really what they grabbed on to and what they thought were fun.

Eileen: So there were things that we heard from students that perhaps we didn't really want to hear, but we heard them.

Joe: Or that we did want to hear: that they did like language. We often don't hear that; we don't get that kind of feedback; we don't solicit it. I guess it's our fault. We don't carry out that kind of research in the classroom typically; we don't solicit their responses; we think we know better. Again, it's sort of top-down teaching; the curriculum is set for us; we teach it; students learn it; and, that's it; this is the way things are. We get entrenched in that process. I guess the standards allow us to breathe some life into what we do and why we do it. And, so the student voices are important in reporting our effectiveness.

Eileen: Did we learn anything about teaching all students, because of course that's another big issue we're dealing with today.

Joe: Absolutely. We go back and forth on this issue of whether all students can learn or not. The inclusion issue is a big one. In the project with minority students (Moore and English), there was a process from which all students could learn; everybody could bond; and, it could be a successful and inclusive language experience.

Dale: Including the teacher learning from the students on how to teach. Again, I refer to the honesty and directness of the voices. If only we listen and reflect on them, I think that we can learn a lot. These projects certainly provide us examples of the voices we need to listen to.

Action Research

Eileen: One of the key elements of the project design was the action research component. Joe, as a classroom teacher, what does the term action research mean to you?

Joe: For us, it generally means something that's done to us or to our students without any form of dialogue. We don't see ourselves as part of action research at all. About research in general, I would say, in fact, we neither accept nor reject the tenets of research; we're simply not involved. The video culture project (Schwartz and Kavanaugh) certainly brought out the fact that the teacher was also an action researcher. I think that's a direction we need to explore, change our minds about, but currently that's not our professional duty.

Eileen: Do you think that on a daily basis we do research, even if it isn't ...

Joe: Absolutely. The minute I think about something I've done, reflect on it (Did this work? Didn't it? What will I try next time?), and modify or change something in a classroom, I'm doing action research in a small way. What I'm doing is participating in professional development, but as teachers we don't see that as part of what we do.

Dale: I think you have hit on two major aspects of action research: reflection and action. This discussion makes me think about a fairly well-known Brazilian educator, Paolo Freire. He talks about this kind of research when a teacher is interacting with students, reflecting on what is taking place, and acting on the reflection (Freire, 1973; and, Freire and Faundez, 1989). The teacher is actually applying what s/he knows to the situation; the action upon the reflection takes into consideration what is known and what is understood of the situation. Together, the action and the reflection indicate that a teacher is actually doing research and applying that research as teaching is taking place. Such action research is qualitative research; these projects are reflective of an ethnographic approach to research. Action research strives to understand what is taking place; it avoids predicting answers as in a quantitative orientation. What I would like to see more of in these projects is the really deep and full description that we need in order to understand what students are doing in language learning. In addition, we need to involve students as much as possible in providing this description. It will help us formulate better questions about the process. The two kinds of research— qualitative and quantitative—provide answers to two different kinds of questions. Quantitative research is convergent, wanting to know a particular answer to a particular question. In many cases we can already predict the answer to the question, but we need to verify it. Qualitative research is divergent, thereby examining the complexity of what it taking place in the classroom, providing us with the opportunity to formulate questions that we might not otherwise ask. We need both kinds of research; they are complementary, not competitive.

Joe: They also show the role of collaboration between the typical researcher and the action researcher in the classroom, something that needs to continue. And that collaboration is something that teachers need to be involved in.

Eileen: Is the type of action research that was carried out in the projects something that is valued at the postsecondary level?

Dale: Well, I think that depends on a particular institution as well as the moment. Twenty years ago in my own institution, a qualitative approach to research was certainly not respected. But today, I think graduate students are doing research with both quantitative and qualitative research; in fact, we're really talking about two kinds of research already mentioned that are really complementary. So, I think the situation is much more open and the world of research is richer and more open. That's a change for the better.

Assessment of Language for Communication

Eileen: That is probably true. But let me change the topic for the moment. These projects are more or less snapshots in time. We know something more about the standards from them than we did previously; yet, we certainly don't know everything. What are some additional questions or additional details that you would have liked to have known as you read about these projects?

Dale: Well I think one of the issues which is not necessarily addressed very well, although it wasn't the purpose of the projects, is assessment. As we move forward with the standards, assessment is obviously going to have to change. The standards direct our attention to communication and using language for a purpose. Therefore, the kinds of measures that we have been using for reading and listening, in particular standardized tests, are going to have to change. If the language of the standards prevails, the focus of assessment should probably be on the uses of language for interpersonal communication, interpretation of oral and visual messages, and presentation of knowledge and information. In this regard, standardized tests are not necessarily going to work very well. So, what kinds of assessments are we going to have to create? This is an area for lots of exploration. And this exploration should not only reflect the standards, but also curriculum and classroom instruction. In this regard, we might look toward authentic assessment as one of the keys to resolve the tension between a shift in the national standards toward more communicative outcomes and traditional measurement assumptions about the assessment of those outcomes.

Joe: From my viewpoint in K–12, there is always the question of who's going to be responsible for the assessment and what happens if the assessment isn't successful. Assessment can show what you've done is or is not good. Will that mean a termination of employment? Will that mean some sort of reprimand? I think that is one of our fears. Whose responsibility is this assessment? And, what does it mean? And then even beyond, where will I get the tools so that I can create the assessment activities?

Dale: I think Joe has a good point. The issue of assessment is one thing for the classroom. It's another matter when thinking about a national assessment. The national standards suggest national assessment. The ways in which we currently assess learning on a national basis is through standardized tests. First of all, how should teachers assess for the standards in classroom to give students feedback on how well they are working with the standards? However, then the next issue is how do we get corporations that prepare national tests to look at this issue as well. National tests and classroom tests have to have things in common so that the purposes for testing are similar on both levels. Currently, the tension between the two gives value to the standardized test. And, of course the tension is caused by the need for standardized tests to be legally defensible. The whole area of assessment is one that needs to have a lot of discussion as we work with the standards.

Joe: Another unanswered question is, what's our long-term commitment to the national standards? What's it going to cost me to work with the national standards in terms of energy and time? Where will I be in twenty years? If we are looking at a snapshot of these projects, I want to see the video, the entire thing. Where are we going to be? Is there going to be another paradigm shift in twenty years? Are we going to say, I can't do this; it takes too much time, too much energy? The standards are voluntary, anyway, are they not? Are they really? If the standards make as much sense as these case studies, if they make as much sense to us intuitively, are they really voluntary? So, what are we going to decide? What are we going to do with all this information, now that we've got it? Where are we going to go?

Dale: I think Joe's questions are indicative of how we have been prepared to think about these issues. National standards are not something that is part of the educational culture. School districts are organized locally; we don't think on a national level. So you are asking a crucial question. You want to know, what is the long-term picture with the standards? They make intuitive sense, but will they be accepted? And that's the question we all want to have answered, and right now. But the answer is not available to us.

Joe: In terms of research, Galloway (1995) makes a point again and again. We work following trends all the time. Is this going to be another trend? We hope not. We hope this is a vision toward which we work so that we'll have a research paradigm, a vision, and a style to what we do; we'll have an end point.

Learning Materials and Instruction

Eileen: Well, certainly textbook publishers are asking the question: "What is the future of textbooks?" especially if we consider projects like those we have just discussed. Where are we going from here with respect to textbooks?

Joe: Often we look at textbooks as the synonym to curriculum, which also drives methodology. We sort of have the whole neat package all done for us. We expect a lot of publishers to provide us with every single bit of materials. We don't buy a textbook now; we buy the textbook package (CD-ROM, cassette tapes, video, learning materials, black line masters, substitute plans). We want the publishers to provide everything. We could simply continue to accept the materials as prepared, saying that they validate what we do; they are for student learning. Or maybe we should say, let us be involved in creating the materials. The materials development project case study (Lorenz and Verdaguer) brought out the possibility of university level and K–12 people collaborating in materials development. In that context, we would be involved in materials development. We could say to publishers what we need because we know what we need; we know we like it; and, we know it will work in K–12.

Eileen: Well, what's interesting to note is that none of the projects used a textbook per se, right?

Dale: Right! I think a couple of things are happening here. First, as a result of action research, teachers are focusing more on what students are doing. And second, as a result of focusing on the student, teaching is changing from an almost total acceptance of method to more of an understanding of the metaphors of "student as learner" and "teacher as coach." I am not saying that materials and concern about instructional approaches are irrelevant, but I am saying that the direction of instruction is changing from a prescriptive application of instructional method to an understanding of how students learn. Howard Gardner's (1993) work on multiple intelligences (MIs) is one approach to learning, including for the development of learning materials. Such an approach focuses directly on the learner. Some students are more oriented toward expressing themselves not only verbally and linguistically, but also bodily, artistically, and musically. For some learners, movement is an important part of learning.

Teachers who have used Total Physical Response know the importance of movement. But how can we get teachers to use other multiple intelligences with materials?

Joe: It's like nailing jelly to a tree sometimes, in teaching and educational materials development.

Dale: I love that metaphor!

Joe: That's the way I look at it. We're trying to nail one little thing. But where is everything else? Where do the multiple intelligences fit in? Are we stimulating the right brain (Waldspurger, 1995)? Are we going to use music? To know how teachers use music in the classroom might actually help in materials development.

Dale: It's not that teachers use multiple intelligences as a method. The real issue here is that teachers help students, coach students, to use their own capacities. The perspective of this kind of teaching is not, "I'll tell you how to learn a language," but rather, "let me work with you so that you can develop your own learning of a language." That's a very different way; that's coaching.

Joe: And publishers can take on the role of coach by providing materials that are appropriate, accessible, and affordable, the three As of materials. But again, they should reflect what we are feeling as a profession. The standards are one way of anchoring us into saying what we know and want. We've got to say what we want. It's got to be a bottom-up instead of a top-down feeling that the textbook is made for us by people who understand what we want. We want to be heard in the area of materials development.

Eileen: Do you think there's a danger just as with proficiency that materials and textbooks will come out labeled as "standards driven textbooks?"

Dale: Sure. It's the nature of the capitalistic society that people want to make a return on their investment. I think it is wrong to label a textbook as a "National Standards Oriented" textbook simply to get people to buy it. But that will surely be done, no question. However, the thinking behind the development of the national standards is much richer and deeper than any of us really understand. And, if you sit down with the standards and think about them seriously and open-mindedly, they lead us far beyond our current thinking. If I were in a language classroom today, I know it would be very difficult for me to say that my students had risen to the case and were mastering the standards.

Joe: We've now mastered the standards!!!

Dale: Right.

Joe: There is also the danger in having publishers produce materials that are couched in terms of reflecting a vision for the 21st century, whatever the standards. Such materials will become prescriptive; there will be one method, one way of "doing it"; our repertoire will not expand. I hope we're not going to say, "this is it; we've arrived; this is what I do; and, this is the only thing that I'll do." Rather, we need to keep the dialogue open among us all in order to say, "I did it in this way; this is why; how can it change?; how can I learn to add to my teaching and the learning and learning styles of my students?"

Dale: Joe has a very important point here. The whole issue of method isn't relevant any more. Instead, we want to examine what are the ways teachers work with learners to reach a goal. It's not a set of prescribed activities; it's not a linear approach to teaching language. There are multiple approaches for multiple learners in the classroom. For example, I think there is a role for audiolingual activities, very narrowly prescribed. And, there is also a role for very wide, very unstructured open activities so that the learner can create with what s/he knows. In this context, we don't need to talk about method; we need to understand the goal, the objectives to be reached, and the help that learners need to reach the objectives and the goal. Ted Higgs has a wonderful phrase that he has used on this subject, namely that the "search for the Holy Grail" is over (Higgs, 1984). Rather, we need to ask the following questions: What are the goals and objectives for *learners*? How do we get them there?

Role of the Teacher

Eileen: I guess that brings us to the important role of the teacher in addressing the standards. Do you think that we're looking at a different kind of preservice teacher preparation to address the standards for the 21st century?

Joe: Yes, I think that before they go into teaching, teachers need to change their mind set. I think preservice programs should focus somewhat on what language learning is and not just giving a method. When I hear about standards, I want to teach to that vision. I don't say, simply give me the method or give me a standards and I'll teach the same way until 2025 when I retire. That's something we have to change. The recursive nature of the standards requires us to spiral, rewrite, and revise as we find out more about our new generation of learners. Will they be more savvy? If indeed they start with a K–12 program and then go on in college, will they be more knowledgeable about what's going on? Will they react differently to the standards than they have in the past? I think we can work with preservice programs, saying that we will work together with you, eliminating the we–they mentality. As a result, we will accept the teachers that postsecondary education sends us; we'll work with everybody so that preservice education will always have constant contact among the different members.

Teacher Development (Pre- and InService)

Eileen: In other words, you are suggesting that the responsibility of preparing teachers will not only be on the shoulders of postsecondary faculty, but also the responsibility of inservice teachers.

Joe: It's our responsibility as K–12 educators to be involved in creating future educators. We can't simply say to those who want to become language majors, what are you going to do with a foreign language? We need to say to them, "We want you to teach! We want you to be a part of who we are!" Inservicing will say, "Here is a standard; let's look at it! What's worked? What hasn't? What knowledge can we share in activities, assessments, and materials that help the learner?" Then the body of knowledge will grow from the bottom up.

Eileen: Let me be real specific and put you on the spot. What kinds of skills will tomorrow's teachers need that they perhaps don't have now to do the job we've been talking about?

Joe: Not only the know-how to deliver instruction, but language ability, as well as a variety of techniques to make sure that the five goals and the eleven standards are met. And, are there goals we haven't thought about? Are there other standards that might be appropriate? So that's one level. Another focus is, can they deliver instruction effectively so that students will feel they are learning? Teachers should feel comfortable within themselves to handle a variety of levels, level one through advanced levels of education. This focus isn't on the teacher per se, but rather on the student. What do teachers know about themselves to say, this instruction is for you? You are the one who's going to be speaking the language, it's not for me. All in all, we need to have competence.

Dale: I think Joe has offered some very good points. I guess I'd like to add a couple of things to them. First, you are talking about the importance of teachers knowing the language and culture. Yet, we do not have any real standards for that. Some of the postsecondary teacher preparation programs have focused on language to some degree. But, with the standards, I think we are moving beyond where we currently are in teacher education. In addition to knowing the language and the culture, it is important to know what to do with students. Notice I didn't say *to* or *for* students, I said *with* students. So teaching is not only working with linguistic principles and cultural knowledge, but also with educational principles. Too often, we have allowed the science of linguistics to get in our way in understanding how we help students learn. I've talked a lot about teaching, knowing, and understanding the metaphors they use. There's more than one! Take narrative as one perspective on teaching. Storytelling is one way in which we incorporate what we know, negotiate meaning, and understand from the narratives of others (See Bruner, 1990; Egan, 1988). The student as learner is another metaphor (See Hall and Davis, 1995) we've talked about. And the learning of foreign languages as multiculturalism (Tedick, Walker, Lange, Paige, and Jorstad, 1993) should be included, not only because we are a multicultural society, but every society whose language we study is multicultural. All you have to do is look at the recent history of France, Germany, or Spain to see that influxes of different peoples affect the nature of culture. And, the metaphor of multiculturalism is another way we can get teachers to think about how they help students learn.

Joe: Look at the metaphors we use for teaching: sage on the stage; guide on the side, etc. We're part of the metaphors which sound like positioning in the classroom. Well, maybe part of preservicing is helping teachers define their role and helping us move toward creating a generation of teachers who are willing to renew constantly rather than say this is what we are only going to do for the next five years. I also think that we move from this to that, from extreme to extreme, or at least we move and we fix. It's sort of a fossilization, not with students, but with teacher education.

Dale: That's interesting, we move and we fix. Why don't we think about moving and incorporating so those are constant. Change is constant in language and in culture. So why isn't change constant in teaching? Change means that we can set aside some things that don't work anymore ... and also, our students are constantly changing. We can't use the same assumptions about students today that we did five or ten years ago. We need to meet students where they are.

Joe: I think that the fixation is problematic. If we say, I've done that standard, we really don't know that to be the case. We have to be like the lava lamps of the '60s; we just keep changing and never being quite the same ever ...

Eileen: Well, I think if we think about the action research projects we'll probably all agree that in order to do these kinds of things in today's classrooms, teachers have to have a high level of linguistic ability and cultural understanding. What do we do about the widespread problem of teachers coming from four- or five-year programs at the intermediate-mid level of proficiency, if they're lucky. For example, neither their speaking or cultural awareness is assessed in any way. There are teachers being prepared in these programs who have not had the opportunity to study abroad. They haven't experienced the culture at all first hand. To me, this is a plaguing problem for the profession. What do we do about that, what can we do to fix that problem?

Dale: I don't think there is any one simple way to address that issue. Individual professorial and program responsibility is one way by which the problem can be addressed. Another is to work through our own professional organizations. AATF, AATG, AATSP, and ACTFL are organizations which should create and agree on teacher education standards. I think it's also important to work with the National Council for the Accreditation of Teacher Education (NCATE). I happen to be a member of the NCATE Board of Examiners. As a result of being on accreditation teams, I know the importance of a visit to an institution and what a visit can generate once the visit has taken place. There are always matters to be worked for the next visit. It's pressure of both an individual and organizational nature that gives impetus to work on continuous improvement. I don't think that teacher education programs can afford to recommend licensure to anyone who cannot perform at the advanced level of the ACTFL Proficiency Guidelines (1986) in speaking. Intermediate-mid is simply not usable any longer. I think it's important that we hold to a standard like advanced. In addition, not only does one have to be proficient in the language and have cultural understanding, one has to have enough experience with teaching and working with kids prior to initial licensure. Joe's statement a little while ago, about the importance of K–12 people working with teacher education, presents a moral responsibility. In collaborations, such as with professional development schools (e.g., the Austin school in Moore and English) where K–12 and postsecondary teacher education work together, the work is extremely difficult. However, the end result is worth every trial and tribulation. You see student teachers not only capable of using the language in the classroom, being culturally aware, and working with learners in these broad areas, but they also understand learners. Their understanding of learners happens because they have sufficient experience, almost a whole year of clinical experiences before they finish their program and are recommended for initial licensure (Lange, 1990).

Joe: I think in the K–12 level, we need a higher degree of commitment to mentoring. Often, we don't share materials; we don't have dialogue with each other, even within the same system, within the same building. I think we hurt ourselves when teachers come from teacher education programs and they *are* prepared. In a typical K–12 sequence, teachers have to handle multilevel classes: German 2, 3, and 4 or Spanish 3 and 4 or Spanish 4 and 5. I have a colleague who is doing Italian 1 and Spanish

5. Imagine the kinds of resources he needs linguistically in both languages.

Eileen: That's amazing. Two different languages ...

Joe: Two different languages in one classroom at the same time.

Eileen: Because after all, there ...

Joe: It's language. I think we've got to do our own promotion, even within our own buildings with administrators, the people who can say, "let me help you; let me help you by sending you to another school to visit, to a university; let me support you by sending you to the Northeast Conference." We don't ask for those things. We never say that. We say, watch each other in the classroom. Our mentality is not let's go back to college. My response is, Where do you think we got our education?

Eileen: And, I think with the whole mentoring issue comes the idea of collaboration. This issue takes us back into the chapters. For example, if you think about the culture video project (Schwartz and Kavanaugh), we had a clear case of true collaboration because the two partners actually team taught. I think that ties in very will with the ongoing professional development project. There was certainly a lot of collaboration taking place with the inservice teachers involved in that project.

Joe: I took away from that article the sense that a process was involved. The curriculum wasn't set, and the process was centered around creating: creation, creator, created. I got the feeling of wanting to do this project again and again so that we make sure something happens in the classroom. We also need to back to the universities and say teach us more, give us more, and how can we work together better?

Eileen: Well, I think it's a two-way street. If you recall from the voices of the postsecondary partners in the project, they learned just as much as the K–12 researchers. So, I think there is a lot to be gained in professional development on both sides. Then, the question arises: What implications or what ideas do we have regarding the ongoing professional development of inservice teachers as we work with them in addressing the standards framework?

Dale: Well, as we address the framework of standards with inservice teachers in the reform of K–12 education, there is one direction, not the only one, which is the continual development of language capacity. The National Board for Professional Teaching Standards is looking toward the competency of teachers in their teaching area, as well as their ability to teach. In this context, language capacity includes the ability to communicate through language; I include the development of cultural sensitivity here, as well. In spite of the fact that I have some problems with the politics of the National Board for Professional Teaching Standards, I think the direction the Board is taking is a way to focus teachers toward a continuing redevelopment of their own capacities in language, communication, and cultural sensitivity. There is also a second direction we can take, as we have seen in these projects, namely collaboration and mentoring. I think these ways provide an opportunity for K–12 teachers to take responsibility within their own districts, schools, and with colleagues for an understanding of the standards and their implications for curriculum and instruction. There is a third direction that can be taken which is for inservice programs to be developed for a particular cadre of teachers, be it a local school or a school district. Postsecondary educators can't do everything, and so a collaboration of K–12 and postsecondary educators could work together for an understanding of the standards. In a fourth direction, in a graduate-level program for teachers, a college/university program would contain elements to prepare inservice teachers for National Board licensure. In such a context, national standards would have to be part of the total understanding of what students need to learn and how to help them learn it. In each direction, there can be a broadening of educational implication of the standards. We need to have an understanding that learning psychology and cognition are as important to language learning as the scientific knowledge about language. Such directions can open up our vision to a better understanding of our role(s), goals, and how we work with learners.

Joe: I think our responsibility as a group is to go to the universities and say: These are our needs. Can you help us meet them? Can we work together to meet them? Can we work together as a profession toward a common vision? We all have a vested interest in having everybody succeed.

Dale: We do, and we have to listen to each other, instead of thinking that you're something less than ...

Joe: Oh, we think of ourselves as top down, definitely. We are told what to do and we do it. Probably the other issues that we haven't addressed is that we're in the mind-set of, "give me the fish, instead of teach me to fish." If you teach me how these standards can be important to my life as a teacher, I can make them important to my students. I want to go back to "culture is life." So is language! So is everything else! We can teach all students to fish. But will they be good language learners? Will they be a generation who can say I learned language; I can still say things; I can still do things? Will they continue to say, I took language and guess what, I can do my dialogue; I'm limited to that?

Dale: Again, I think this metaphor of teaching "them" how to fish is not just important for language; it's important for any school subject. If that metaphor were to be applied, what a turnaround that could make!

Joe: Maybe that's why we stop! We don't know where to go to fish, I guess ...

Dale: Well, we're all fishing. We need to work together to find out how to fish better.

The Future of the Standards

Eileen: Let's think about the future and standards in perhaps a broader sense, beyond these projects. Is there a danger that we may address the standards in too superficial a manner?

Joe: You know, if we say we accept them superficially, we can also reject them very easily, too. They are not embedded in what we do. Again, we'll create that unit mentality of this is my three-day unit on standard 1.3, on communication. Or, "been there, done that, bought the T-shirt, bye!" ...

Eileen: Too many metaphors ...!

Joe: Yes, but we need to realize that the standards are part of what we do and that they can revolutionize student attitudes and actually change our collective mentality. So if we accept the standards superficially, we can also reject them. We hope they don't become fluff. That rather they shape how we are going to do things.

Dale: I think the standards provide us with an opportunity to think about curriculum differently. The curriculum can be organized thematically in a recursive way so that themes can be revisited in a slightly different orientation. And, these themes come back so that the learner gets a broader perspective and more experience with the language learned and the cultural content that was first introduced. If we're thinking about developing the five Cs, we have to think about curriculum differently; a recursive thematic organization can deal with the weave of the standards (See Standards, pp. 27–34).

Joe: Yes, and are we going to change curriculum? That's our next commitment. Are we going to change the curriculum to reflect the standards? How will that have an impact on the classroom? How will it impact publishers and the materials they produce for us? Or, are we again going to use the textbook as the standard in the classroom? We hope not. We hope this has changed a little bit.

Dale: As we know them at the present moment, I think the standards provide us with direction for the future. And, yet, we need to constantly examine them to know that they lead toward the future. In my own critical analysis of the standards, I am concerned about the issue of comparisons. To some degree, I believe that comparison and contrast may get us into an older mode of thinking about learning. Contrast and comparison has been used in language analysis, but its use in standards could be considered problematic. Why? Well, it is actually being used in the standards as a learning device to predict what to learn in the areas of language and culture when learning is a much more individualistic endeavor. Contrast and comparison is an incomplete way of determining what students need to learn and how they need to learn it.

Eileen: Do you think that's where future research would come into play? It's certainly important.

Dale: I think that's really important. What we're learning from these projects, as well as from other avenues, suggests that the a major focus needs to be placed on the learner. If you look at all the strategies research, the learner is the focus. And, we need to expand our focus on the learner. One way that we can get data and develop research questions is through observation of classrooms and participating as teacher researchers. Thus, I think the standards provide us with a model for the examination of the future.

Eileen: Of course, the standards document was never written to stand for years and years; it's intended to be a constantly changing framework to reflect research and what's taking place in classes with our students.

Joe: I look at the standards as making order out of linguistic and cultural chaos. It makes order, but it changes things. When things are ordered, they change from what they were before. We've got to move with that and say, "OK, now what do we do? Now where do we go?" And, there's the danger that, if we accept the standards too readily, we might look at them as prescriptive. I don't think they are prescriptive; I hope they're descriptive of what we do and where we are going. But again, as things change, we need to change with them.

Dale: I think teachers need to look at the standards as directional, not prescriptive, but visionary. With these standards, I can't see over the hill yet. I can get to a particular point, and I can see the light coming toward me, but I can't fully understand what that means yet. So for me, I'm certainly looking at the standards critically, but I also see that the provide an important nudge toward the future.

Joe: I feel the last two standards probably bring that out most clearly in that I cannot know that students will have a personal enjoyment of learning. However, I can plant the seeds right now. Later, the students will recognize something read or heard as language learned in school.

Eileen: Well, Dale, let me ask if you had a crystal ball and could see over that hill, what would you see in the future?

Dale: Well, you catch me off guard at this point. It's very difficult to predict the future, but I think I hope that certain things can happen. I certainly look toward language learning and language teaching as a much more collaborative endeavor. Teachers and students work together to help each other construct the future. I think that's indicative of what the standards are attempting to do. I think that the curriculum needs to be more collaboratively negotiated and thematic. It should relate to learners' needs and desires. And, I hope the curriculum for language learning will be recursive, experiential, open, and will allow for creativity for both learners and teachers. In these ways, the language learning curriculum will be responding to the vision of the standards. You can't have a divergent, creative, open response to a convergent perspective and the standards present a diverging perspective on communication and cultural sensitivity. Finally, the standards will create many questions with concern for assessment. How can we deal with assessment in a diverging context that is fair and relates to our expectations for student learning?

Eileen: What do you think of that, Joe?

Joe: Well, I see a kind of halo effect. We need to be open to the fact that there will be successes and failures with the standards. We have to be realistic. We need to look at all the parameters here: What's going on? What are the factors? If we can look at the K–12 situation more collaboratively and think of ourselves as involved in the profession, that may be the key to revise the standards, to look at them more realistically, and to create learners who want to learn. The motto for our school system is "learning for a lifetime." I think that's reflected in the standards. But the acceptance of the standards isn't going to happen overnight. This is a long-term, lifetime process. And so at the end of it, what will we have accomplished? I think if we're more involved, that'll be something, a direction for us.

Eileen: Well, I'd like to thank you very much for your valuable contributions to the conference and the volume. You've helped analyze the projects, make sense out of them as they relate to the goal areas, and you've helped us think through the key issues addressing the new national standards framework. I think you've given us a great deal to continue to talk about and to explore. We can only hope that this kind of discussion among professionals will continue to take place throughout the profession as we work to move forward and have good things happen "over the hill."

Note

[1]A special thanks to Sister Phillip Mary Reilly and Rosary College for hosting the taping session and for providing their equipment.

References

American Council on the Teaching of Foreign Languages (ACTFL). (1987). ACTFL proficiency guidelines, 1986. In H. Byrnes & M. Canale, (Eds.), *Defining and developing proficiency: Guidelines, implementations and concepts* (pp. 15–24). The ACTFL Foreign Language Education Series. Lincolnwood, IL: National Textbook.

Bruner, J. (1990). *Acts of meaning.* Cambridge, MA: Harvard University Press.

Egan, K. (1988). *Teaching as story telling: An alternative approach to teaching and Curriculum in the elementary school.* Chicago: University of Chicago Press.

Freire, P. (1973). *Education for critical consciousness.* New York: Continuum.

Freire, P., & Faundez, A. (1989). *Learning to question: A pedagogy of liberation.* New York: Continuum.

Galloway, V. (1995). From control to chaos: Reflections on an "unstylish" research paradigm. In M. Haggstrom, L. Morgan, & J. Wieczorak (Eds.). *The foreign language classroom: Bridging theory and practice* (pp. 211–220). New York: Garland Press.

Gardner, H. (1993). *Multiple intelligences: The theory in practice, a reader.* New York: Basic Books.

Gardner, H. (1993). *Frames of mind: The theory of multiple intelligences.* [Tenth-Anniversary edition of original publication, 1983.] New York: Basic Books.

Hall, J. K., & Davis, J. (1995). Voices from the traditional classroom: Learner reflections. In T. Dvorak (Ed.), *Voices from the field: Experiences and beliefs of our constituents* (pp. 1–32). Northeast Conference Reports. Lincolnwood, IL: National Textbook.

Higgs, T. V. (1984). Language teaching and the quest for the Holy Grail. In T. V. Higgs, (Ed.), *Teaching for proficiency, the organizing principle* (pp. 1–9). ACTFL Foreign Language Education Series. Lincolnwood, IL: National Textbook.

Lange, D. L. (1990). A blueprint for a teacher development program. In J. C. Richards & D. Nunan (Eds.), *Second language teacher education* (pp. 245–268). Cambridge: Cambridge University Press.

National Standards in Foreign Language Education Project. (1996). *Standards for foreign language learning: Preparing for the 21st century.* Yonkers, NY: Author.

Tedick, D. J., Walker, C. L., Lange, D. L., Paige, R. M., and Jorstad, H. L. (1993). Second language education in tomorrow's schools. In G. Guntermann (Ed.), *Developing language* teachers for a changing world (pp. 43–75). ACTFL Foreign Language Education Series. Lincolnwood, IL: National Textbook.

Waldspurger, T. (1995). Stimulating the right brain in the second-language classroom. In M. Haggstrom, L. Morgan, & J. Wieczorak (Eds.). *The foreign language classroom: Bridging theory and practice* (pp. 89–98). New York: Garland Press.

Northeast Conference on the
Teaching of Foreign Languages
Video Guide

Collaborations:
Meeting New Goals, New Realities

This *Video Guide* is designed for use with the video which accompanies this *1997 Reports* volume. The video illustrates examples of classroom scenarios from the five research projects described in the volume. Each classroom scenario with its corresponding project focuses on one of the five goal areas of the *National Standards for Foreign Language Learning* (1996). Since the video is based upon the projects described in the volume, the most productive use of this package is to read the chapters before viewing the video.

The following series of discussion questions were designed to accompany the classroom scenarios presented for each goal area. These questions will help you to reflect on the scenarios and to share your ideas with your colleagues. We hope that the discussion that follows from viewing this video will enhance your collaboration with colleagues as you address our new foreign language standards.

Copies of the video can be obtained by contacting the Northeast Conference on the Teaching of Foreign Languages, Dickinson College, P.O. Box 1773, Carlisle, PA 17013-2896 (717/245-1977). Copies of the *1997 Reports* can be obtained by contacting the National Textbook Company, 4255 West Touhy Ave., Lincolnwood, IL 60646-1975 (1-800-323-4900).

The Board of Directors of the 1997 Northeast Conference
Eileen W. Glisan, 1997 Chair

*I. Communication Goal: Meaning Making
through a Whole Language Approach*

1. How can the PACE model be used to address the three modes of communication—interpersonal, interpretive, presentational?
2. How does the PACE strategy compare to a traditional approach to teaching grammar?
3. What role do the following play in the PACE model: meaning, grammar, the teacher, the students?
4. For the French lesson you just viewed, brainstorm several extension activities in which students could practice using interpersonal and presentational communication.

II. Cultures Goal: Using Video to Explore Perspectives, Practices, and Products of Guatemalan Culture

1. How has culture traditionally been taught in language classrooms?
2. Given what you have seen about this unit on Guatemalan culture, how does this approach to teaching culture differ from a traditional approach?
3. This unit was designed for a ninth-grade Level III class. How might it be adapted for use in a lower-level class?
4. In addition to the Cultures Goal, what other goal areas are addressed in this unit?

III. Connections Goal: Making New Connections through Interdisciplinary Lessons

1. How does this lesson address the Connections Goal?
2. What follow-up activities might you plan to reinforce the cultural aspects of this lesson?
3. How could you adapt this lesson for use in a non-immersion foreign language class at the middle or high school level?
4. What other curricular areas could be connected to this particular lesson?

IV. Comparisons Goal: Using Linguistic and Cultural Comparisons to Help Students Succeed in Learning

1. According to what you have seen in these video segments, what insights did students gain about language and culture as a result of their experience learning Arabic?
2. What do students' comments reveal about their attitudes toward learning a foreign language?
3. What kinds of questions would you ask these students to help them compare their cultures to the Arab culture?
4. What other goal areas are addressed in this project?

V. Communities Goal: Using a Foreign Language to Connect with the Community

1. How does this project address the Communities Goal?
2. What other goal areas does this segment address?
3. What might you do with these students as a follow-up to the bakery visit?
4. What other strategies might you use to enable students to use the target language beyond the classroom in order to gain greater cultural awareness?

Special thanks to Dr. Kurt P. Dudt and students in the Dept. of Communications Media at Indiana University of Pennsylvania for their work in producing this video.

Northeast Conference Reports 1954–1996

Foreign Language Teachers and Tests.
*Hunter Kellenberger, editor. Committee on
the Qualifications of Foreign Language
Teachers,* Stephen A. Freeman, Chairman;
Theodore Andersson, Finis E. Engleman, E.
Duncan Grizzell, John Holden, Kathryn L.
O'Brien, T. M. Stinnett: *Committee on For-
eign Language Instruction in Elementary
Schools,* Arthur M. Selvi, Chairman, Lillian
S. Adams, Nelson Brooks, Dorothy Cham-
berlain, Vincenzo Cioffari, Ann Foberg,
Howard Garey, Manuel H. Guerra, Victoria
Lyles, Mary P. Thompson, Olga Scherer Vir-
ski: *Committee on Tests,* Nelson Brooks,
Chairman; Frederick B. Agard, Anne-Marie
de Commaille, Howard Garey, Archibald T.
MacAllister, Kathryn L. O'Brien, Henry B.
Richardson, Edith A. Runge, Stanley M.
Sapon, Paula Thibault: *Committee on the
Teaching of Literature,* Norman L. Torrey,
Chairman; Esther M. Eaton, Archibald T.
MacAllister, Olga Scherer Virski, Donald D.
Walsh: *Committee on the Role of Foreign
Languages in American Life,* Theodore An-
dersson, Chairman; Leon Dostert, Herbert
G. Espy, Stephen A. Freeman, Henri Peyre,
Henry Lee Smith, Wilmarth H. Starr: *Com-
mittee on Linguistic Aids,* Richard H.
Walker, Chairman; F. B. Agard, William N.
Locke, Edmond A. Meras, Robert Politzer,
Fred H. Tone, W. Freeman Twaddell: and
The Foreign Language Program, speech
given by W. R. Parker. 1954

Culture, Literature and Articulation.
*Germaine Brée, editor. Committee on the
Role of Literature in Language Teaching,*
Archibald T. MacAllister, Chairman; Mrs.
Germaine Cressey, Edwin M. Faust, Joseph
Genna, Joseph Stookins, Olga Scherer Vir-
ski: *Committee on the Place of Culture and
Civilization,* Laurence Wylie, Chairman;
Joseph B. Casagrande, A. Irving Hallowell,
John B. Hughes, Otto Klineberg, Mrs. Dol-
ores Andújar de MacDonald, David C.
McClelland, Albert H. Marckwardt, Eric
Rosenbaum, William C. Sayres, Mrs. Rose
Scheider, Elbridge Sibley, Theodore C.
Wright: *Committee on Foreign Language
Instruction in Elementary Schools,* Mary P.
Thompson, Chairman; Sandra Adler, Julius
Arnold, Joseph Astman, Marion Digisi,
Marguerite Eriksson, James Grew, Lucrecia
Lopez, Susan Scott, Sylvia Smith, Alex
Szogyi, Olga Scherer Virski: *Committee on
Foreign Languages in Secondary Schools,*
Robert G. Mead, Jr., Chairman; Louis Gon-
zález, Audrey Havican, Joseph LoBue,
Louise Theurer: *Classical and Modern For-
eign Languages: Common Areas and Prob-
lems,* Barbara P. McCarthy, Chairman;
Josephine P. Bree, Helen E. Bridey, Austin
M. Lashbrook, Alice Nesta Lloyd Thomas,
C. Arthur Lynch, Edmond A. Meras: *Com-
mittee on Tests,* Nelson Brooks, Chairman;
Ramona Beeken, Anne-Marie de Com-
maille, Durand Echeverria, Sarah W. Lorge,
Kathryn L. O'Brien, Edith Runge, Stanley
Sapon, James Stephens, Paula Thibault:
*Committee on the Preparation of Foreign
Language Teachers,* Alonzo G. Grace,
Chairman; Stephen Freeman, Henry Herge,
John R. Matthew, Arthur Selvi: *Committee
on Teaching Aids and Techniques,* Jeanne
Varney Pleasants, Chairman; Douglas W.
Alden, Armand Bégué, Jean Benoît-Levy,
Pierre Crénesse, Renée Jeanne Fulton,
Daniel Girard, Pierre Guédenet, Robert M.
Hankin, Sylvia N. Levy, Sister Margaret
Thérèse, Richard H. Walker, Ruth Hirsch
Weinstein, Edward Williamson: *Committee
on the Role of Foreign Languages in Ameri-
can Life,* Wilmarth Starr, Chairman; Theo-
dore Andersson, Lilian Avila, Yaroslav

Chyz, Leonard Covello, Rachel DuBois, Joseph Monserrat, Alfred Pellegrino, Nora Wittman. 1955

Foreign Language Tests and Techniques. *Margaret Gilman, editor. Committee on Teaching Aids and Techniques,* Frederick D. Eddy, Chairman; John B. Archer, Grace A. Crawford, Kathryn Fellows, Daniel P. Girard, Karl Kellermann, E. Wesley O'Neill, Hubert S. Packard, Fred B. Painter, Tilla Thomas, Mrs. Ruth Hirsch Weinstein, Mrs. Margaret V. Wojnowski, Mrs. Jeanne Varney Pleasants: *Committee on Tests,* Stanley M. Sapon, Chairman; Simon Belasco, Nelson Brooks, Charles Choquette, Paula Thibault: *Committee on Foreign Language Instruction in Elementary Schools,* Mary P. Thompson, Chairman; Joyce Greene, Paul F. Poehler, Mrs. Ina C. Sartorius, Katherine Scrivener, Sylvia Smith: *Committee on Foreign Language Instruction in Secondary Schools,* Mrs. Ruth P. Kroeger, Chairman; Joseph LoBue, Alexander D. Gibson, Blanche A. Price, Frank M. Soda, Elizabeth White, Alfred J. Wright: *Committee on the Teaching of Classical and Modern Foreign Languages, Common Areas and Problems,* Josephine P. Bree, Chairman; Allan Hoey, Sister Marie Louise, Barbara P. McCarthy, Kenneth Meinke, Esther Tabor, Ralph Ward: *Committee on the Role of Literature in Language Teaching,* Robert J. Clements, Chairman; Annette Emgarth, Laurent LeSage, Grace Myer, Charlotte Pekary, Sanford Shepart, Adeline Strouse, Floyd Zulli: *Committee on the Place of Culture and Civilization in Foreign Language Teaching,* John B. Carroll, Chairman; William C. Sayres, Otto Klineberg, William G. Moulton, Mrs. Rose M. Scheider, Gerald E. Wade, Theodore C. Wright: *Committee on the Role of Foreign Languages in American Life,* Wilmarth Starr, Chairman; Yaroslav Chyx, Leonard Covello, Rachel DuBois, Joseph

Monserrat, Alfred Pellegrino, Nora Wittman. 1956

The Language Classroom. *William F. Bottiglia, Editor. Committee on Materials and Methods for Teaching Literature in Secondary School in Preparation for Admission to College with Advanced Standing,* Blanche A. Price, Chairman; Morton W. Briggs, Georgette Galland, DeVaux de Lancey, Marthe Lavallée, Edward P. Morris, Rose Presel, Olga S. Virski: *Committee on Tests,* Nelson Brooks, Chairman; Stanley M. Sapon, Simon Belasco, Charles Choquette, Fernand Marty, Paula Thibault: *Committee on the Place of Grammar and the Use of English in the Teaching of Foreign Languages at Various Levels,* James Grew, Chairman; Nelson Brooks, Elliott Grant, Paul Gropp, Paul S. Hennessey, Emilie Margaret White: *Committee on the Drop-Out of Students in High School Language Classes,* Renée J. Fulton, Chairman; Thomas V. Banks, Josephine R. Bruno, A. Louise Carlson, Emilio Guerra, Alice F. Linnehan, Nita Willits Savage, Mary M. Stavrinos: *Committee on the Philosophy of the Language Laboratory,* John B. Archer, Chairman; Frederick D. Eddy, Mrs. Lois S. Gaudin, Joyce E. Greene, Sister Julie, S.N.D., Rudolph V. Oblum, Geneviève Wantiez, Mrs. Margaret V. Wojnowski: *Committee on Teaching Aids and Techniques,* Jeanne Varney Pleasants, Chairman; Pierre Capretz, Kathryn F. Fellows, Manuel H. Guerra, Paul King, Theodore Mueller, William Nemser, Marcella Ottolenghi, Pierre Oustinoff, S. E. Schmidt, Richard H. Walker, Elizabeth Young. 1957

The Language Teacher. *Harry L. Levy, Editor. Committee on the Teaching of Writing,* Jeannette Atkins, Chairman; Jeane-Pierre Cossnard, Elliott M. Grant, Mrs. Glenda G. Richards: *Committee on Single*

Verses Multiple Languages in Secondary Schools, James H. Grew, Chairman; Thelma B. DeGraff, Arthur Howe, Jr., William N. Locke, Paul H. Phaneuf, A. Marguerite Zouck: *Committee on the Foreign Language Program, Grades 3–12,* Margaret E. Eaton, Chairman; Dorothy Chamberlain, Janet Jones, Filomena C. Peloro, Elizabeth H. Ratte, Mrs. Anne Slack, Emily L. Snow: *Committee on Patterns as Grammar,* Mrs. Dorothy Brodin, Chairman; Sidney D. Braun, J. Donald Bowen, Nelson Brooks, Catherine Davidovitch, Naomi Goldstein, Frederick Kempner: *Committee on "The Ghosts in the Language Classroom,"* Donald D. Walsh, Chairman; Nelson Brooks, Margaret Gilman, S. A. Kendrick, Oliver A. Melchior, Archibald K. Shields: *Committee on Means of Meeting the Shortage of Teachers,* Carolyn E. Bock, Chairman; Mrs. Genevieve S. Blew, William Brunt, Grace A Crawford, Otis N. Jason, William J. Nelligan, Carl A. Tyre, Mrs. Eleanor Young. 1958

The Language Learner. *Frederick D. Eddy, Editor. Modern Foreign Language Learning: Assumptions and Implications,* Wilmarth H. Starr, Chairman; Alfred G. Pellegrino, Frederick H. Dedmond, James H. Grew, Elizabeth H. Ratte, Clyde Russell; *A Provisional Program to Implement the Report of Committee I: A Six-Year Sequence from Grade Nine Through the Second Year of College,* Gordon R. Silber, Chairman; Jeannette Atkins, Paul M. Glaude, Richard R. Miller, Jauquina Navarro, W. Napoleon Rivers, Nita W. Savage: *Elementary and Junior High School Curricula,* Filomena C. Peloro, Chairman, Alexander S. Hughes, J. Donald Bowen, Doris Dunn, Mary Lou Washburn, Isamael Silva-Fuenzalida: *Definition of Language Competences Through Testing,* Nelson Brooks, Chairman; James M. Ferrigno, Charles A. Choquette, Esther M. Eaton, Mary E. Hayes, Maxim New-

mark, Perry Sturges: *Committee on Resolutions,* Harry L. Levy, Chairman; Archibald T. MacAllister, Mary P. Thompson. 1959

Culture in Language Learning. *G. Reginald Bishop, Jr., Editor. Working Committee I: An Anthropological Concept of Culture,* Ernestine Friedl, Chairman; Edward M. Bruner, Regina Flannery Herzfeld: *Working Committee II: Language as Culture,* William E. Welmers, Chairman; Alexander Hull, Eva Douglas, Dan Desberg: *Working Committee III: Teaching of Western European Cultures,* Ira Wade, Chairman; Joseph M. Franckenstein, Daniel Girard, Maria Sora, Fernand Vial: *Working Committee IV: Teaching of Classical Cultures,* Doris E. Kibbe, Chairman; Moses Hadas, Ralph Marcellino, Irene E. Stanislawczyk, John Rowe Workman: *Working Committee V: Teaching of Slavic Cultures,* Leon I. Twarog, Chairman; Edward J. Brown, William E. Harkins, Alfred E. Senn, Johannes Van Straalen, Wiktor Weintraub. 1960

Modern Language Teaching in School and College. *Seymour L. Flaxman, Editor. Working Committee I: The Preparation of Secondary School Teachers,* Genevieve S. Blew, Chairman; Wesley Childers, Alice A. Arana, Philip E. Arsenault, Anna Balakian: *Working Committee II: The Preparation of College and University Teachers,* Jack M. Stein, Chairman; Helen M. Mustard, Patricia O'Connor, Francis Rogers, Wilmarth Starr: *Working Committee III: The Transition to the Classroom,* Evangeline Galas, Chairman; Remunda Cadoux, Sister Margaret Pauline, Robert Serafino, Herbert Schueler: *Working Committee IV: Coordination Between Classroom and Laboratory,* Guillermo del Olmo, Chairman; Jeannette Atkins, Dora S. Bashour, Pierre Capretz, Clark A. Vaughan. 1961

Current Issues in Language Teaching.
William F. Bottiglia, Editor. Working Committee on Linguistics and Language Teaching, Robert A. Hall, Jr., Chairman; Raleigh Morgan, Jr., Josephine R. Bruno, Paul M. Glaude, William D. Ilgen, James P. Soffietti, Seymour O. Simches: *Working Committee on Programmed Learning,* Alfred S. Hayes, Chairman; Harlan L. Lane, Theodore Mueller, Waldo E. Sweet, Wilmarth H. Starr: *Panel on FLES Practices,* Mary A. Brophy, Chairman; Nancy V. Alkonis, Alice Arana, Randall Marshall, Andre Paquette, Laurence G. Paquin, Beverly Sherp, Mary P. Thompson: *Panel on Televised Teaching,* M. Jeannette Atkins, Chairman; Dorothy Brodin, Robert W. Cannaday, Jr., Benito L. Lueras, Robert Serafino. 1962

Language Learning: The Intermediate Phase. *William F. Bottiglia, Editor. Working Committee on the Continuum: Listening and Speaking,* Simon Belasco, Chairman; Eleanor Bingham, Dan Desberg, Stanley M. Sapon, Albert Valdman, Filomena Peloro Del Olmo: *Working Committee on Reading for Meaning,* George A. C. Scherer, Chairman; Delvin Covey, Sharon Entwistle, Wallace E. Lambert. Dean H. Obrecht, Betty Robertson, Alfred S. Hayes: *Working Committee on Writing as Expression,* Marina Prochoroff, Chairman; Richard Burgi, Jacques Ehrmann, George Krivobok, Mary P. Thompson. 1963

Foreign Language Teaching: Ideals and Practices. *George Fenwick Jones, Editor. Working Committee I: Foreign Languages in the Elementary School,* Conrad J. Schmitt, Chairman; Marjorie P. Bowen, Janice S. Calkin, Gladys Lipton, Protase E. Woodford, Seymour O. Simches: *Working Committee II: Foreign Languages in the Secondary School,* Milton R. Hahn, Chairman; Colette Garimaldi, Jack B. Krail,

James F. McArthur, Arnold Tauber, Joseph Tursi, Russell Webster, M. Jeannette Atkins: *Working Committee III: Foreign Languages in Colleges and Universities,* Roger L. Hadlich, Chairman; Harlan P. Hanson, James H. Harris, Robert J. Nelson, Arthur M. Selvi, Ralph L. Ward, Delvin L. Covey. 1964

Foreign Language Teaching: Challanges to the Profession. *G. Reginald Bishop, Jr., Editor. A Discussion Panel - The Case for Latin,* William R. Parker, Chairman; Clara West Ashley, Margaret Gill, John F. Latimer, Edward A. Robinson, Edward D. Sullivan: *Working Committee I: Study Abroad,* Stephen A. Freeman, Chairman; Donald Bigelow, Leonard Brisley, George E. Diller, John A. Garraty, Francis Rogers: *Working Committee II: The Challenge of Bilingualism,* A. Bruce Gaarder, Chairman; Joshua A. Fishman, Wallace E. Lambert, Elizabeth Anisfeld, Gerard J. Brault, Pauline M. Rojas, Louis L. Curcio, Norman D. Kurland: *Working Committee III: From School to College: The Problem of Continuity,* Micheline Dufau, Chairman; Miriam M. Bryan, John W. Kurtz, Theodore Nuzzi, Josephine Bruno Pane. 1965

Language Teaching: Broader Contexts. *Robert G. Mead, Jr., Editor. Discussion Panel - Research and Language Learning,* Edward D. Sullivan, Chairman; John B. Carroll, Noam Chomsky, Charles A. Furguson, with comments by Harlan L. Lane, W. Freeman Twaddell, Douglas C. Sheppard: *Working Committee I: Content and Crossroads: Wider Uses for Foreign Languages,* Brownlee Sands Corrin, Chairman; William F. Bottiglia, Cleophas W. Boudreau, James H. Grew, W. Roy Phelps, Helen P. Warriner: *Working Committee II: Coordination of Foreign Language Teaching: A Contemporary View of Professional Leadership,* Genevieve S. Blew, Chairman;

John W. Gartner, Sister Charlotte Marie, Frank M. Soda, June U. Stillwell, Marilyn E. Wolf. 1966

Foreign Languages: Reading Literature Requirements. *Thomas E. Bird, Editor. Working Committee I: The Teaching of Reading,* William G. Moulton, Chairman; Hugh Campbell, Doris E. Kibbe, Albert M. Reh, Dorothy S. Rivers, Kimberly Sparks: *Working Committee II: The Times and Places for Literature,* F. Andre Paquette, Chairman; Anna Benjamin, Hugh M. Davidson, Gladys Lipton, Chris N. Nacci, Filomena Del Olmo, Robert H. Spaethling, James P. Ward: *Working Committee III: Trends in FL Requirements and Placement,* John F. Gummere, Chairman; Robert L. Hinshalwood, Mrs. Herbert F. McCollom, Gordon R. Silber. 1967

Foreign Language Learning: Research and Development. *Thomas E. Bird, Editor. Working Committee I: Innovative FL Programs,* Oliver Andrews, Jr., Chairman; Carolyn E. Bock, Grace A. Crawford, A. Bruce Gaarder, Elton Hocking, Paul C. McRill, Mabel W. Richardson, George E. Smith: *Working Committee II: The Classroom Revisited,* Seymour O. Simches, Chairman; Josephine Bruno Pane, Richard M. Penta, James R. Powers, Dorothy S. Rivers, Marigwen Schumacher, Symond Yavener: *Working Committee III: Liberated Expression,* Mills F. Edgerton, Jr., Chairman; Dwight Bolinger, Thomas W. Kelly, Gail E. Montgomery, Donald G. Reiff. 1968

Sight and Sound: The Sensible and Sensitive Use of Audio-Visual Aids. *Mills F. Edgerton, Jr., Editor. Non-Projected Visuals* by Brenda Frazier: *Sound Recordings* by Jermaine Arendt (Using Taped Material in Studying Goethe's *Faust* in High School: A Slide-Tape Demonstration - by Margaret

Shryer): *Slides and Filmstrips* by Rev. Hilary Hayden, O.S.B. (*Combray:* A Multi-Media Introduction to the World of Marcel Proust by Pierre Capretz): *The Overhead Projector* by James J. Wrenn, *Motion Pictures* by Allan W. Grundstrom (Motion-Picture Film: A Demonstration - by Mills F. Edgerton, Jr.): *Television* by Joseph H. Sheehan (Demonstration of the Use of Television in the Training of Foreign-Language Teachers - by Joseph Sheehan and Robert Willis): *Let us Build Bridges* by Stephen A. Freeman. 1969

Foreign Languages and the "New" Student. *Joseph A. Tursi, Editor. A Relevant Curriculum: An Instrument for Polling Student Opinion,* Robert P. Serafino, Chairman; Joan L. Feindler, F. André Paquette, John J. Reilly and consultant Leon A. Jakobovits: *Motivation in Foreign-Language Learning,* Robert J. Nelson, Chairman; Leon A. Jakobovits, Filomena Peloro Del Olmo, Rev. Daniel R. Kent, Wallace E. Lambert, Elaine C. Libit, Jane W. Torrey, G. Richard Tucker: *Foreign Languages For All Students?,* Eleanor L. Sandstrom, Chairman; Paul Pimsleur, Michael E. Hernick, Gertrude Moskowitz, Frank Otto, Frederick J. Press, Mary L. Robb, Pearl M. Warner: *The Rung and the Ladder* by Nelson Brooks. 1970

Leadership for Continuing Development. *James W. Dodge, Editor. Professional Responsibilities,* James R. Powers, Chairman; Nelson Brooks, A. Bruce Gaarder, Stowell C. Goding, John F. Latimer, John P. Nionakis, Rebecca Valette, and consultants Frank Di Giammarino, Frederick D. Eddy, Ronald Fitzgerald: *Inservice Involvement in the Process of Change,* Jerome G. Mirsky, Chairman; Edward H. Bourque, Jerald R. Green, Norma Enea Klayman, Gladys C. Lipton, Harriet Norton: *Innovative Trends in Foreign-Language Teaching,* François Hugot, Chairman; Genelle Caldwell, Nancy-anne Fitzgibbons, Judith Le Bovit, Frank Otto, Ferdinand Ruplin, Brother Dean Warthen, C.F.X.: *Literature for Advanced Foreign-Language Students* by Harry L. Levy. 1971

Other Words, Other Worlds: Language-in-Culture. *James W. Dodge, Editor. On Teaching Another Language as Part of Another Culture* by Joey L. Dillard, Mary R. Miller and William A. Stewart: *Sociocultural Aspects of Foreign-Language Study* by G. Richard Tucker and Wallace E. Lambert: *Ancient Greek and Roman Culture* by Samuel Lieberman: *France* by Gerard J. Brault: *Some Suggestions for Implementing the Report on France* by Joan L. Feindler: *Quebec: French Canada* by Marine Leland: *An Approach to Courses in German Culture* by Harry F. Young: *Italy and the Italians* by Joseph Tursi: *Japan: Spirit and Essence* by Walter J. Odronic: *The Soviet Union* by Irina Kirk: *Spain* by John W. Kronik: *Spanish America: A Study in Diversity* by Frank N. Dauster: *Some Suggestions for Implementing the Report on Spanish America* by Jerome G. Mirsky: *Teaching Foreign Languages: A Brief Retrospect and Prospect* by Robert G. Mead, Jr.: *Individualizing Instruction through Team Teaching* by Frank Otto: *La Révolte des jeunes or An Experiment in Relevancy* by Michael Agatstein. 1972

Sensitivity in the Foreign-Language Classroom. *James W. Dodge, Editor. Interaction in the Foreign-Language Class,* Gertrude Moskowitz, Chairman; Jacqueline Benevento, Norma Furst: *Teaching Spanish to the Native Spanish Speaker,* Herman La-Fontaine, Chairman; Evelyn Colón, Marco Hernández, Awilda Orta, Muriel Pagan, Carmen Pérez, Nathan Quiñones, Sonia Rivera: *Individualization of Instruction,*

Ronald L. Gougher, Chairman; Howard B. Altman, John F. Bockman, Aline C. Desbonnet, Philip D. Smith, Lorraine A. Strasheim and consultants Tora T. Ladu and Alfred D. Roberts: *Meditations on Being a Foreign-Language Teacher* by Freeman Twaddell: *The Audio-Motor Unit: A Listening Comprehension Strategy That Works* by Theodore B. Kalidova, Genelle Morain and Robert J. Elkins. 1973

Toward Student-Centered Foreign-Language Programs. *Warren C. Born, Editor. Training for Student-Centered Language Programs,* Annette S. Baslaw, Co-Chairwoman, Joan S. Freilich, Co-Chairwoman; William E. De Lorenzo, Thomas H. Geno, Charles R. Hancock, Robert R. Sherburne and consultants Howard B. Altman, Leo Benardo and Barbara E. Elling: *Implementing Student-Centered Foreign-Language Programs,* Anthony Papalia, Chairman; Peter Boyd-Bowman, Dale V. Lally, Jr., Helene Loew, Stefano Morel, Roland Obstfeld, Anne Slack, Harry Tuttle and consultant Toby S. Tamarkin: *Careers, Community, and Public Awareness,* René L. Lavergneau, Chairman; Marguerite D. Bomse, Beverly Butler Lavergneau, Diane F. Menditto, Richard W. Newman, Toby S. Tamarkin, Blanca G. Wright and consultant Doris Marks: *Curriculum Perspectives: The Need for Diversified Services* by Emma Birkmaier: *Penetrating the Mass Media: A Unit to Develop Skill in Reading Spanish Newspaper Headlines* by H. Ned Seelye and J. Laurence Day. 1974

Goals Clarification: Curriculum Teaching Evaluation. *Warren C. Born, Editor. Committee on Curriculum,* Stephen L. Levy, Chairman; Muriel H. Goldstein, Mark Levine, June K. Phillips, Pearl M. Warner, and consultants Gladys C. Lipton, Helen Z. Loew, Rose Marie Roccio: *Committee on*

Teaching, Ann A. Beusch, Chairman; Jane M. Bourque, Roberta Cohen, William E. De Lorenzo, and consultant Philip Arsenault: *Committee on Evaluation,* John L. D. Clark, Chairman; Virginia S. Ballard, John P. Nionakis, Richard C. Ten Eyck, and consultant Brenda Frazier Clemons: *Gladly Teche ... and Gladly Lerne* by Donald D. Walsh: *Fusion of the Four Skills: A Technique for Facilitating Communicative Exchange* by Robert J. Elkins, Theodore B. Kalivoda and Genelle Morain. 1975

Language and Culture: Heritage and Horizons. *Warren C. Born, Editor. Committee on the Classics,* Grace Crawford, Chairperson; Marigwen Schumaker, William Ziobro, and consultants Marie Cleary, John Latimer, Meyer Reinhold: *Committee on the French-Speaking,* Normand C. Dube, Chairperson; Gerard J. Brault, Guy F. Dubay and consultants Madeleine D. Giguere, Roger Grindle, Roger Paradis: *Committee on the German-Speaking,* Helene Z. Loew, Chairperson; Barbara Elling, LaVern J. Rippley, William I. Schreiber: *Committee on the Spanish-Speaking,* John M. Darcey, Chairperson; Milagros Carrero, Rosemary Weinstein Dann, John Leach, Toby Tamarkin, Penny A. Zirkel and consultants, Janet Baird, Janie L. Duncan, Dora Kennedy: *Retrospect and Prospect* by Nelson Brooks: *Changing Goals for Foreign Language Education* by Ted T. Grenda: *The Imaginative Use of Projected Visuals* by Thomas P. Carter. 1976

Language: Acquisition, Application, Appreciation. *Warren C. Born, Editor. Working Committee on Acquisition,* Pierre F. Cintas, Chairperson; Nelson Brooks, Yvonne Escola, Robert C. Gardner, John S. Rohsenow, Ernest A. Scatton and consultant Seok Choong Song: *Working Committee on Application,* Kenneth Lester, Chairperson; Merriam Moore, Flora O'Neill, Symond

Yavener and consultant Philip Arsenault: *Working Committee on Appreciation,* Germaine Brée, Chairperson; Claude Chauvigne, Micheline Dufau, Enrique H. Miyares: *The Link Between Language and Ethnicity: Its Importance for the Language Teacher* by Joshua A. Fishman: *Affective Learning Activities* by Clay Benjamin Christensen. 1977

New Contents, New Teachers, New Publics. *Warren C. Born, Editor. Working Committee on New Contents,* Rebecca M. Valette, Chairman; Pietro Frassica, Gesa Kandeler, Gene S. Kupferschmid, Cathy Linder, Helene B. Mensh, Elaine V. Uzan, Freidrich Winterscheidt and consultant Peter A. Eddy: *Working Committee on New Teachers,* William E. De Lorenzo, Chairman; Ann A. Beusch, Yvonne Escola, Charles R. Hancock, Anthony Mistretta, Sara Schyfter and consultants Peter A. Eddy, James S. Greenberg and Dora Kennedy: *Working Committee on New Publics,* Joseph A. Tursi, Chairman; Ruth L. Bennett, Alain Blanchet, Richard I. Brod, Helene Z. Loew, Anita Monsees and consultant Peter A. Eddy: *Interaction Activities in the Foreign Language Classroom, or How to Grow a Tulip-Rose* by Christina Bratt Paulston. 1978

The Foreign Language Learner in Today's Classroom Environment. *Warren C. Born, Editor. The View on the Way Up: A Wider Perspective* by Wilga M. Rivers: *Educational Goals: The Foreign Language Teacher's Response* by Wilga M. Rivers: *Cindy: A Learner in Today's Foreign Language Classroom* by Carol Hosenfeld: *The Second Language Teacher: Reconciling the Vision with the Reality* by Gilbert A. Jarvis: *The Combining Arrangement: Some Techniques* by I.S.P. Nation, New Zealand. 1979

Our Profession/Present Status & Future Directions. *Thomas H. Geno, Editor. Present Status of Foreign Language Teaching: A Northeast Conference Survey* by Peter A. Eddy: *Toward an Articulated Curriculum* by Robert C. Lafayette: *Competence in a Foreign Language: A Valuable Adjunct Skill in the Eighties* by Mills F. Edgerton, Jr.: *Educational Technology* by James W. Dodge: *New Approaches to Assessment of Language Learning* by Helen L. Jorstad: *The American Language Association: Toward New Strength, Visibility, an Effectiveness as a Profession* by David P. Benseler: *Diagnosing and Responding to Individual Learner Needs* by Diane W. Birckbichler and Alice C. Omaggio. 1980

New Cases for Foreign Language Study. [A special publication project.] *Compiled by June K. Phillips. Language and Global Awareness* by George W. Bonham: *Escalating the Campaign Against Provincialism* by S. Frederick Starr: *Why Study Foreign Languages?* by F. Andre Paquette: *We Think We Are "Evening in Paris", But We're Really "Chanel"* by Gilbert A. Jarvis: *Educational Goals: The Foreign Language Teacher's Response* by Wilga M. Rivers: *Developing Foreign Language Curriculum in the Total School Setting: The Macro-Picture* by Robert S. Zais: *Defending the FL Requirement in the Liberal Arts Curriculum* by Thomas J. Bugos: *Views on the Foreign Language Requirement in Higher Education* by Norma Enea Klayman: *The Resurgence of Foreign Language Study* by John K. Primeau: *Special Curricula for Special Needs* by Barbara Elling: *Rationales for Foreign Language Study: What Are Our Goals?* by Gerd K. Schneider: *Views of Secondary School Superintendents on Foreign Language Study: A Support-Constraint Analysis* by Dominick DeFilippis: *Students' Beliefs on the Importance of Foreign Lan-*

guages in the School Curriculum by Anthony Papalia: *Why Study Foreign Languages? A Junior Orientalist's Perspective* by John Buscaglia. 1981

Foreign Language and International Studies—Toward Cooperation and Integration. *Thomas H. Geno, Editor. A Chronicle: Political, Professional, and Public Activities Surrounding the President's Commission on Foreign Language and International Studies* by Thomas H. Geno: *Global Responsibility: The Role of the Foreign Language Teacher;* Donald H. Bragaw, Helene Z. Loew, Judith S. Wooster: *Exchanges and Travel Abroad in Secondary Schools* by Claudia S. Travers: *Toward an International Dimension in Higher Education* by Richard C. Williamson: *International Training* by Lucia Pierce. 1981

The Foreign Language Teacher: The Lifelong Learner. *Robert G. Mead, Jr., Editor. Less Frequently Taught Languages: Basic Information and Instruction: American Sign Language* by Marilyn Conwell and April Nelson; *Chinese* by David N. Gidman; *Japanese* by Jean-Pierre Berwald and Toshiko Phipps; *Latin* by Marie Cleary; *Portuguese* by Rosemarie Pedro Carvalho; *Russian* by Robert L. Baker; *Comtemporary Cultures: Issues and Answers: La France Comtemporaine* by Pierre Maubrey; *Die Bundesrepublik Deutschland heute-zeitgemäBe Betrachtungen* by Barbara Elling and Karl Elling; *L'Italia Contemporanea* by Romo J. Trivelli; *La España de Hoy* by John M. Darcey; *La Cultura Contemporánea de Hispanoamérica* by Frank Dauster: *Methodology and Evaluation: Merging Methods and Texts: A Pragmatic Approach* by Elizabeth G. Joiner and June K. Phillips: *Proficiency Testing in Second Language Classrooms* by Judith E. Liskin-Gasparro and Protase E. Woodford: *Technology and the*

Foreign Language Classroom: Audiovisual Materials and Techniques for Teaching Foreign Languages by Carolyn Parks: *Applications of Computer Technology in Foreign Language Teaching and Learning* by John S. Harrison. 1982

Foreign Languages: Key Links in the Chain of Learning. *Robert G. Mead, Jr., Editor. Elementary School Foreign Language: Key Link in the Chain of Learning,* Myriam Met, Chair; Helena Anderson, Evelyn Brega, Nancy Rhodes: *Foreign Language in the Secondary School: Reconciling the Dream with the Reality,* Alice C. Omaggio, Chair; Anthony J. DeNapoli, Paul T. Griffith, Dora F. Kennedy, Stephen L. Levy, Gladys Lipton, Helene Z. Loew: *"Nuturing the Ties that Bind": Links Between Foreign Language Departments and the Rest of the Post-secondary Educational Enterprise,* Claire Gaudiani, Chair; Patricia Cummins, Humphrey Tonkin: *Foreign Language and the "Other" Student* by Vicki Galloway: *Toward a Multidimensional Foreign Language Curriculum* by H. H. Stern: *Thirty Years of the Northeast Conference: A Personal Perspective* by Jane McFarland Bourque. 1983

The Challenge for Excellence in Foreign Language Education. *Gilbert A. Jarvis, Editor. For Teachers: A Challenge for Competence* by Barbara H. Wing: *The Challenge of Proficiency: Student Characteristics* by Diane W. Birckbichler: *Testing in a Communicative Approach* by Michael Canale: *Of Computers and Other Technologies* by Glyn Holmes: *The Challenge for Excellence in Curriculum and Materials Development* by Christine L. Brown. 1984

Proficiency, Curriculum, Articulation: The Ties that Bind. *Alice C. Omaggio, Editor. Designing the Proficiency-Based Cur-*

riculum by Frank W. Medley, Jr.: *The Development of Oral Proficiency* by Jeannette D. Bragger: *Teaching Toward Proficiency: The Receptive Skills* by Heidi Byrnes: *Teaching and Testing Proficiency in Writing: Skills to Transcend the Second-Language Classroom* by Sally Sieeloff Magnan: *Toward Cultural Proficiency* by Wendy W. Allen: *A Continuing Chronicle of Professional, Policy, and Public Activities in Foreign Languages and International Studies* by J. David Edwards and Melinda E. Hanisch. 1985

Listening, Reading, and Writing: Analysis and Application. *Barbara H. Wing, Editor. Listening in the Native Language* by Carolyn Gwynn Coakley and Andrew D. Wolvin: *Listening in the Foreign Language* by Elizabeth G. Joiner: *Reading in the Native Language* by Michael L. Kamil: *Reading in the Foreign Language* by Elizabeth B. Bernhardt: *Writing in the Native Language* by Kathryn K. Osterholm: *Writing in the Foreign Language* by Trisha Dvorak. 1986

The Language Teacher: Commitment and Collaboration. *John M. Darcey, editor. The Importance of Collaboration* by Claire L. Gaudiani: *Grassroots and Treetops: Collaboration in Post-secondary Language Programs* by Humphrey Tonkin: *Incorporating and International Dimension in Education Reform: Strategies for Success* by Gordon M. Ambach: *Baltimore's Foreign Language Mandate: An Experiment That Works* by Alice G. Pinderhughes: *Commitment to Excellence: Community Collaboration in Pittsburgh* by Richard C. Wallace, Jr., Mary Ellen Kirby and Thekla F. Fall: *Parents: The Child's Most Important Teachers* by Madeline Ehrlich: *Canadian Parents for French: Parent Action and Second Official Language Learning in Canada* by Carolyn E. Hodych: *The Role of the Foreign Lan-*

guage Teacher in American Corporate Edu- cation by Badi G. Foster. 1987

Toward a New Integration of Language and Culture. *Alan J. Singerman, editor. Language and Culture at the Crossroads* by Peter Patrikis: *Semiotic and Sociolinguistic Paths to Understanding Culture* by Angela Moorjani and Thomas T. Field: *Integrating the Teaching of Culture into the Foreign Language Classroom* by Robert C. Lafayette: *The Cultural Discourse of Foreign Language Textbooks* by Claire J. Kramsch: *Mass Media and Authentic Documents: Language in Cultural Context* by Jean-Pierre Berwald: *Integrating Language and Culture Through Video: A Case Study from the Teaching of Japanese* by Seiichi Makino: *Linguistic and Cultural Immersion: Study Abroad for the Younger Student* by Aleidine J. Moeller: *Linguistic and Cultural Immersion: Study Abroad for the College Student* by Norman Stokle: *Learning Culture through Local Resources: A Hispanic Model* by Barbara Lotito and Mireya Pérez-Erdélyi. 1988

Shaping the Future: Challenges and Opportunities. *Helen S. Lepke, editor. Teacher Education: Target of Reform* by June K. Phillips: *Elementary School Foreign Languages: Obstacles and Opportunities* by Carol Ann Pesola and Helena Anderson Curtain: *The Secondary Program, 9-12* by Helen P. Warriner-Burke: *Re-shaping the "College-level" Curriculum: Problems and Possibilities* by Dorothy James: *The Less Commonly Taught Languages in the Context of American Pedagogy* by Galal Walker: *Beyond the Traditional Classroom* by Emily L. Spinelli. 1989

Shifting the Instructional Focus to the Learner. *Sally Sieloff Magnan, editor. Attending to the Affective Domain in the For-*

eign Language Classroom by Elaine K. Horwitz: *Language Learning Strategies and Beyond: A Look at Strategies in the Context of Styles* by Rebecca L. Oxford: *Child Development and Academic Skills in the Elementary School Foreign Language Classroom* by Nancy Rhodes, Helena Curtain and Mari Haas: *The Exploratory Years: Foreign Languages in the Middle-Level Curriculum* by Anne G. Nerenz: *Learning Foreign Language in High School and College: Should It Really Be Different?* by Thomas Cooper, Theodore B. Kalivoda and Genelle Morain: *Foreign Language Proficiency and the Adult Learner* by Katherine M. Kulick. 1990

Building Bridges and Making Connections. *June K. Phillips, editor. Adapting an Elementary Immersion Approach to Secondary and Postsecondary Language Teaching: The Methodological Connection* by Eileen W. Glisan and Thekla F. Fall: *ESL and FL: Forging Connections* by Diane Larsen-Freeman: *Higher-Level Language Abilities: The Skills Connection* by Karen E. Breiner-Sanders: *Building Multiple Proficiencies in New Curricular Contexts* by Barbara Schnuttgen Jurasek and Richard T. Jurasek: *Linking the Foreign Language Classroom to the World* by Juliette Avots: *Connecting Testing and Learning in the Classroom and on the Program Level* by Elana Shohamy. 1991

Languages for a Multicultural World in Transition. *Heidi Byrnes, editor. Societal Multilingualism in a Multicultural World in Transition* by Ofelia García: *The Role of the Foreign Language Teaching Profession in Maintaining Non-English Languages in the United States* by Guadalupe Valdés: *Area Studies for a Multicultural World in Transition* by Claire Gaudiani: *Toward a Cultural Reading of Authentic Texts* by Vicki Galloway: *The Changing Goals of Language In-*

struction by John M. Grandin, Kandace Einbeck and Walter von Reinhart: *Technology at the Cutting Edge: Implications for Second Language Learning* by Clara Yu. 1992

Reflecting on Proficiency From the Classroom Perspective. *June K. Phillips, editor. Proficiency-Oriented Language Learning: Origins, Perspectives, and Prospects* by Alice Omaggio Hadley: *Proficiency as a Change Element in Curricula for World Languages in Elementary and Secondary Schools* by Robert LaBouve: *Using Foreign Languages to Learn: Rethinking the College Foreign Language Curriculum* by Janet Swaffar: *Proficiency as an Inclusive Orientation: Meeting the Challenge of Diversity* by Marie Sheppard: *Perspectives on Proficiency: Teachers, Students, and the Materials that They Use* by Diane W. Birckbichler and Kathryn A. Corl: *On Becoming a Teacher: Teacher Education for the 21st Century* by Anne Nerenz: *Forty Years of the Northeast Conference: A Personal Perspective* by Stephen L. Levy. 1993.

Teaching, Testing, and Assessment: Making the Connection. *Charles R. Hancock, editor. Teaching, Testing, and Assessment: Conceptualizing the Relationship* by Rebecca M. Valette: *Developments in Foreign Language Testing and Instruction: A National Perspective* by Charles W. Stansfield: *Toward More Authentic Assessment of Language Performances* by Grant Wiggins: *Assessing the Speaking Skill in the Classroom: New Solutions to an Ongoing Problem* by Peggy Boyles: *Listening Skills: Acquisition and Assessment* by Donna Reseigh Long and Janice Lynn Macián: *Authentic Assessment: Reading and Writing* by James J. Davis: *The Portfolio and Testing Culture* by Zena T. Moore: *Affective Considerations in Developing Language Tests for Secondary Students* by Pat Barr-Harrison and Elaine K. Horwitz: *Assessment in Foreign Language Teacher Education* by Leslie

L. Schrier and JoAnn Hammadou: *Glossary of Selected Terms* by Charles R. Hancock: *Annotated Bibliography* by Graduate Students at Ohio State University. 1994

Voices From the Field: Experiences and Beliefs of Our Constituents. *Trisha Dvorak, editor. Voices from the Field: An Introduction* by Rebecca R. Kline: *Voices from the Traditional Classroom: Learner Reflections* by Joan Kelly Hall and Jackie Davis: *Voices from Beyond the Classroom: Foreign Language Learners in Non-Traditional Environments* by Gwendolyn Barnes-Karol: *Native Speakers as Language Learners* by María Teresa Garretón: *Voices from Down the Hall: The Reflections of Non-Foreign Language Teachers* by Frank B. Brooks: *Voices Outside Academia: The View from the Center* by Susan Terrio and Mark Knowles: *Venerable Voices* by Dolly Jesúsita Young and Mary M. Kimball: *Voices from the Field: Conclusion* by Trisha Dvorak. 1995.

Foreign Languages for All: Challenges and Choices. *Barbara H. Wing, editor. Foreign Languages for All: Challenges and Choices—An Introduction* by Barbara H. Wing: *The Case for Multilingual Citizens in the 21st Century* by Jeffrey J. Munks: *Starting Early: Foreign Languages in the Elementary and Middle Schools* by Barbara H. Wing: *Meeting the Challenges of the Diverse Secondary School Population* by Emily Spinelli: *Choices in Postsecondary Foreign Language Programs* by Susan M. Bacon: *National Standards and the Challenge of Articulation* by Claire W. Jackson: *Technological Choices to Meet the Challenges* by Sue K. Otto and James P. Pusack: *R(T)eaching All Students: Necessary Changes in Teacher Education* by Diane J. Tedick and Constance L. Walker: *State Foreign Language Standards Projects—A Sampling* by S. Paul Sandrock. 1996

Northeast Conference Reports
Editors and Authors 1954–1996

Adams, Lillian S. 1954
Adler, Sandra 1955
Agard, Frederick B. 1954
Agatstein, Michael 1972
Alden, Douglas W. 1955
Alkonis, Nancy V. 1962
Allen, Wendy W. 1985
Altman, Howard B. 1973, 1974
Ambach, Gordon M. 1987
Anderson, Helena 1983
Andersson, Theodore 1954, 1955
Andrews, Oliver, Jr. 1968
Anisfeld, Elizabeth 1965
Arana, Alice A. 1961, 1962
Archer, John B. 1956, 1957
Arendt, Jermaine 1969
Arnold, Julius 1955
Arsenault, Philip E. 1961, 1975, 1977
Ashley, Clara West 1965
Astman, Joseph 1955
Atkins, Jeannette M. 1958, 1959, 1961, 1962, 1964
Avila, Lilian 1955
Avots, Juliette 1991
Bacon, Susan M. 1996
Baird, Janet 1976
Baker, Robert L. 1982
Balakian, Anna 1961
Ballard, Virginia S. 1975
Banks, Thomas V. 1957
Barnes-Karol, Gwendolyn 1995
Barr-Harrison, Pat 1994
Bashour, Dora S. 1961
Baslaw, Annette S. 1974
Beeken, Ramona 1955
Bégué, Armand 1955
Belasco, Simon 1956, 1957, 1963
Benardo, Leo 1974
Benevento, Jacqueline 1973
Benjamin, Anna 1967
Bennett, Ruth L. 1978

Benoît-Levy, Jean 1955
Benseler, David P. 1980
Bernhardt, Elizabeth B. 1986
Berwald, Jean-Pierre 1982, 1988
Beusch, Ann A. 1975, 1978
Bigelow, Donald 1965
Bingham, Eleanor 1963
Birckbichler, Diane W. 1980, 1983, 1984
Bird, Thomas E. Ed. 1967, Ed. 1968
Birkmaier, Emma 1974
Bishop, G. Reginald, Jr. Ed. 1960, Ed. 1965
Blanchet, Alain 1978
Blew, Genevieve S. 1958, 1961, 1966
Bock, Carolyn E. 1958, 1968
Bockman, John F. 1973
Bolinger, Dwight 1968
Bomse, Marguerite D. 1974
Bonham, George W. 1981
Born, Warren C. Ed. 1974, Ed. 1975, Ed. 1976, Ed. 1977, Ed. 1978, and Ed. 1979;
Bottiglia, William F. 1957, Ed. 1962, Ed. 1963, 1966
Boudreau, Cleophas W. 1966
Bourque, Edward H. 1971
Bourque, Jane McFarland 1975, 1983
Bowen, J. Donald 1958, 1959
Bowen, Marjorie P. 1964
Boyd-Bowman, Peter 1974
Boyles, Peggy 1994
Bragaw, Donald H. 1981
Bragger, Jeannette D. 1985
Brault, Gerard J. 1965, 1972, 1976
Braun, Sidney 1958
Brée, Germaine Ed. 1955, 1977
Bree, Josephine P. 1955, 1956
Brega, Evelyn 1983
Breiner-Sanders, Karen E. 1991
Bridey, Helen E. 1955
Briggs, Morton W. 1957
Brisley, Leonard 1965
Brod, Richard I. 1978

Lavergneau, René L. 1974
Le Bovit, Judith 1971
Leach, John 1976
Leland, Marine 1972
Lepke, Helen S. Ed. 1989
LeSage, Laurent 1956
Lester, Kenneth 1977
Levine, Mark 1975
Levy, Harry L. Ed. 1958, 1959, 1971
Levy, Stephen L. 1975, 1983, 1993
Levy, Sylvia N. 1955
Libit, Elaine C. 1970
Lieberman, Samuel 1972
Linder, Cathy 1978
Linnehan, Alice F. 1957
Lipton, Gladys C. 1964, 1967, 1971,
    1975, 1983
Liskin-Gasparra, Judith E. 1982
LoBue, Joseph 1955, 1956
Locke, William N. 1954, 1958
Long, Donna Reseigh 1994
Lopez, Lucrecia 1955
Lorge, Sarah W. 1955
Lotito, Barbara 1988
Lueras, Benito L. 1962
Lyles, Victoria 1954
Lynch, C. Arthur 1955
MacAllister, Archibald T. 1954, 1955,
1959
Macián, Janice Lynn 1994
Magnan, Sally Sieloff 1985, Ed. 1990
Makino, Seiichi 1988
Marcellino, Ralph 1960
Marckwardt, Albert H. 1955
Marks, Doris 1974
Marshall, Randall 1962
Marty, Fernand 1957
Matthew, John R. 1955
Maubrey, Pierre 1982
McArthur, James F. 1964
McCarthy, Barbara P. 1955, 1956
McClelland, David C. 1955
McCollom, Mrs. Herbert F. 1967
McRill, Paul C. 1968
Mead, Robert G., Jr. 1955, Ed. 1966, 1972,

Ed. 1982, Ed. 1983
Medley, Frank W., Jr. 1985
Meinke, Kenneth 1956
Melchior, Oliver A. 1958
Menditto, Diane F. 1974
Mensh, Helene B. 1978
Meras, Edmond A. 1954, 1955
Met, Myriam 1983
Miller, Mary R. 1972
Miller, Richard R. 1959
Mirsky, Jerome G. 1971, 1972
Mistretta, Anthony 1978
Miyares, Enrique H. 1977
Moeller, Aleidine 1988
Monsees, Anita 1978
Monserrat, Joseph 1955, 1956
Montgomery, Gail E. 1968
Moore, Merriam 1977
Moore, Zena T. 1994
Moorjani, Angela 1988
Morain, Genelle 1973, 1975, 1990
Morel, Stefano 1974
Morgan, Raleigh 1962
Morris, Edward P. 1957
Moskowitz, Gertrude 1970, 1973
Moulton, William G. 1956, 1967
Mueller, Theodore 1957, 1962
Munks, Jeffrey J. 1996
Mustard, Helen M. 1961
Myer, Grace 1956
Nacci, Chris N. 1967
Navarro, Jauquina 1959
Nelligan, William J. 1958
Nelson, April 1982
Nelson, Robert J. 1964, 1970
Nemser, William 1957
Nerenz, Anne G. 1990, 1993
Newman, Richard W. 1974
Newmark, Maxim 1959
Nionakis, John P. 1971, 1975
Norton, Harriet 1971
Nuzzi, Theodore 1965
O'Brien, Kathryn L. 1954
O'Connor, Patricia 1961
O'Neill, E. Wesley 1956

O'Neill, Flora 1977
Oblum, Rudolph V. 1957
Obrecht, Dean H. 1963
Obstfeld, Roland 1974
Odronic, Walter J. 1972
Hadley, Alice C. Omaggio 1980, 1983,
    Ed. 1985, 1993
Orta, Awilda 1973
Osterholm, Kathryn K. 1986
Otto, Frank 1970, 1971, 1972
Otto, Sue K. 1996
Ottolenghi, Marcella 1957
Oustinoff, Pierre 1957
Oxford, Rebecca L. 1990
Packard, Hubert S. 1956
Pagan, Muriel 1973
Painter, Fred B. 1956
Pane, Josephine Bruno 1965, 1968
Papalia, Anthony 1974, 1981
Paquette, F. Andre 1962, 1967, 1970, 1981
Paquin, Laurence G. 1962
Paradis, Roger 1976
Parker, William R. 1954, 1965
Parks, Carolyn 1982
Patrikis, Peter 1988
Paulston, Cristina Bratt 1978
Pekary, Charlotte 1956
Pellegrino, Alfred 1955, 1956, 1959
Peloro, Filomena C. 1958, 1959
Penta, Richard M. 1968
Pérez, Carmen 1973
Pérez-Erdélyi, Mireya 1988
Pesola, Carol Ann 1989
Peyre, Henri 1954
Phaneuf, Paul H. 1958
Phelps, W. Roy 1966
Phillips, June K. 1975, 1981, 1982, Ed.
    1991, Ed. 1993, Ed. 1997
Phipps, Toshiko 1982
Pierce, Lucia 1981
Pimsleur, Paul 1970
Pinderhughes, Alice G. 1987
Pleasants, Jeanne Varney 1955, 1956, 1957
Poehler, Paul F. 1956
Politzer, Robert 1954

Powers, James R. 1968, 1971
Presel, Rose 1957
Press, Frederick J. 1970
Price, Blanche A. 1956, 1957
Primeau, John K. 1981
Prochoroff, Marina 1963
Pusack, James P. 1996
Quiñones, Nathan 1973
Ratte, Elizabeth H. 1958, 1959
Reh, Albert M. 1967
Reiff, Donald G. 1968
Reilly, John J. 1970
Reinhold, Meyer 1976
Rhodes, Nancy 1983, 1990
Richards, Glenda G. 1958
Richardson, Henry B. 1954
Richardson, Mabel W. 1968
Rippley, LaVern J. 1976
Rivera, Sonia 1973
Rivers, Dorothy S. 1967, 1968
Rivers, W. Napoleon 1959
Rivers, Wilga M. 1979
Robb, Mary L. 1970
Roberts, Alfred D. 1973
Robertson, Betty 1963
Robinson, Edward A. 1965
Roccio, Rose Marie 1975
Rogers, Francis 1961, 1965
Rohsenow, John S. 1977
Rojas, Pauline M. 1965
Rosenbaum, Eric 1955
Runge, Edith A. 1954, 1955
Ruplin, Ferdinand 1971
Russell, Clyde 1959
Sandrock, S. Paul 1996
Sandstrom, Eleanor L. 1970
Sapon, Stanley M. 1954, 1955, 1956, 1957,
    1963
Sartorius, Ina C. 1956
Savage, Nita Willits 1957, 1959
Sayres, William C. 1955, 1956
Scatton, Earnest A. 1977
Scheider, Rose 1955, 1956
Scherer, George A. C. 1963
Schmidt, S. E. 1957

Schmitt, Conrad J. 1964
Schneider, Gerd K. 1981
Schreiber, William I. 1976
Schrier, Leslie L. 1994
Schueler, Herbert 1961
Schumacher, Marigwen 1968, 1976
Schyfter, Sara 1978
Scott, Susan 1955
Scrivener, Katherine 1956
Seelye, H. Ned 1974
Selvi, Arthur M. 1954, 1955, 1964
Senn, Alfred E. 1960
Serafino, Robert P. 1961, 1962, 1970
Sheehan, Joseph H. 1969
Shepart, Sanford 1956
Sheppard, Douglas C. 1966 (consultant)
Sheppard, Marie 1993
Sherburne, Robert R. 1974
Sherp, Beverly 1962
Shields, Archibald K. 1958
Shohamy, Elana 1991
Shryer, Margaret 1969
Sibley, Elbridge 1955
Silber, Gordon R. 1959, 1967
Silva-Fuenzalida, Isamael 1959
Simches, Seymour O. 1962, 1964, 1968
Singerman, Alan J. Ed. 1988
Sister Charlotte Marie 1966
Sister Julie, S.N.D. 1957
Sister Margaret Pauline 1961
Sister Margaret Thérèse 1955
Sister Marie Louise 1956
Slack, Anne 1958, 1974
Smith, George E. 1968
Smith, Henry Lee 1954
Smith, Philip D. 1973
Smith, Sylvia 1955, 1956
Snow, Emily L. 1958
Soda, Frank M. 1956, 1966
Soffietti, James P. 1962
Song, Seok Choong 1977
Sora, Maria 1960
Spaethling, Robert H. 1967
Sparks, Kimberly 1967
Spinelli, Emily L. 1989, 1996

Stanislawczyk, Irene E. 1960
Stansfield, Charles W. 1994
Starr, S. Frederick 1981
Starr, Wilmarth H. 1954, 1955, 1956, 1959, 1961, 1962
Stavrinos, Mary M. 1957
Stein, Jack M. 1961
Stephens, James 1955
Stern, H. H. 1983
Stewart, William A. 1972
Stillwell, June U. 1966
Stinnett, T.M. 1954
Stokle, Norman 1988
Stookins, Joseph 1955
Strasheim, Lorraine A. 1973
Strouse, Adeline 1956
Sturges, Perry 1959
Sullivan, Edward D. 1965, 1966
Swaffar, Janet 1993
Sweet, Waldo E. 1962
Szogyi, Alex 1955
Tabor, Esther 1956
Tamarkin, Toby S. 1974, 1976
Tauber, Arnold 1964
Tedick, Diane J. 1996
Terrio, Susan 1995
Theurer, Louise 1955
Thibault, Paula 1954, 1955, 1956, 1957
Thomas, Alice Nesta Lloyd 1955
Thomas, Tilla 1956
Thompson, Mary P. 1954, 1955, 1956, 1959, 1962, 1963
Tone, Fred H. 1954
Tonkin, Humphrey 1983, 1987
Torrey, Jane W. 1970
Torrey, Norman L. 1954
Travers, Claudia S. 1981
Trivelli, Romo J. 1982
Tucker, G. Richard 1970, 1972
Tursi, Joseph A. 1964, Ed. 1970, 1972, 1978
Tuttle, Harry 1974
Twaddell, W. Freeman 1954, 1966, 1973
Twarog, Leon I 1960
Tyre, Carl A. 1958

Northeast Conference Officers and Directors since 1954

Abbott, Martha G., Fairfax County (VA) Public Schools, Director 1994-97.

Alexander, Elizabeth, Burlington (VT) HS, Director 1997-2000.

Anderson, Nancy E., ETS, Director 1990-93, ACTFL Representative 1994, Consultant to the Chair 1996.

Andersson, Theodore†, [Yale U]* U of Texas, Director 1954-56.

Andrews, Oliver, Jr., U of Connecticut, Director 1971-74.

Arndt, Richard, Columbia U, Director 1961.

Arsenault, Philip E., Montgomery County (MD) Public S, Local Chair 1967, 1970; Director 1971, 1973-74; Vice Chair 1975; Conference Chair 1976.

Atkins, Jeannette, Staples (Westport, CT) HS, Director 1962-65.

Baird, Janet, U of Maryland, Local Chair 1974.

Baker, Robert M.†, Middlebury C, Director 1987-90.

Bashour, Dora, [Hunter C], Secretary 1963-1964; Recording Secretary 1965-68.

Baslaw, Annette S., [Teachers C], Hunter C, Local Chair 1973.

Bayerschmidt, Carl F., [Columbia U], Conference Chair 1961.

Bennett, Ruth, Queens C, Local Chair 1975-76.

Bertin, Gerald A., Rutgers U, Local Chair 1960.

Berwald, Jean-Pierre, U of Massachusetts-Amherst, Director 1980-83.

Bird, Thomas E., Queens C, Editor 1967-68; Director 1969.

Bishop, G. Reginald, Jr., Rutgers U, Editor 1960, 1965; Director 1961-62, 1965, 1968; Vice Chair 1966; Conference Chair 1967.

Bishop, Thomas W., New York U, Local Chair 1965.

Born, Warren C., [ACTFL], Editor 1974-79.

Bostroem, Kyra, Westover S, Director 1961.

Bottiglia, William F., MIT, Editor 1957, 1962-63; Director 1964.

Bourque, Jane M., [Stratford (CT) Public S], Mt. Vernon (NY) Public S, Director 1974-75; Vice Chair 1976; Conference Chair 1977.

Brée, Germaine, [New York U, U of Wisconsin], Wake Forest U, Conference Chair 1955; Editor 1955.

Brennan, Judith, Virginia Beach Public S, Director 1995-98

Bressler, Julia T., Nashua (NH) Public S, Director 1991-94; Vice Chair 1995, Conference Chair 1996.

Brod, Richard I., MLA, Consultant to the Chair, 1983; Director 1985-88.

Brooks, Nelson†, [Yale U], Director 1954-57, 1960-61; Vice Chair 1959.

Brooks-Brown, Sylvia R., [Baltimore (MD) City S], Baltimore County (MD) Public S, Director 1988-92; Vice Chair 1993, Conference Chair 1994.

Brown, Christine L., [West Hartford (CT) Public S], Glastonbury (CT) Public S, Director 1982-85; Vice Chair 1986; Conference Chair 1987.

Byrnes, Heidi, Georgetown U, Director 1985-88; Vice Chair 1989; Conference Chair 1990; Editor 1992.

Cadoux, Remunda†, [Hunter C], Vice Chair 1969; Conference Chair 1970.

Campbell, Hugh, [Roxbury Latin S], Rocky Hill Country Day S, Director 1966-67.

Cannon, Adrienne G., Prince George's Co (MD) Public S, Director 1993-96.

Carr, Celestine G., Howard County (MD) Public S, Director 1993-96.

Churchill, J. Frederick, Hofstra U, Director 1966-67; Local Chair 1971-72.

Ciotti, Marianne C., [Vermont State Department of Education, Boston U], Barre (VT) Public S, Director 1967.

Cincinnato, Paul D., Farmingdale (NY) Public S, Director 1974-77; Vice Chair 1978; Conference Chair 1979.

Cintas, Pierre F., [Dalhousie U], Pennsylvania State U-Ogontz, Director 1976-79.

Cipriani, Anita A., Hunter C Elem S, Director 1986-89.

Clark, John L.D., [CAL], DLI, Director 1976-78; Vice Chair 1979; Conference Chair 1980.

Clark, Richard P., Newton (MA) HS, Director 1967.

Clemens, Brenda Frazier, [Rutgers U, U of Connecticut], Howard U, Director 1972-75.

Cobb, Martha, Howard U, Director 1976-77; Recording Secretary 1978.

Covey, Delvin L., [Montclair State C], Spring Arbor C, Director 1964-65.

Crapotta, James, Barnard C, Director 1992-95.

Crawford, Dorothy B., Philadelphia HS for Girls, Conference Chair 1956.

Dahme, Lena F., Hunter C, Local Chair 1958; Director 1959.

Darcey, John M., West Hartford (CT) Public S, Director 1978-81; Vice Chair 1982; Conference Chair 1983; Editor 1987.

Dates, Elaine, Burlington (VT) HS, Recording Secretary 1991.

Del Olmo, Filomena Peloro, [Hackensack (NJ) Public S], Fairleigh Dickinson U, Director 1960-63.

De Napoli, Anthony J., Wantagh (NY) Public S, Local Chair 1980-82, 1987; Director 1982-85.

Di Donato, Robert, MIT, Consultant to the Chair 1986.

Díaz, José M., Hunter C HS, Director 1988-91; Vice Chair 1992; Conference Chair 1993; Consultant to the Chair 1995 and 1997.

Didsbury, Robert, Weston (CT) JHS, Director 1966-69.

Dodge, James W.†, [Middlebury C], Editor 1971-73; Secretary-Treasurer 1973-89.

Dodge, Ursula Seuss, Northeast Conference Secretariat, Interim Secretary-Treasurer 1990.

Donato, Richard, U of Pittsburgh, Director 1993-96, Vice Chair 1997.

Dostert, Leon E., [Georgetown U], Occidental C, Conference Chair 1959.

Duclos, Marie, Nashua (NH) Public S, Newsletter Editor 1996.

Dufau, Micheline†, U of Massachusetts, Director 1976-79.

Dvorak, Trisha, U of Michigan, Editor 1995.

Dye, Joan C., Hunter C, Local Chair 1978.

Eaton, Annette, Howard U, Director 1967-70.

Eddy, Frederick D.†, [U of Colorado], Editor 1959; Director 1960.

Eddy, Peter A., [CAL/ERIC], CIA Language S, Director 1977-78.

Edgerton, Mills F., Jr., Bucknell U, Editor 1969; Director 1970; Vice Chair 1971; Conference Chair 1972.

Elkins, Robert, West Virginia U, Director 1991-94.

Elling, Barbara E., SUNY-Stony Brook, Director 1980-83.

Feindler, Joan L., East Williston (NY) Public S, Director 1969-71; Vice Chair 1972; Conference Chair 1973.

Flaxman, Seymour, [New York U], City C of New York, Editor 1961; Director 1962.

Freeman, Stephen A., [Middlebury C], Director 1957-60.

Fulton, Renee J., New York City Board of Education Director 1955.

Gaarder, A. Bruce, [USOE], Director 1971-74.

Galloway, Vicki B., [ACTFL], Georgia

Technological U, Consultant to the Chair 1985.

Geary, Edward J., [Harvard U], Bowdoin C, Conference Chair 1962.

Geno, Thomas H., U of Vermont, Director 1975-76; Vice Chair 1977; Conference Chair 1978; Recording Secretary 1979; Editor 1980-81.

Gilman, Margaret†, Bryn Mawr C, Editor 1956.

Glaude, Paul M., New York State Dept of Education, Director 1963-66.

Glisan, Eileen W. Indiana U of Pennsylvania, Director 1992-95, Vice Chair 1996, Conference Chair 1997.

Golden, Herbert H., Boston U, Director 1962.

Goldfield, Joel, Fairfield U, Director 1995-98.

Grew, James H., [Phillips Acad], Director 1966-69.

Gutiérrez, John R., Pennsylvania State U, Director 1988-91.

Hancock, Charles R., The Ohio State University, Editor 1994

Hartie, Robert W., Queens C, Local Chair 1966.

Harrison, John S., Baltimore County (MD) Public S, Local Chair 1979, 1983; Director 1983-86; Recording Secretary 1988-89.

Harris-Schenz, Beverly, [U of Pittsburgh], U of Massachusetts-Amherst, Director 1988-91.

Hayden, Hilary, OSB, St. Anselm's Abbey S, Vice Chair 1970; Conference Chair 1971.

Hayes, Alfred S.†, CAL, Vice Chair 1963; Conference Chair 1964.

Hernandez, Juana A., Hood C, Director 1978-81.

Holekamp, Elizabeth L., Executive Director 1990-95.

Holzmann, Albert W.†, Rutgers U, Director 1960.

Hurtgen, André, St. Paul's School (NH), Director 1992-95.

Claire Jackson, Brookline (MA) Public S, Director 1996-99.

Jalbert, Emile H., [Thayer Acad], Berkshire Comm C, Local Chair 1962.

Jarvis, Gilbert A., Ohio State U, Editor 1984.

Jebe, Suzanne, [Guilford (CT) HS], Minnesota Dept of Education, Director 1975-76; Recording Secretary 1977.

Johnston, Marjorie C., [USOE], Local Chair 1964.

Jones, George W., Jr.†, Norfolk (VA) Public S, Director 1977-80.

Kahn, Timothy M., S Burlington (VT) HS, Director 1979-82.

Kassen, Margaret Ann. Catholic U of America, Director 1997-2000.

Keesee, Elizabeth, [USOE], Director 1966-70.

Kellenberger, Hunter†, [Brown U], Conference Chair 1954, Editor 1954.

Kennedy, Dora F., Prince George's County (MD) Public S, Director 1985-88; Recording Secretary 1990; Consultant to the Chair 1991.

Kesler, Robert, Phillips Exeter Acad, Director 1957.

Kibbe, Doris E., Montclair State C, Director 1968-69.

Kline, Rebecca, [Dickinson C], Pennsylvania State U, Director 1990-93, Vice-Chair 1994, Conference Chair 1995, Executive Director 1995-.

Koenig, George, State U of New York-Oswego, Recording Secretary, 1993.

Kramsch, Claire J., [MIT], Cornell, Director 1984-87.

La Follette, James E., Georgetown U, Local Chair 1959.

La Fountaine, Hernan, New York City Board of Education, Director 1972.

Lenz, Harold, Queens C, Local Chair 1961.

Lepke, Helen S., [Kent State U], Clarion U

of Pennsylvania, Director 1981-84; Vice Chair 1985; Conference Chair 1986; Editor 1989.

Lester, Kenneth A., Connecticut State Dept of Education, Recording Secretary 1982.

Levy, Harry†, [Hunter C], Fordham U, Editor 1958; Director 1959-61; Conference Chair 1963.

Levy, Stephen L., [New York City Board of Education], Roslyn (NY) Public S, Local Chair 1978, 1980-82, 1984-85, 1987-present; Director 1980-83; Vice Chair 1984; Conference Chair 1985; Consultant to the Chair 1994.

Lieberman, Samuel, Queens C, Director 1966-69.

Lipton, Gladys C., [New York City Board of Education, Anne Arundel County (MD) Public S], U of Maryland-Baltimore County, Director 1973-76; *Newsletter* Editor 1993-95.

Liskin-Gasparro, Judith E., [ETS], Middlebury C, Recording Secretary 1984; Director 1986-89; Vice Chair 1990; Conference Chair 1991.

Lloyd, Paul M., U of Pennsylvania, Local Chair 1963.

Locke, William N.†, MIT, Conference Chair 1957; Director 1958-59.

MacAllister, Archibald T.†, [Princeton U], Director 1955-57, 1959-61.

Magnan, Sally Sieloff, University of Wisconsin-Madison, Editor 1990.

Masciantonio, Rudolph, School District of Philadelphia, Director 1969-71.

Mead, Robert G., Jr.†, U of Connecticut, Director 1955; Editor 1966; Vice Chair 1967; Conference Chair 1968; Editor 1982-83.

Medley, Frank W. Jr., West Virginia U, Director 1996-99.

Mesnard, Andre, Barnard C, Director 1954-55.

Micozzi, Arthur L., [Baltimore County (MD) Public S], Local Chair 1977, 1979,

1983, 1986; Director 1970-82.

Mirsky, Jerome G.†, [Jericho (NY) SHS], Shoreham-Wading River (NY) HS, Director 1970-73; Vice Chair 1974; Conference Chair 1975.

Nelson, Robert J., [U of Pennsylvania], U of Illinois, Director 1965-68.

Neumaier, Bert J., Timothy Edwards (S Windsor, CT) MS, Director 1988-92.

Neuse, Werner†, [Middlebury C], Director 1954-56.

Nionakis, John P., Hingham (MA) Public S, Director 1984-87; Vice Chair 1988; Conference Chair 1989.

Obstfeld, Roland, Northport (NY) HS, Recording Secretary 1976.

Omaggio, Alice C., U of Illinois, Editor 1985.

Owens, Doris Barry, West Hartford (CT) Public S, Recording Secretary 1983.

Pane, Remigio U., Rutgers U, Conference Chair 1960.

Paquette, Andre, [Middlebury C], Laconia (NH) Public S, Director 1963-66; Vice Chair 1968; Conference Chair 1969.

Parks, Carolyn, [U of Maryland], French International S, Recording Secretary 1981.

Peel, Emily S., Wethersfield (CT) Public S, Director 1991-94.

Perkins, Jean, Swarthmore C, Treasurer 1963-64; Conference Chair 1966.

Petrosino, Vince J., Baltimore (MD) City S, Local Chair 1986.

Phillips, June K., [Indiana U of Pennsylvania, Tennessee Foreign Language Institute, US Air Force Acad], Weber State U, Director 1979-82; Vice Chair 1983; Conference Chair 1984; Consultant to the Chair 1986, 1989, 1990, 1992; Editor 1991, 1993, 1997.

Prochoroff, Marina, [MLA Materials Center], Director 1974.

Ramos, Alicia, Indiana U of Pennsylvania, *Newsletter* Editor 1995-97.

Reilly, John H., Queens C, Local Chair

1968-69; Director 1970.

Remillard, Vincent., St. Francis C (PA), Recording Secretary 1997.

Renjilian-Burgy, Joy, Wellesley C, Director 1987-90; Vice Chair 1991; Chair 1992.

Reutershan, Donald H., Jr., Maine Dept. of Ed., Director 1997-2000.

Riley, Kerry, U of Maryland, Consultant to the Chair 1986.

Riordan, Kathleen M., Springfield (MA) Public S, Director 1988-91; Recording Secretary 1992.

Rochefort, Frances A., Cranston (RI) Public S, Director 1986-89.

Rosser, Harry L., Boston College, Director 1994-97.

Russo, Gloria M., [U of Virginia], Director 1983-86.

Sandstrom, Eleanor L., [School District of Philadelphia], Director 1975-78.

Selvi, Arthur M., Central Connecticut State C, Director 1954.

Senn, Alfred, U of Pennsylvania, Director 1956.

Serafino, Robert, New Haven (CT) Public S, Director 1969-73.

Sheppard, Douglas C., [SUNY-Buffalo], Arizona State U, Director 1968-71.

Shilaeff, Ariadne, Wheaton C, Director 1978-80.

Shrum, Judith, Virginia Tech U, Director 1996-99.

Shuster, George N.†, [U of Notre Dame], Conference Chair 1958.

Simches, Seymour O., Tufts U, Director 1962-65; Vice Chair 1965.

Sims, Edna N., U of the District of Columbia, Director 1981-84.

Singerman, Alan J., Davidson C, Editor 1988.

Sister Margaret Pauline, [Emmanuel C], Director 1957, 1965-68; Recording Secretary 1969-75.

Sister Margaret Therese, Trinity C, Director 1959-60.

Sister Mary Pierre, Georgian Court C, Director 1961-64.

Sousa-Welch, Helen Candi, West Hartford (CT) Public S, Director 1987-90.

Sparks, Kimberly, Middlebury C, Director 1969-72.

Starr, Wilmarth H., [U of Maine], New York U, Director 1960-63, 1966; Vice Chair 1964, Conference Chair 1965.

Steer, Alfred G., Jr., Columbia U, Director 1961.

Stein, Jack M.†, [Harvard U], Director 1962.

Stracener, Rebecca J., Edison (NJ) Public S, Director 1984-87.

Tamarkin, Toby, Manchester (CT) Comm C, Director 1977-80; Vice Chair 1981; Conference Chair 1982; Recording Secretary 1987.

Thompson, Mary P., [Glastonbury (CT) Public S], Director 1957-62.

Trivelli, Remo J., U of Rhode Island, Director 1981-84.

Tursi, Joseph, [SUNY-Stony Brook], Editor 1970; Director 1971-72; Vice Chair 1973; Conference Chair 1974.

Valette, Rebecca, Boston C, Director 1972-75.

Vasquez-Amaral, Jose, Rutgers U, Director 1960.

Walker, Richard H., Bronxville (NY) HS, Director 1954.

Walsh, Donald D.†, [MLA], Director 1954; Secretary-Treasurer 1965-73.

Walton, A. Ronald†, U of Maryland, Director 1990-93.

Warner, Pearl M., New York City Public S, Recording Secretary 1985.

Webb, John, Hunter College HS, Consultant to the Chair 1993; Director 1995-98.

White, Arlene, Salisbury State U, Recording Secretary 1994.

White, Emile Margaret, [District of Columbia Public S], Director 1955- 58.

Williamson, Richard C., Bates C, Director 1983-86; Vice Chair 1987; Conference

Chair 1988.

Wing, Barbara H., U of New Hampshire, Editor 1986; *Newsletter* Editor 1987-93; Recording Secretary 1995; Editor 1996.

Woodford, Protase E., ETS, Director 1982-85.

Yakobson, Helen B., George Washington U, Director 1959-60.

Yu, Clara, Middlebury College, Director 1994-97.

Zimmer-Loew, Helene, [NY State Education Dept], AATG, Director 1977-79; Vice Chair 1980; Conference Chair 1981.

Copies of the Reports issued since 1992 may be ordered from National Textbook Co. Reports issued 1954–91 may be obtained from Northeast Conference at Dickinson College, P.O. Box 1773, Carlisle, PA 17013-2896. Please write for ordering information.